The author has made every effort to ensure that the information in this book is accurate and up to date at the time of publication. However, policies, deadlines, requirements, costs, and admissions practices may change. Readers should verify all information directly with colleges, universities, and official sources before making decisions.

This book is based on publicly available information, independent research, and the author's work in college counseling. It does not contain confidential, proprietary, or nonpublic information from the University of California or any other college. Any views expressed are solely those of the author.

ISBN: 979-8-234-07193-4
Library of Congress Control Number: 2026912461
Copyright registration: pending

Published by Periwinkle Tide Publishing
www.missionaccepted.international

PRAISE for *The California College Playbook*

"**I love this book!** I help manage a Bay Area program that brings volunteer mentors into our local public high school to help first-generation students navigate the college admissions process. This book will be a great resource. It's easy to read, well-organized, and covers all the important info one needs to apply to schools in California. Highly recommended!"

— *Dale T., Board Member, Non-Profit College Access Organization*

"*The California College Playbook* is a practical, accessible guide to navigating California's college systems and admissions processes. The topics are well **organized, easy to follow, and thoroughly covered**. Any student considering California colleges should read this incredible resource!"

— *Shannon K., Independent Educational Consultant*

"If you are a junior or senior, this book is **a must**."

— *Alex P., California High School Student*

"Navigating college admissions in California can feel overwhelming, but this book maps it out perfectly. It gives you **real, practical strategies** for the UC, CSU, and community college tracks. It fills a massive gap in college counseling and is a must-have resource for anyone navigating this for the first time and looking toward higher education in the Golden State."

— *Renu B., California Parent*

"*The California College Playbook* is a **concise, well-written** and **very thorough** guide to the California college ecosystem. Even those with a good amount of college experience will learn a lot from this book. In addition to covering the "facts" of the college system, Ms. Hees shows students how to approach the college journey with minimum emotion and maximum logic. There is no fat in this book, so it may take several readings of some chapters to really understand everything that is covered. Students and parents will get the most benefit if they read this guide in 9th or 10th grade. I highly recommend this book for determined students, their parents and anyone else who want/need to know more about the CA college system."

— *Lisa E., California Parent*

"This book is extremely well structured, with multiple layers providing depth of information. Highly **recommend this book** to every student and parent who is considering applying for California colleges.

— *Reena A., California Parent*

"This book is a valuable resource for students and families considering California colleges. It offers great insight into the California college system in **a much more organized way than the internet** can provide. Even reading it after having been through college application cycles, I found useful information that I wish I had known while applying for college."

— *Joy X., UC Transfer Student*

"*The California College Playbook* is the **ultimate college admissions guide** for anybody learning about university admissions in the Golden State. Easy to read and accessible to experts, students and their families alike, Hees' work reflects her deep knowledge of the California tertiary education landscape, California's unique allure as an economic powerhouse with a three-tiered public higher education structure, and her overall expertise with college admissions guidance."

— *Christopher K., International School College Counselor*

"*The California College Playbook* is like having a **private college counselor in your back pocket**! Christine Hees breaks down the daunting task of applying to California universities into manageable chunks, using easy to follow advice, with helpful examples and tips so that anyone can approach college application season **feeling confident**. [...] As an AVID teacher with over 15 years of experience helping first-generation students navigate college applications, I found this book easy to follow, thorough, and reassuring. I wish I had *The California College Playbook* when I was first beginning my career!"

— *Arantxa A., California High School Teacher*

"*The California College Playbook* demystifies the complex public and private collegiate system in California and provides practical guidance that equips students with the tools to navigate the unique process for admission to California colleges and universities and craft applications designed to **maximize their chances of admission**. An essential primer for anyone thinking about applying to school in California!"

— *Cathy M., California Parent*

"Christine outlines an **invaluable roadmap** for California college applicants. She breaks down complex college systems into **easy-to-understand** language, offering the exact strategies, resources, and examples students and parents need to navigate the California college application process with confidence."

— *Regina P.-I., Independent College Counselor*

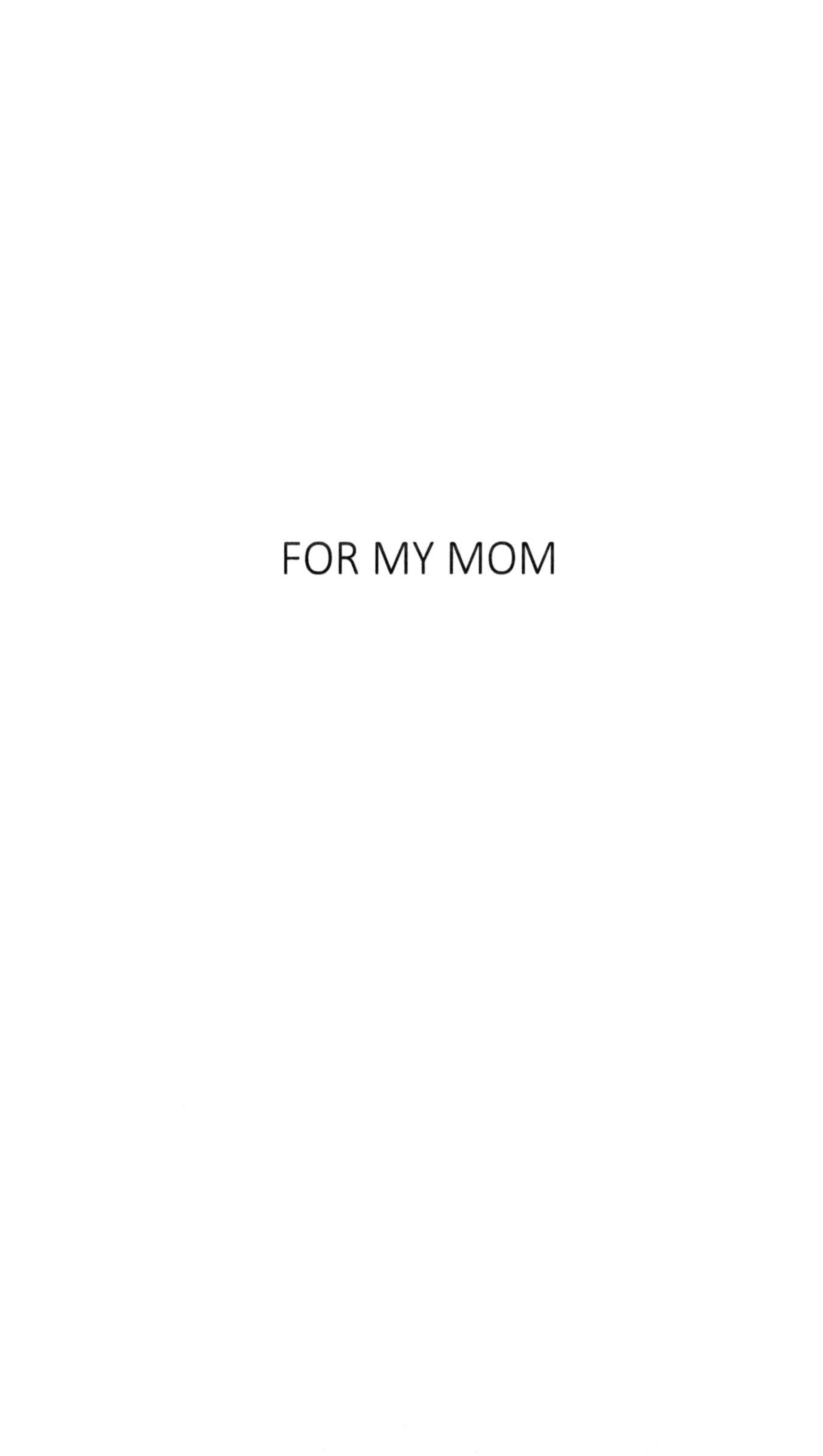

FOR MY MOM

Content

The Big Picture

1 | California College Landscape

Why College Admissions Works Differently in California

Ask any Californian: The Golden State is different. Its geography, economy, innovation culture, and diversity create a state unlike any other. So, it should come as no surprise that applying to college in California is fundamentally different from applying anywhere else in the country (or the world). Not just a little different. Structurally different in ways that can make the whole process feel confusing, even unpredictable.

If you are a high school student or parent going through this, you have probably sensed it already. Perhaps you know someone with a perfect GPA who was rejected from Stanford. Maybe you have heard that UCLA is now harder to get into than some Ivy League schools. You might be wondering why admission rates seem to get more intimidating every year. The answer has nothing to do with students being less qualified or admissions officers being arbitrary. The answer is California itself.

California Is a Global Force.

If California were its own country, it would have one of the ten largest economies in the world. The gross state product approaches four trillion dollars ($ 4,000,000,000,000!), larger than most nations. California competes economically with countries like Germany, the United Kingdom, and Japan.

This matters for college admissions because **economic power attracts** people. Families move here for jobs in tech, entertainment, healthcare, and countless other industries. International students are drawn for the same reasons. California's colleges are not just educating California kids. They sit at the center of global talent pipelines. California colleges feed Silicon Valley, Hollywood, major research hospitals, biotech companies, and public institutions that operate at world-class levels.

The state itself is massive and incredibly diverse. Nearly **40 million people** live here, spread across different environments: beach towns, agricultural valleys, sprawling cities, mountain communities, desert regions. Students applying to California colleges come from wealthy Silicon Valley suburbs. They come from rural farming towns in the Central Valley. And they come from bustling Los Angeles neighborhoods, and literally every country on Earth. No other state faces this combination of **internal diversity** and **external demand** at the same time.

The Core Problem

Universities cannot expand nearly as fast as interest grows. Think about what expanding a university requires. More classroom buildings. More student housing. More faculty members. More lab space. More dining halls. More parking. More funding. Physical campuses cannot double in size overnight, and state budgets do not automatically increase when application numbers go up. Hiring new faculty takes months, and construction takes years.

Meanwhile, the number of qualified applicants keeps rising. More California high school students graduate each year. More out-of-state students want to move here. More international students see California schools as gateways to their American Dream. This explains why California admissions feels so competitive.

The dilemma
Too many qualified students are competing for a limited number of seats that cannot grow fast enough to meet the growing demand.

Application Numbers Keep Rising

UCLA is now the **most applied-to university** in the United States. For Fall 2025, UCLA received 173,297 applications and admitted just 12 percent of applicants. And in 2026, 4,000 additional students applied to UCLA (177,317 total). UC Berkeley received over 150,000 applications with a 13 percent acceptance rate in 2025. Stanford's acceptance rate sits around 3 to 4 percent, and Caltech admits a similar fraction of applicants. This is the new California normal: skyrocketing application numbers, sinking acceptance rates.

Even within the University of California system, almost every campus is seeing **record application numbers** year after year. Surprisingly, the biggest growth happened in the Central Valley: For Fall 2025, UC Merced received over 51,000 applications, a 45 percent increase from the year before. The good news, however, is that California residents saw a 97 percent acceptance rate at UC Merced and a 71 percent acceptance rate at UC Santa Cruz, showing that the UC system still offers accessible options alongside its highly selective campuses.

California's Three-Tier System

To make sense of California college admissions, we need to understand how the state deliberately designed its public university system. California created a three-tier model to balance **access, quality, and scale**. Let us have a first look at the three options now; we will cover each in more detail later.

The University of California

> **The UC system is California's research powerhouse**
> All UC campuses are R1 research institutions, the highest designation for research activity in the United States.

The UC campuses are built around research, scholarship, and graduate education. They employ world-renowned faculty and run major research labs. They contribute significant discoveries in medicine, technology, and countless other fields.

Because of this research focus and practical space limitations, the UC campuses must **limit undergraduate enrollment**. Research labs have finite capacity, and professors split their time between teaching and research. Popular majors like computer science, biology, or engineering face especially intense competition because demand far exceeds what these programs can accommodate.

This explains why UC admissions are **selective** and **holistic** (they look at your whole application, not just your grades). The UCs are not just filling seats randomly; they are building cohorts of students who can thrive in research-intensive environments. Your choice of major can significantly impact your chances because some programs are simply more popular than others.

The California State University

The California State University prepares students for the workforce. The CSU system is the largest four-year public university system in the United States. Schools like San Diego State, Cal Poly San Luis Obispo, San José State, and Long Beach State focus on teaching, applied learning, and **career readiness**. This is the reason why you will find **business majors** at almost all CSUs but only at a few UCs. The CSU's learning approach is more hands-on, while UCs focus on academic theory and research.

Taken together, the CSU campuses educate nearly twice as many undergraduate students as the nine UC campuses. For Fall 2025, the CSUs enrolled over 416,000 students while the UC system counted about 236,000 undergraduates. The CSU system is designed for broad access. Its admission relies heavily on numbers, using GPA thresholds and eligibility formulas rather than a holistic review. This approach reflects a mission optimized for serving large numbers of California students. Many CSU programs are excellent, and some (like Cal Poly's engineering programs) are extremely competitive. But the system as a whole is structured to be **more accessible than the UCs**.

California Community Colleges

This is the **foundation** of the entire system, and people often misunderstand it. California's community colleges are not just fallback options; they are a core part of how the state provides educational opportunity.

Community colleges are **open admission**, meaning anyone can enroll regardless of high school grades. They serve students who need to save money or were not ready to attend a four-year university right after high school. They also serve working students and those who want to explore different fields before committing to a major.

Here is the part people often miss: California has built official **transfer pathways** from community colleges right into the UC and CSU campuses. For many students, this is a **strategic advantage**. Complete two years at a community college, then transfer into a UC as a junior. Transfer admission rates are often significantly higher than freshman admission rates, and you save a lot of money in the process. This is not a backdoor or a loophole; this is how the system was designed to work.

Private Universities: A Different Game

While California's public system dominates the conversation because of sheer scale, the Golden State is also home to some of the most selective private universities in the world. These schools operate under completely **different rules**. Stanford University and the California Institute of Technology (Caltech) are the most obvious examples. These are not just excellent schools; they are elite institutions that compete with Harvard, MIT, and Princeton for the best students and faculty worldwide.

> **Stanford rejects 96% of its applicants**
> Stanford's acceptance rate hovers around 3-4 percent. That means roughly 96 to 97 out of every 100 applicants are denied. Caltech is similar.

These numbers are not inflated by mass applications from unqualified students. The applicant pools are self-selecting. Most students who apply to Stanford or Caltech are already exceptional by conventional measures.

What makes these schools different from the UCs? Everything.

Private schools have **no public mission**. As private institutions, Stanford and Caltech do not owe California residents any preference. They can admit whoever they want from wherever they want. In practice, they draw students from every state and dozens of countries, building classes based entirely on institutional priorities rather than legislative mandates.

Private universities often have enormous resources. Stanford's **endowment** exceeds $30 billion. Caltech's endowment is smaller but still substantial, and the school operates at an incredibly high level of research funding per capita. These resources allow them to offer generous financial aid, attract top faculty, and maintain some of the lowest student-to-faculty ratios in the country. Money creates options that public universities, dependent on state budgets and tuition, simply do not have.

Private schools can also be **smaller** than public ones. Caltech enrolls fewer than 1,000 undergraduates and Stanford around 7,000. Compare that to UCLA, which has more than 30,000 undergraduates. Small enrollment means these schools can (and must) be incredibly selective. They are not trying to serve the many. They are trying to cultivate the few.

Private schools are also not required to be transparent about how they make admissions decisions. The University of California publishes detailed information about how they evaluate applicants, allowing applicants to understand their admissions criteria. Private universities are under no such obligation. Their admissions decisions are essentially **black boxes.** They can prioritize legacies, recruited athletes, children of major donors, or any other institutional interest without public accountability.

Just recently, Stanford University demonstrated this independence. In 2025, California passed a law banning legacy admissions at schools that receive state funding. Rather than comply, Stanford withdrew from the state-funded Cal Grant program entirely. The university now covers about $4 million in state aid with its own money so it can continue considering legacy and donor connections. Private schools can simply **opt out of public requirements** when those requirements conflict with their priorities.

Beyond Stanford and Caltech, California has several other selective private schools that operate in this same space. The University of Southern California (**USC**) has grown increasingly competitive, with acceptance rates now in the single digits. The **Claremont Colleges** (Pomona, Claremont McKenna, Harvey Mudd, Scripps, Pitzer) are small liberal arts colleges with strong reputations and selective admissions. Occidental College, the University of San Diego, Santa Clara University, and Pepperdine all have their own niches and draw national applicant pools.

The private universities also shift how families think about cost. Because schools like Stanford have massive endowments, they can offer generous **need-based financial aid** that sometimes makes them cheaper than public universities. A student who qualifies for maximum aid at Stanford might pay less than they would at UCLA, even though Stanford's sticker price is much higher

Private colleges have their own rules
They follow different rules, serve different missions, and make admissions decisions based on different criteria.

Getting into Stanford is not comparable to getting into UC Berkeley, even though both are extremely selective. The comparison is like saying climbing Everest and climbing Denali are the same because both are hard. The difficulty is real, but the nature of the challenge is different.

Why Admissions Outcomes Feel Unpredictable

When we put all this together, we start to understand why California admissions outcomes often feel frustrating or confusing. Application numbers keep rising. Every year, more students apply to California colleges, and the trend shows no signs of stopping. UCLA received around 80,000 applications a decade ago. Now that number exceeds 177,000. UC Berkeley, UC San Diego, and other campuses have seen similar growth. More applications mean **more competition** for the same number of seats. Even if you are as qualified as someone who got in five years ago, your odds are worse simply because you are competing against a lot more people.

Acceptance rates do not reflect the quality of applications. When a school rejects more than 90 percent of applicants, it does not mean these applicants were unqualified. It basically means there were ten qualified applicants for every available seat, and the university had to turn away thousands of students who could have succeeded there.

In addition, your **major matters** enormously. Applying as a computer science major at a UC is vastly more competitive than applying as a humanities major, even at the same campus. Some programs receive five times as many applicants as others. Engineering, computer science, biology, business economics, and similar fields face brutal competition because so many students want them. Less popular majors have far better odds, not because standards are lower, but simply because fewer people apply.

Being qualified may not be enough. You can be an objectively strong student and still face denials. Not because you are lacking in any way but because demand exceeds supply by enormous margins. A 4.0 GPA was never a guarantee to get in. Now, with application numbers climbing every year, even exceptional students face uncertain outcomes.

A few public schools act like highly selective private schools. UCLA and UC Berkeley are public universities, but their selectivity now rivals elite private institutions. They still have public missions (prioritizing California residents, for example), but their admissions outcomes look like those of schools that do not have those obligations. UC campuses were not designed to be this selective. The selectivity is a consequence of **demand overwhelming capacity**, not a goal the system set out to achieve.

What This Means for You

Understanding this changing landscape is the first step to navigating it successfully. California admissions is not about proving you are 'worthy'. You need to understand a complex, capacity-limited system that operates at a global scale. I believe in the **power of knowledge**. When you understand how California's college systems work, why they make the decisions they make, and what constraints they are operating under, you can build smarter strategies.

You can make informed choices about where to apply, what majors to consider, and how to present yourself effectively. This book will deliver exactly that: a playbook to understanding California college admissions from the ground up.

Shifting Your Mindset

Context matters more than comparisons. Do not compare California admissions to other states. This is genuinely a different landscape. And do not compare your outcome to someone else's. You do not know their full application details, essays, and personal background. Comparison is the thief of joy. In life and in college admissions.

Strategic planning is essential. Understanding the three-tier system, major impaction, transfer pathways, finances, and how colleges evaluate applications will help you build a smarter college list and a stronger application.

There are many paths forward. California's public system was intentionally designed with multiple entry points. Starting at a community college, attending a CSU, or choosing a less-impacted major are all legitimate strategies.

Now that we have a broad view of California's higher education landscape, the real work begins. Knowledge is power, and the chapters ahead are designed to give you plenty of both. You start by building your **college strategy** before you ever touch an application: constructing a balanced college list, thinking carefully about your major, and understanding what strong applications actually look like from the inside.

From there, we go **deep into each system**. The UC and CSU chapters walk you through how admissions works at each, how to apply correctly, and how to avoid the mistakes that trip up even strong applicants. Keep them handy as a reference before and while you fill out your applications. The community college chapters lay out why starting at a CCC and transferring is, for many students, the smartest path to a four-year degree. After looking at California's public schools, we will discuss the great variety of private institutions.

The final chapter covers **financial aid** and **choosing the school that works best for you**. Getting in is not the goal. The goal is finding a college and major that fits your interests and situation, where you can build the foundation for a career that is both successful and meaningful. That is what this book is about.

Application Strategy

2 | Building a Balanced College List

From Exploration to Shortlist

'Where are you applying?' is a question high school students hear everywhere. At family dinners, school events, even from strangers at the grocery store. Meanwhile, your mailbox fills with glossy brochures, and college emails swamp your inbox. But you are not even sure where to start. There are over 4,000 colleges in the United States. California alone has more than 400.

How do you narrow that down to a manageable list of schools to apply to? I like to think of this process like a **funnel**. You will start with broad exploration and gradually narrow your options based on what matters most to you. Success comes from finding colleges that fit you, not chasing the highest-ranked names. This chapter walks you through a **systematic approach** to building a balanced college list. We will cover how to define what 'best fit' means for your family, use research tools effectively, categorize schools by admission probability, and verify affordability before you even apply.

What Does 'Best Fit' Mean?

Before going down the rabbit hole of researching colleges, you need to understand what you are looking for. Finding the right fit is a three-part evaluation that should guide every decision you make.

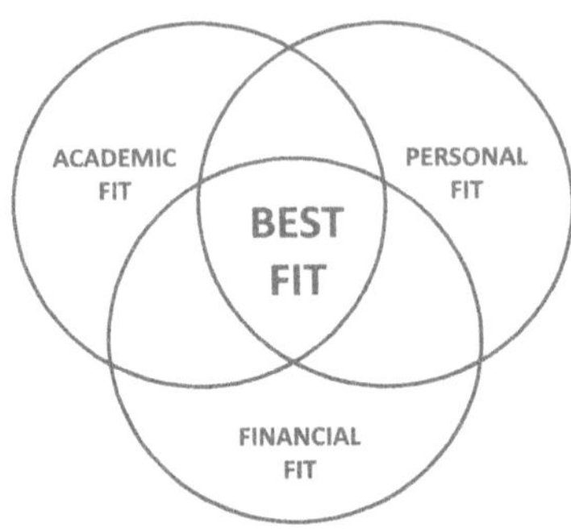

First, **academic fit** means finding schools where you can excel academically and pursue your interests. Does the school offer your intended major? If you are undecided, does it offer multiple major options you are considering? Does the academic rigor match your preparation level? Will class sizes suit your learning style? Are there research or internship opportunities? Can you explore or change majors if needed? A school might have a great computer science program, but if it is impossible to transfer into it, it is not a good fit if you are entering undecided.

Social fit encompasses the overall campus environment and culture. Consider campus size. Do you want to know most people in your major, or prefer the anonymity of a large university? Think about location and setting. Would you thrive on an urban campus, in a college town, or in a rural setting with a defined campus bubble? Student culture, housing options, residential life, extracurricular activities, and the general vibe all matter. You will spend four years in this place. The academics might be stellar, but if you are miserable outside the classroom, it is not a good fit for you.

Last but not least, there is **financial fit**. This is not negotiable. A school is not a good fit if your family cannot afford it without taking on crushing debt. Consider the total cost of attendance: tuition, fees, room, board, books, transportation, and personal expenses. Factor in the financial aid package you are likely to receive. Will you need to chase merit aid to afford a four-year degree?

Discuss your budget early
Research financial fit before you apply. Even if it is uncomfortable, discuss your family's college budget early in the process.

Waiting until decision time to have an honest conversation about money can lead to heartbreak that could have been avoided. If a college is exciting but unaffordable, it is not a good fit for you. If it is affordable but you would be miserable there, it is also not a good fit.

A strong but balanced college list includes schools where **all three fit points overlap**. Understanding these three dimensions helps you ask better questions. Instead of asking 'Is this school good?' you can ask 'Is this the kind of place where I would succeed academically, socially, and financially?'

The Funnel: From Hundreds to a Handful

I like to think of college list building as a funnel. You **start broad** and **gradually narrow down** based on what matters most. This is not a weekend project; it is a process that typically unfolds over several months, often beginning in sophomore or junior year and continuing into senior year.

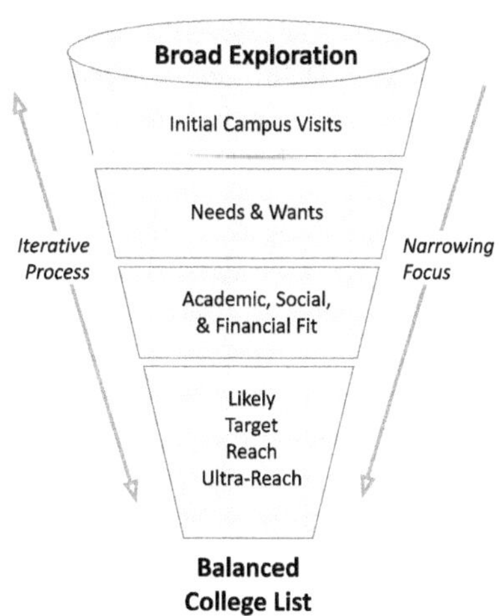

At the top of the funnel is **broad exploration**. This is where you cast a wide net and explore different types of institutions without immediately ruling anything out. You are gathering information, either online or with a campus visit. Based on this, you reflect on what is important to you and build a list of what a college must have (**your needs**) and which criteria are nice to have (**your wants**).

In the middle stage, you start **researching and sorting schools** more carefully. You compare each college to your needs and wants, use tools like the Common Data Set and Net Price Calculators, and check admission stats. Then, you sort the colleges into different **categories** based on your chances of admission. By removing schools that do not meet your criteria, you narrow your list to a realistic number. This is usually an **iterative process**, with colleges added or removed as you learn more.

The result of this process is your **balanced college list**. The schools all meet your academic, social, and financial criteria, where you have a reasonable chance at admission, and where you would genuinely be happy to attend. Let us look at each phase in more detail.

Exploration Phase

Many students begin their college search by looking at **rankings.** U.S. News, Forbes, Money, Princeton Review, Niche… Rankings are everywhere. They can give you a starting point for schools to research and can introduce you to colleges you had not heard of. However, rankings cannot tell you where *you* will thrive. That is why they should never be the primary driver of your college list. Let us have a closer look at how college rankings work.

Different ranking systems use **different criteria**, which means a school can be #15 on one list and #85 on another. For example, the Forbes ranking uses factors like alumni salary, debt levels, graduation rates, and counts of notable alumni. Money Magazine emphasizes economic mobility, how effectively colleges serve lower-income students, and how quickly graduates earn more than they paid for their degrees. And U.S. News includes reputation surveys, basically asking university presidents and admissions deans to rate the academic quality of peer institutions.

Let us think about that for a moment. Some college rankings reflect what university administrators think about their competition! Would you consider a soda ranking based on what Coca-Cola® thinks about Pepsi®? Probably not so much...

Which ranking is right?
Rankings measure what their creators prioritize. Your goal is to find colleges that fit you and your individual circumstances, not someone else's.

It is okay to use rankings as **one data point** in your early research. If you see a highly ranked school that interests you, add it to your list to investigate further. But make sure to also look beyond the top-ranked names.

Early Campus Visits

Rankings can help you discover options, but they cannot tell you what matters to you personally. To find that out, you should **visit two or three** nearby **colleges**, even if you are not seriously considering them. The goal is to experience different campus environments and figure out what feels right. Walk around when school is in session, if possible. Sit in the student union. Check out the dining halls and even the dorms if you can. Talk to current students.

Does the campus feel too big? Too small? Do you like being steps away from city life, or does a traditional college town appeal to you? Can you see yourself walking these paths for four years? Do the students look happy? What clubs are available? These visits help you develop your **personal criteria** for what matters most to you. They are not about deciding where to apply; your first campus visits are about learning what is important to you.

Defining Your Needs and Wants

After visiting a few campuses and doing initial online research, sit down and create two lists. The first list contains your **needs,** the factors that are non-negotiable. These might include things like staying within a few hours of home, having your intended major, staying within budget, or campus safety. If a school does not meet your needs, it is out.

On your second list, write down the aspects of college life that you consider nice to have. These **wants** are preferences that would enhance your experience but are not deal-breakers. Perhaps you would prefer a school with Greek life, or you would love a campus with strong study-abroad programs. Wants can help you choose between similar schools, but they should not eliminate otherwise strong options.

This framework keeps you grounded. When you are looking at that highly ranked school with the beautiful campus, you can check it against your criteria. Does it have your major? Is it affordable? If a school fails on the needs, it does not belong on your list, no matter how prestigious it seems. Your needs and wants are your filters as you move through the college funnel. As you build your longlist and begin evaluating schools more critically, you will **eliminate schools** that do **not meet your needs**. Combined with admission probability categories, these filters help you narrow hundreds of possibilities down to a manageable shortlist.

Research Phase: Data Sources

Once you have identified your needs and wants, you need the right tools to help you filter colleges. Several free resources provide comprehensive, reliable data directly from the colleges themselves. Others help you get a broad overview of what different colleges offer. Here are some of the most useful.

Useful research tools

College Navigator[1] offers searchable data on virtually every college in the U.S. You can filter by location, size, program offerings, and more. The data comes directly from the colleges' reports to the federal government.

College Scorecard[2] focuses on outcomes and affordability. It shows you average costs after financial aid, graduation rates, and median earnings of graduates by field of study. This is invaluable for understanding the return on investment for different schools and majors.

---

1 nces.ed.gov/collegenavigator

2 collegescorecard.ed.gov

BigFuture[3] lets you search and compare colleges, explore majors and careers, and estimate costs. It is particularly useful for getting a sense of whether your academic profile aligns with a school's admitted student statistics.

Niche[4] provides college rankings, student reviews, and detailed information about campus life, academics, and outcomes. While you should take individual student reviews with a grain of salt, Niche can help you get a sense of what current students value about their schools.

Printed guidebooks like the **Fiske Guide to Colleges** provide detailed profiles that go beyond just statistics.

If you are unsure about your future career, the **Interest and Career Finder**[5] and **Explore Careers tools**[6] help you explore careers based on your interests and see what education is required for different paths. The **Career Statistics**[7] gives detailed information about what different careers involve day-to-day, typical education requirements, and job outlook projections.

These tools help you narrow down potential career paths, which in turn helps you identify colleges offering the right programs. But your college experience will not happen in a spreadsheet. You need to understand campus culture, student life, and what it feels like to be at these schools. That is where qualitative research comes in.

Research Phase: Qualitative Context

Visiting every college on your early list is usually not realistic. Distance, time, and cost make in-person visits impossible for most families. Fortunately, **virtual resources** have improved dramatically. Almost all colleges now offer

---

[3] bigfuture.collegeboard.org

[4] niche.com

[5] mynextmove.org/

[6] careeronestop.org/ExploreCareers/explore-careers.aspx

[7] bls.gov/ooh/

virtual tours on their websites. Some provide full 360-degree experiences that let you 'walk' through campus. Many admission offices host virtual information sessions, major-specific panels, and online Q&A sessions throughout the year. Check college websites for their virtual event calendars.

YouTube is surprisingly useful. Current students post dorm tours, day-in-the-life videos, and honest reviews of their experiences. Search '[School Name] college tour' or '[School Name] student review' to see what comes up. Take individual opinions with a grain of salt, but recurring themes across multiple videos can give you a sense of campus culture. Look for those patterns, not individual student opinions.

Check out the school's official **social media accounts** and student-run accounts on Instagram, TikTok, and other platforms. What kind of content do they share? What do students seem excited about? Does the vibe appeal to you? Subreddits for specific colleges can also be eye-opening. Students ask questions and share experiences, both positive and negative. Just remember that people are more likely to post when they are upset about something, so do not let a few negative comments scare you off. However, do pay attention to **recurring themes** or concerns. The goal is not to get a complete picture from virtual resources. That is impossible. The goal is to gather enough information to decide whether the school belongs on your list and warrants further investigation.

Using AI

Artificial intelligence (AI) tools like ChatGPT, Claude, and Copilot have become popular resources. These tools can be helpful at the very beginning of the college search, while you are still exploring options and trying to see what is out there.

> **Helpful early on**
> AI can help you widen your search before you start narrowing your list.

How helpful AI is depends largely on how you use it. Short, vague prompts usually lead to generic answers; **clear, detailed prompts** work much better.

If you decide to use AI as a brainstorming partner, start by sharing the basics of your **academic profile**. Include your GPA, your classes, and how rigorous your coursework has been. If you have test scores, include them, too.

Next, describe what you want to study. If you are undecided, list a few possible **majors** or fields you are considering. This helps AI avoid suggesting schools that do not offer strong programs or where switching majors later is difficult. Add your **needs and wants**, which you defined earlier. Sharing both helps AI understand what matters to you. It also helps to mention campuses you have visited or researched and explain what you liked or did not like about them. For example, saying that you liked the feel of a college-town campus but did not enjoy a dense urban campus gives AI a much clearer sense of your preferences than asking for a 'good fit.'

Good use of AI

AI can help you generate ideas and uncover schools worth researching further. But it is not meant to produce a final college list.

When I tested AI college list recommendations, the tools generated different lists based on the student's gender. They also misunderstood local admissions realities and got some of the facts wrong. For that reason, use AI only as a starting point for ideas and verify everything with reliable data sources.

Categorization Phase: Probability Buckets

Building a balanced list requires you to be realistic about your **admission chances**. If you only apply to schools where you face long odds, you may end up with very few or no acceptances at all. A list loaded with Ivies and ultra-competitive programs is not balanced. The 'balanced' part means categorizing schools based on your *individual* probability of admission. Creating a balanced list ensures you have genuine options come spring.

The Categories

You have probably heard people refer to colleges as **safety, target,** and **reach** schools. Instead of the term safety, I prefer 'likely schools' for two reasons.

First, nothing in college admissions is truly safe; the term is quite misleading. Second, safety implies you are settling for something less desirable. Yet every school on your list should be a place you would genuinely be **excited to attend**. If a school truly feels like settling, remove it from your list.

Likely schools are institutions where your academic profile places you at the top of previously admitted students. Your GPA and test scores (if used) are stronger than those of most students the school typically admits, typically above the **75th percentile**. For example, if your GPA is 4.0 and the school's 75th percentile GPA is 3.7, you are a strong candidate. While no school is guaranteed, you should feel confident about your chances if you submit a strong application.

Target schools are institutions where your **academic profile aligns** with that of admitted students, roughly between the 50th and 75th percentiles. You are academically competitive, and admission is possible, but not assured. If your GPA is 3.6 and the school's 50th percentile range is 3.5 to 3.7, you fall squarely in their target range. These schools usually form the core of your college list.

Reach schools are institutions where your academic profile falls below the 50th percentile. If your GPA is 3.3 and the school's average GPA is 3.5, you are below where most students are admitted. Admission is uncertain.

Ultra-reach schools are highly selective institutions (think Ivy League, UCLA, Stanford) that admit fewer than 20 percent of applicants. For everyone, regardless of their profile, admission is **highly uncertain**. Even students with perfect grades and test scores face long odds at these schools.

How to Categorize Schools

So, how can you tell if a school is a likely, target, or reach for you? We start with what we know. In their admissions process, many colleges consider not only academics but also qualitative factors like essays, letters of recommendation, and extracurricular activities. Those qualitative factors matter, but you cannot measure them or know how heavily they will count in admissions. However, what you do know is your GPA, your test scores (if considered), and the published ranges for each school's admitted students.

What are your likely-target-reach schools?
Likely, target, and reach categories are determined by comparing your GPA and test scores to a college's published admission statistics.

Begin by noting down your unweighted and weighted GPA and SAT or ACT scores, if you plan to submit them. Remember that UCs and CSUs are test-blind, ignoring SAT and ACT scores entirely. Both systems also recalculate your GPA using their own formulas (which we will cover later in more detail). For UC and CSU schools, use that recalculated GPA when categorizing, not your high school's GPA.

Next, let us briefly review how **percentiles** work. If 100 students are admitted to a college and you line them up by GPA from lowest to highest, each student occupies a position in that line. The student with the lowest GPA is the first student in line, the one with the second lowest GPA stands next to them, and so on. The 50th percentile is the student with the median GPA, standing right in the middle. And the student with the highest GPA is the 100th student in line. When a college reports that the middle 50th percentile of admitted students had GPAs between 3.5 and 3.7, half of all admitted students had GPAs in that range. One quarter (25 percent) had a GPA below 3.5, and one quarter (25 percent) had a GPA above 3.7. Using the same approach, you can also assess SAT and ACT scores.

Worked Example:
Comparing Your GPA With the Middle 50th Percentile

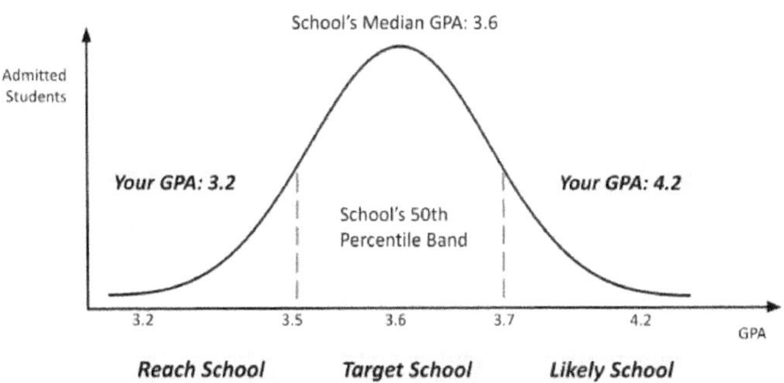

Here is how your placement in these percentile ranges determines your **school category**: In our example, when the school's median GPA is 3.6 and your GPA is 4.2, you can consider the school likely to admit you; your academic profile is stronger than those of their typical students. If your GPA is between 3.5 and 3.7, it is a target school. If your GPA falls below 3.5, this college is a reach school as your profile is less competitive than those of previously admitted students. Schools with admission rates below 20 percent are ultra-reaches for everyone, regardless of published GPA and test scores. Seeing how useful these admissions statistics are, the next question is obvious: where do we find this data?

Your Core List-Building Source

The Common Data Set (CDS) is the **most comprehensive source** of standardized college information. Almost all colleges publish a CDS or similar data. If you cannot find it on the college's website directly, search '[School Name] Common Data Set.' Some schools make you dig for it or call it by another name, but the data exists.

Section C in the CDS tells you the total number of first-year applicants, admitted students, enrolled students, admission rates, and which factors are considered in admission decisions. It also tells you the GPA and test score ranges of previously admitted students.

> **Determine the school category**
> To see where this school fits on your college list, compare your GPA and test scores with the middle 50th percentile range for admitted students.

Reading Section C helps you understand not just whether you are academically competitive, but also what the **school values**. If demonstrated interest is listed as important, you need to visit or engage with admission events. If the school considers rigor of secondary school record, your course selection matters in addition to your GPA. If character/personal qualities or essays are marked as important, you need to deliver top-notch essays. This document shows what a school values in admissions. This is powerful information, and we will discuss later how to use it strategically.

Naviance Scattergrams

If your high school uses a student information system like Naviance®, you have access to another valuable tool for predicting your admission chances: scattergrams. These graphs show at which colleges students from your high school have been admitted, denied, or waitlisted, plotted by GPA and test scores. Colleges admission teams **evaluate** you in the **context** of your high school. Not all high schools offer the same resources, so admission standards can vary between high schools. Naviance data is **often more useful** than national statistics because it shows actual outcomes for students at your high school.

A scattergram shows you the reality of **past outcomes**. You can see the lowest GPA and test score combination that got in a particular college and where denials cluster. Maybe everyone from your school with a 3.3 GPA got into a certain CSU, making it a strong likely school. Or maybe a private university waitlisted a lot of strong applicants from your high school, suggesting it is more of a reach than the CDS would indicate. Use Naviance scattergrams alongside the Common Data Set, not instead of it. Both data points together give you the best picture of where you stand.

Major-Specific Selectivity

But overall admit rates and Naviance data only go so far. College admissions is more nuanced. Check major-specific selectivity whenever that information is available. Engineering, computer science, nursing, and business programs are often significantly more competitive than a college's general admission rate. At many schools, **admission** is **by major** or by college within the university. UC Berkeley might have a 12 percent overall acceptance rate, but engineering and computer science are a lot more competitive. UCLA's nursing program has a one percent admit rate! Whenever you can find major-specific admission data, use that to categorize the school for your intended program, not just the campus-wide statistics.

When researching colleges, keep track whether this school **admits by major**. If you are applying to a competitive major, what are the program specific admission statistics? If you are admitted to the university but not your first-choice major, how difficult is it to transfer into that major later? Some schools make internal transfers nearly impossible.

This is especially important if you plan to apply as **undecided**. It is normal not to know what you want to major in, and many students change majors in college. Still, flexibility varies at the different schools. You might be accepted without a declared major, but it may be nearly impossible to switch into engineering later. For each school, take a note of how hard it is to switch majors, and what potential backup majors are available.

Understanding how majors affect admission is so important that we dedicate the next chapter to it. It will walk you through the strategic decisions around choosing a major, understanding capacity constraints, and evaluating whether you are prepared for your major. For now, just know that your choice of major is not separate from list building but a **key part** of it.

Setting Your Budget

Affordability should be part of your list building from the beginning, not something you address when acceptance letters arrive in the spring. Set a **realistic family budget** early. Have an honest conversation about what college will cost and what your family can realistically afford. This includes understanding how much your family can contribute from current income, how much you have saved for college and are willing to borrow, and what your Student Aid Index might be based on the FAFSA. This conversation might feel uncomfortable, but it is essential. Waiting until April of senior year to discover that your dream school is unaffordable creates unnecessary heartbreak.

How do you know what a college will cost you? Since many students get financial aid, it does not make sense to use a school's published sticker price. You need to understand how much you are likely to pay, based on your family's unique financial situation.

Run the Net Price Calculator

Every college is required by federal law to have a Net Price Calculator on its website. The NPC estimates what you will likely pay after grants and scholarships, based on your family's financial information.

The NPC is not perfect, but it gives you a realistic estimate of your likely cost of attendance. Never skip this step! The sticker price you see in college marketing materials is meaningless for many families. What matters is your net price after aid. A generous school with a $70,000 sticker price might cost your family $15,000 after financial aid, while a school with a $35,000 sticker price might cost you $30,000 if they offer little aid.

To use the NPC effectively, gather your family's household income and assets including savings and investments. Then visit each school's financial aid website and find the NPC. You will input your family's information, and the calculator will estimate your expected net price after typical aid.

Run the **NPC for every school** you are seriously considering (before you apply). This prevents heartbreak later when you discover that your 'dream' school is unaffordable. If the estimated net price is beyond your family's budget, you have two choices: remove the school from your list or keep it if there are other merit-based scholarships you might qualify for.

Remember that NPCs are **estimates, not guarantees**. Your actual financial aid package may vary somewhat from the estimate. However, for most families, the NPC provides a reasonably accurate picture of what you can expect to pay. If you have unusual financial circumstances (parents are divorced, family owns a business, significant assets), the NPC may be less accurate. In this case, you should reach out to the financial aid office.

Merit Aid Strategy: Going Down a Tier

Understanding the net price is the first step in understanding affordability. If you need significant merit aid to afford a four-year degree, your college list will look different. It will include **more likely schools** where you are a strong candidate, or schools that offer automatic merit aid based on GPA or test scores. Merit aid is awarded for academic or other achievements, not financial need, and is often used to attract strong applicants.

You are most likely to receive meaningful merit aid at private schools where you are in the **top tier** of their **applicant pool**. If your GPA or test scores place you at or above the 75th percentile of admitted students, you are a desirable applicant. Merit scholarships are a common way how schools entice strong students to enroll. Keep in mind that the most prestigious colleges usually do not offer merit aid at all. Instead, they provide generous need-based financial aid.

Middle Class Trap

Many middle-class families do not qualify for need-based aid yet cannot cashflow four years of college out-of-pocket. If this applies to you, schools with merit aid should play a large role in your college list.

Research merit aid early. Look at each school's website and the Common Data Set for scholarship information. In the **CDS**, merit aid appears in **Section H** (Financial Aid). This section shows how many first-year students receive non-need-based institutional aid and the average award amount. While it does not list individual scholarships or eligibility cutoffs, it helps you see whether a school offers merit aid broadly or only to a small group of students. Some merit aid is automatic if you meet certain criteria, while other awards require separate applications, essays, or interviews.

Other Considerations

Once you have a solid working list, a few additional strategic lenses can help you refine it further. These considerations do not replace your core criteria of fit, affordability, and admission probability, but they can strengthen your list and improve the quality of your final options.

In-state versus out-of-state

California residents have excellent in-state options, but if your family is comfortable with distance and cost, consider out-of-state schools as well. Remember that public universities in other states typically offer little to no financial aid to out-of-state students, and many prioritize in-state applicants. For example, the University of North Carolina at Chapel Hill is required by state law to enroll at least 82 percent North Carolina residents, making admission extremely **competitive for out-of-state** applicants. Keeping a mix of in-state and out-of-state schools (and their limitations) in mind can be an additional factor when building your list.

WUE schools

The Western Undergraduate Exchange (WUE) program allows California residents to attend participating colleges in other Western states at 150 percent of that state's resident tuition, rather than full out-of-state tuition. This can help make out-of-state public universities more affordable than paying the nonresident tuition. In Chapter 17, we take a closer look at WUE schools and the financial implications for your family.

Public versus private

As discussed, public and private colleges have different pricing structures and financial aid approaches. Public universities have lower sticker prices for in-state students. Private schools often have higher total costs but may offer more generous need-based aid to qualifying families. Run the net price calculators for both types of schools to compare your real cost.

Assembling Your Final List

At this point, you have done something many students rush or even skip. You took the time to explore colleges, define your needs and wants, check your chances of admission, and think seriously about affordability. That effort is not busywork. It is one of the **most important steps** in the entire college process.

Why this research is worth while

Your college list quietly determines your options later. You cannot attend a school you did not apply to, and you will not apply to schools that never made your list. But your college list is only as good as the research and knowledge behind it.

Remember that your college list is not carved in stone. It is work in progress, and it is normal for it to change over time. Colleges may be added, removed, and sometimes re-added as you learn more, visit campuses, run the NPC, or rethink your priorities. That **back-and-forth** is part of the process. So, pause and ask yourself: does your list give you real options you would be happy with? If not, this is the moment to fix it. The time you spend refining your college list is time well spent.

> **How many schools?**
> A balanced list typically includes around **12 to 15 schools** distributed across the probability spectrum.

Some students apply to fewer, especially if they have strong likely options or are not pursuing highly competitive majors. A common structure for a longer list looks like this: about **three to four likely** schools where admission is probable, **five to six target** schools where you are competitive, **three to four reach** schools where admission is uncertain but possible, and **one or two ultra-reach** schools if you are genuinely interested.

These numbers are guidelines, not rules. If your grades and course rigor place you above the 75th percentile at many schools, your list may lean more heavily toward targets. If you are applying to impacted majors like engineering, computer science, or nursing, you will need more likely schools to ensure real options in the spring.

Application Logistics and Workload

Finally, we need to consider logistics and application workload. Each application takes time and energy. Essays, supplements, portfolios, and interviews add up quickly. Your **list** should be **manageable** enough so that you can submit strong, thoughtful applications to every school. Fewer well-prepared applications often lead to better outcomes than a long list rushed at the last minute.

Most families count multiple CSU campuses as one application since they all use the same portal. The same applies to the nine UC campuses, which share one application. Even so, each school should earn its place on your list based on fit, affordability, and realistic admission chances (not just because it is easy to apply).

Application deadlines are also part of this logistical reality and should factor into how you build your college list. Ideally, your list includes schools with a range of deadlines so that your work is spread out over time instead of piling up all at once. The application calendar breaks the process into natural phases.

Working in chunks

Work on Early Decision/Action applications first. UC and CSU applications are due by November 30, and private schools with Regular Decision in January.

Working in manageable chunks keeps your focus narrow and your work quality high. Submitting a few applications early can also **reduce stress** and help you improve later applications as you gain experience. Earlier deadlines can provide peace of mind as well. Locking in one or two options early can take pressure off the rest of the season and give you more confidence moving forward.

Putting It All Together

A balanced college list is not just a numbers exercise. It is the result of layering multiple filters on top of each other and checking whether the final group of schools still makes sense as a whole. Start by looking only at schools that meet your **needs**. If a college does not meet your academic, social, or financial needs, it does not belong on your list, no matter how prestigious it is. This step alone often removes schools that students feel emotionally attached to but realistically should not apply to.

Next, within the schools that meet your needs, compare how well they match your **wants**. This is where your preferences help you decide between similar options. You might keep two target schools with similar admission chances but drop the one whose campus environment or location does not feel right. At this stage, you are shaping a list that reflects you, not just your statistics.

Then step back and check your **admission probability** for each school and across the entire list. A balanced college list includes schools where admission is likely, some targets, and a few stretches where admission is uncertain. A list filled mostly with reach schools creates both stress and risk. A list filled only with a few likely schools can limit choice and excitement. You are aiming for options that will work for you.

Now check **affordability** across the list, not just school by school in isolation. Ask yourself whether you could realistically attend all the schools on your list if admitted. If your list includes only one affordable option, it is not balanced, even if the admission categories look right on paper. You want multiple schools that work financially, not just one fallback.

Finally, check the **workload.** A balanced college list also needs a balanced calendar. If you use up all your energy in an early application chunk, the later applications may suffer, and your carefully balanced college list may become unbalanced. Your winter applications deserve the same energy and care as the ones you submit in fall.

By the end of this process, your college list should feel both **realistic and exciting**. You should be able to picture yourself at all these colleges. Keep in mind that building your list is just the beginning. The schools you choose and the majors you select work together to determine your real admission chances. In the next chapter, we will examine how to strategically choose a major.

3 | Strategically Choosing a Major

Impaction, Preparedness, and Reading the System

On paper, choosing a major seems like a straightforward exercise in self-discovery. What do you like? What are you good at? What kind of problems do you want to solve? In college applications, your major sometimes serves as a gatekeeper. At many California colleges, applying to a highly competitive major means facing an additional hurdle. The same student, with the same profile, can be admitted or denied depending solely on which major they pick.

For example, let us assume that two students with (nearly) identical applications apply to the same UC campus. Same grades, same course rigor, similar activities, and both students share insightful essays. Student A applies to sociology. Student B applies to computer science. Student A gets admitted. Student B does not. **What separated them? Their major.**

In the previous chapter, we discussed how to build a balanced college list using probability categories: likely, target, reach, and ultra-reach schools. This chapter takes it one step further. We will examine how majors work structurally at different types of institutions, look at how you can evaluate whether you are prepared for your major, and how to test whether your backup plans will work. By the end, you will understand how to layer major strategy on top of your college list to create a plan that actually works.

What 'Impacted' Means

When a program becomes very popular, colleges respond by **limiting access**. You will see different labels, including impacted, capped, selective, high demand, or restricted majors. They all mean the same thing. The department has set a maximum number of students who can enter or declare that major.

This cap exists because the department cannot accommodate unlimited enrollment. The constraint might be limited faculty, lab space, clinical placements, advising capacity, course seats, or accreditation requirements. Access gets managed through competitive processes such as higher GPA requirements, separate application reviews, or point systems. Meeting minimum **eligibility does not guarantee admission**.

The CSU campuses use the term 'impaction' when too many eligible students apply for the seats and resources available. The UC often refers to 'selective' or 'capped' programs, but the reality remains the same.

Many colleges have very **different admit rates by major**. At UCLA, the overall acceptance rate runs approximately nine to ten percent. For their School of Nursing, the rate drops to only one percent, and for computer science, the rate is roughly three percent. At UC Berkeley, the overall rate hovers around eleven to twelve percent. Computer science drops to approximately two to four percent. At UC Irvine, where the overall acceptance rate is approximately 26 percent, the nursing program admits only one percent of applicants.

These gaps represent **different levels of selectivity** happening inside the same institution. When you categorize schools as likely, target, or reach, you should use major-specific data alongside campus-wide statistics. A school that looks like a target for your overall profile can quickly turn into a reach school once you factor in your intended major (and sometimes it may even become an ultra-reach!).

Pipeline vs. Foundation

Before you commit to a major, you need to understand what kind of major you are choosing. Not just what the name says, but what the major includes and actually does for your future career. Ask yourself whether a major functions as a pipeline or a foundation.

Pipeline majors connect directly to licensure, certification, or external approval. Nursing, certain engineering fields, architecture, and teaching fall into this category. These majors have fixed entry points, strict course sequences, and limited flexibility. If you want one of these careers, you need to choose a campus and major where that pipeline opens from the start. Switching into these majors later often is **restricted** or **impossible**. Pipeline majors do not allow for 'I will figure this out later.'

Foundation majors build skills that support **many future careers** rather than licensing you for a specific job. Medicine, law, policy, data science, consulting, and many technology roles fall into this category. Graduate schools and employers care much more about what you can do than what your major was called. Political science, history, and English all work for law school. Biology is a common major for medical school, but chemistry, biochemistry, neuroscience, public health, and even physics work, too, as long as you complete the prerequisite courses. Data science, Computer Science, and Applied Mathematics can all lead to careers in tech.

Reality Check

Before selecting a major, I recommend doing a quick reality check. Look at what you will be studying for four years. Most colleges publish recommended course plans, sample four-year schedules, or major roadmaps on their websites. These show the specific courses required to graduate in a particular major, often broken-down semester. This is one of the most valuable and **most overlooked research tools** available to you.

The major you imagine and the actual content sometimes look very different. A student interested in business might assume that the courses focus primarily on strategy, marketing, and leadership. Then they look at the **actual**

coursework and degree requirements. The first two years weigh heavily toward calculus, statistics, accounting, and economics. Many students are surprised by this.

Similarly, a student drawn to sociology might envision studying social movements and cultural trends. Then they discover that many sociology programs require statistics, research methods, and data analysis as core components. Again, this creates no problem if you know going in. Problems arrive when you show up unprepared or discover halfway through that the major differs from what you expected.

Looking at actual **degree requirements** helps you answer several important questions. Does this major require more math, science, or writing than I expected? Are there specific prerequisite sequences I need to start immediately as a first-year student? How much flexibility do I have to explore other interests or take electives outside the major? If I am not completely certain about this major, will the required courses still be useful if I switch to something related?

This step also reveals warning signs about **course availability** and **sequencing**. If a major requires you to take courses in a strict sequence (Course A before Course B before Course C), and those courses only get offered once per year, delayed entry into the major could mean delayed graduation. If many required courses stay restricted to declared majors, switching into the major later might prove difficult, even if the department allows switching in theory. Do this research before you apply, not after you get admitted. A title like 'Introduction to Data Science' could mean a programming-heavy course, a statistics-heavy course, or a conceptual overview. Read the description or syllabus to understand what the course actually entails.

This step takes time, but the investment pays off. You are committing four years, effort, and a significant amount of money. Spending an hour per school researching the content of your major is a small investment compared to discovering two years later that you chose the wrong program or were not prepared for the work.

Switching Majors

Before we discuss how to enter a major or switch between majors, let us review where majors live within a university. Most majors belong to a larger academic home: a college, department, or school. For example, Psychology often gets housed in the College of Letters & Science, and Engineering majors live in the School of Engineering. That academic home matters because switching majors may require you to switch colleges or schools. Within the **same college** or department, **switching** usually is **straightforward** because you stay inside the same administrative structure. For example, at UCLA, you do not need to petition for a major change within the College of Letters & Science. You simply work with departmental advising.

Across colleges, switching becomes **much harder** as you need approval from that college. You are no longer making a simple major change but are applying to transfer from one academic division to another. Switching often runs backwards.

Switching down from a capped major into a less restricted major, especially within the same college, usually works. **Switching up** into a capacity-constrained major or switching 'across' into an impacted school like Engineering or Business, tends to be much harder. For example, UC Berkeley's College of Engineering does not allow switching into the Electrical Engineering & Computer Science majors. But how do colleges admit their students? Most institutions use one (or more) of four basic entry models.

Four Ways to Enter

While policies vary, most institutions rely on four entry models. Think of these as four doors. The door you enter shapes your access to coursework, your ability to change direction, and the risks you take on after enrollment.

Direct Admission

In this model, you are admitted directly into a **declared major** within a larger college or school. For example, you might be admitted as a Sociology major within a College of Letters and Science, or as a Mechanical Engineering major within the College of Engineering. You arrive with a declared major and have immediate access to the required coursework. This pathway is common and straightforward.

Admission to a College, with Major Declaration Later

This pathway is designed to support **exploration**. Students are admitted to a broader academic unit or to the institution itself rather than to a specific major. Formal **major declaration** happens **later**, often after completing prerequisite coursework and typically by the end of the sophomore year.

Pre-Major Status

In this model, applicants are admitted with the intention of pursuing a specific major, but **without guaranteed entry** into that major. Students must complete defined coursework, often with minimum GPA requirements, before being allowed to declare the major. This model appears most often in high-demand or professionally licensed programs, such as nursing or certain STEM fields. However, this model is **risky**.

Pre-major risks
If a student does not meet the advancement criteria, they may be required to choose a different major or leave the institution.

Because of this, pre-major pathways require an honest **backup plan.** Ask yourself in advance what major you would pursue if you do not make it into your original major. If there is no acceptable alternative, pre-major status may represent a much higher-risk option than it appears on the surface.

Undeclared

Undeclared status means being admitted **without a declared major**. This pathway can be a smart choice when you are genuinely exploring multiple uncapped majors within the same college. For example, a student choosing between Sociology, Political Science, and Economics within the College of Letters & Science may be able to explore different courses before settling on one specific major. Undeclared becomes **risky** when a student's likely majors are capacity-constrained, require direct admission, or restrict access to prerequisite courses. It also is risky when majors require a fixed sequence in the first year. In those cases, delayed entry can make it difficult or impossible to stay on track for a four-year graduation.

These four pathways are **not interchangeable.** A student admitted directly to Sociology in Letters & Science is not in the same position as a student admitted to the same college as undeclared, hoping to become an engineer. The entry pathway determines what doors remain open once you start your classes. When researching colleges, verify what admission model they use.

Campus-Specific Examples

To understand how major choice works in practice, it helps to look at a few concrete examples.

UC Example #1: Proposed Major at UC Santa Cruz

At UC Santa Cruz, most first-year students arrive with a **proposed major.** Students typically declare their major after completing qualification requirements, usually in their sixth academic quarter. For many students, this structure allows real exploration during the first two years.

But that flexibility has **limits.** UCSC warns that many students applying to Computer Science are admitted with their alternate majors as proposed major. These students cannot later switch into CS. In other words, exploration exists, but the system does not distribute opportunities evenly across all majors. Some doors remain open, and others close permanently once an admissions decision is made.

UC Example #2: CS at UC San Diego

At UC San Diego, Computer Science operates as a **capped major** with a fixed limit on how many students may declare the major. Some applicants get admitted directly into CS as incoming freshmen, others are admitted with their alternate major. Enrolled students who later want to change into Computer Science must go through a **separate, competitive process.**

All major changes are reviewed using a point system. Students can earn up to four points total: one point for achieving a 3.0 GPA or higher in screening courses, one point for California residency, one point for Pell Grant eligibility, and one point for first-generation college student status. Students with the highest point totals get selected until all available spaces are filled. Ties get broken through random selection. UC San Diego is very transparent about the limitations of switching into CS.

UC Example #3: Direct Admit at UC Berkeley

At UC Berkeley (and UCLA), admissions decisions are based solely on the first-choice major listed on the UC application. Alternate majors receive no consideration during the admissions review (read: do not your waste time researching and listing an alternate major at either campus!).

At Berkeley, this limitation is especially consequential for Engineering. The **College of Engineering** does not accept change-of-college applications for Electrical Engineering & Computer Science and related joint majors. This means students not admitted directly have **no pathway to switch** in later.

Berkeley's **Haas School of Business** is another example. All Haas undergraduate Business programs are direct admit. Applicants must list Haas as their first-choice major to be considered. These policies significantly limit the usefulness of undeclared, pre-major, or delayed-declaration pathways for majors such as Engineering, Computer Science, Nursing, and Business across the UC system. In these fields, access after enrollment may be competitive or unavailable, even for strong students.

CSU Example: Impaction Point System at San José State University

At San José State University (SJSU), **impaction** is a central part of how the campus manages enrollment. SJSU is one of several CSUs which are campus-wide impacted, meaning the entire campus faces higher admission standards than minimum CSU eligibility requirements. Located in the heart of Silicon Valley, SJSU faces huge demand for programs such as Computer Science, Software Engineering, and many Engineering disciplines.

Admission depends not just on meeting the minimum eligibility requirements, but on how **applicants rank relative** to one another within each major. For freshman applicants, the SJSU-specific impaction point system determines eligibility. Applicants get points for: A-G coursework GPA (calculated as 800 × your A-G GPA), local admission area status for Santa Clara County high schools (200 points), application fee waiver eligibility (40 points), military status (40 points), and first-generation college status (40 points).

Here is how the calculation works. Consider a student with a 3.75 A-G GPA who graduates from a local high school, qualifies for the fee waiver, and is first-generation.

Example: Impaction point calculation
3,000 points (800 * 3.75 GPA) + 200 points (local) + 40 points (fee waiver) + 40 points (first-gen) = 3,280 points.

Whether 3,280 points proves sufficient depends on the major and the year. SJSU publishes impaction results after each admission cycle, indicating the minimum point totals required for each major. These numbers serve as **guidance** for applicants in the following year.

For **Engineering programs**, SJSU adds an additional factor: their math coursework GPA (calculated as 400 × math GPA). This places additional weight on math preparation and can push engineering applicants above typical cutoffs even with the same overall GPA as applicants to other majors.

Let us consider three students, each one with a 3.75 A-G GPA and a 3.8 math GPA. All students meet the baseline CSU eligibility index (2,000 points). Student A scores 3,000 and by far exceeds the Sociology threshold. Student B scores 3,280 including all bonus points but falls short of the CS threshold. Student C benefits from the additional math points and scores exactly the needed 4,800 points for Mechanical Engineering. The three candidates have the same academic profile, but different admission outcomes based on their chosen major!

Impaction Points at SJSU

	Student A	Student B	Student C
Major	**Sociology**	**Computer Science**	**Mech. Engineering**
A-G GPA (points)	3.75 (3.75 x 800 = 3,000)	3.75 (3.75 x 800 = 3,000)	3.75 (3.75 x 800 = 3,000)
Math GPA (points)	3.8	3.8	3.8 (3.8 x 400 = 1,520)
Local high school	No	Yes (+ 200)	Yes (+ 200)
Fee waiver	No	Yes (+ 40)	Yes (+ 40)
First-generation	No	Yes (+ 40)	Yes (+ 40)
Impaction Points	3,000	3,280	4,800
Typical major cutoff	~ 2,000	~3,440	~ 4,800
Eligible?	**Yes**	**No**	**Yes**

SJSU advises students to **apply directly to the major** they intend to complete. Post-admission changes depend on space availability and departmental approval. In practice, students who do not get admitted directly into impacted majors often find that switching later becomes extremely difficult, even with strong academic performance.

Private College Example #1: Institutional Admission at Stanford

Stanford University operates using yet another model. Students apply to Stanford as a university, not to a specific major or school. All students get admitted **without a declared major**. They typically spend their first year exploring before declaring a major during or after their sophomore year.

This applies even to Engineering. Students do not apply to Stanford Engineering as high school seniors. They do not face a second competitive admissions process to enter Engineering majors after enrollment. Instead, major choice gets handled through advising, course planning, and sequencing, not through capacity-based screening at the point of declaration.

Private College Example #2: Open Declaration at Pomona

At Pomona College, students get admitted to the college rather than to a specific major. Pomona encourages broad exploration. Students typically declare a major near the end of their sophomore year, and departments plan to accommodate student interest. Pomona is a small liberal arts college that funds and runs its departments differently than public universities. Departments focus on teaching undergraduates, not managing huge numbers of students. If you discover a new academic interest after you arrive, you can usually pursue it. You just need to finish the requirements before you graduate. This model offers **genuine flexibility**. Students often assume that the freedom they see at private colleges will also exist at UC or CSU campuses. As we have seen that assumption may not always be correct.

When Undeclared Makes Sense

Many students worry that they must apply with a specific major, even if they are not sure about what they are truly interested in. Applying undeclared works well in specific situations. You might be genuinely exploring between multiple majors that are **uncapped** and live in the same college. The campus should explicitly support exploration and keep **access open** to your potential majors. Having a **strong academic basis** across multiple subject areas helps. Look for majors that allow flexible entry without fixed timelines or cohort requirements.

On the other hand, applying undeclared becomes **risky** in several situations. First, when your likely majors face capacity constraints or require **direct admission.** Computer science, Engineering, Nursing, and Business typically fall into this category. Second, when **prerequisite courses** are restricted to students already declared in the major. You may not be getting the classes needed to graduate in time. Being undeclared is also risky when the new major requires you to complete a specific **sequence of courses** by a certain point to graduate in four years. Finally, undeclared does not work as a **procrastination** strategy. If you are using it to avoid making a decision, you are setting yourself up for problems later.

Are You Ready for the Major?

The goal of college admission **goes beyond getting in**. You want to graduate successfully, ideally in four years. How well you are academically prepared for college determines whether you can realistically do that. Being prepared means building the academic foundation during high school. You cannot address this in senior year when building your college list; preparation starts in ninth and tenth grade, when you choose your courses.

Colleges expect high school students to **challenge themselves** academically. Rigor matters, but performance matters, too. Taking courses that you can handle well beats chasing the hardest possible schedule if it means sacrificing your grades. Sustained engagement in **core academic subjects** is part of that balance. Continuing math, science, English, social studies, and world language through senior year demonstrates continuity and academic depth. When students stop practicing skills early, they often arrive at college rusty in ways that matter once coursework accelerates.

For students applying to UC and CSU campuses, this preparation sits **on top of the A-G** course requirements, which define minimum eligibility. We will discuss them in more detail later. Meeting A-G makes you admissible but does not guarantee you are prepared for (or admitted!) to a specific major.

For math-heavy majors (Engineering, Computer Science, Economics, Physical Sciences), being prepared usually means completing advanced high school math through at least Precalculus or **Calculus**, earning strong grades, and handling multi-step problem solving independently. Strong signals include success in honors or AP math courses, sitting for the AP Calculus exam (ideally earning a 4 or 5), and consistent performance across multiple years.

At UC San Diego, faculty recently raised concerns that a growing share of incoming students arrive **not mathematically prepared** for college-level coursework, even when their high school transcripts suggest otherwise. Internal analyses found that many first-year students struggle with foundational skills such as fractions, algebraic manipulation, and proportional reasoning.

High school course titles alone provide an unreliable signal of readiness. A student might earn strong grades in a high school course called 'Calculus' and still lack the understanding required to succeed in college math. Taking AP Calculus and **sitting for the AP exam** provides a more reliable self-check. The exam represents a standardized assessment aligned with college expectations. Performance on the AP exam, especially earning a score that places you into college Calculus, offers concrete evidence of readiness that high school grades alone cannot provide.

For lab-based sciences such as Biology, Chemistry, and Physics, preparation is built through both coursework and **hands-on scientific practice**. Strong readiness signals include taking science through junior and senior year, doing well in classes with regular lab reports, and joining activities where data analysis, troubleshooting, or experimentation played a real role.

Writing- and reading-intensive majors such as History, Political Science, Sociology, and Philosophy require a different kind of preparation. Students should show that they are comfortable with **heavy reading, analytical writing**, and **complex ideas**. This might come through advanced English or humanities courses, frequent essay assignments, independent reading of primary or scholarly sources, or activities such as debate, Model UN, or journalism.

Before selecting a major, **honestly assess** your level of preparation and compare it with the first-year expectations of the major itself. In competitive systems, being academically prepared can be the difference between graduating on time and falling behind. If you are reading this as a sophomore or junior and realize your preparation does not align with your intended major, you still have time to adjust your course selection. If you are reading this as a senior, use this lens to evaluate whether you are genuinely ready for the majors on your college list.

Picking a Less Competitive Major

At this point, some students wonder: what if I choose a less competitive major to get into the campus I want, and then **switch** into my real target major **later**? This approach can work if, and only if, you are genuinely interested in the alternate major and would be willing to complete that major if switching turns out to be impossible. Some students know they want to attend a specific campus for reasons, such as location, cost, family connections, or career opportunities. Others dream of attending UC Berkeley or Stanford (or fill in the blank), regardless of the major. If the **campus** itself is a **key priority**, choosing a less competitive major can indeed improve your admission chances.

For example, a student interested in studying human behavior might apply to Sociology (often uncapped) instead of Psychology (very popular). A student interested in technology might apply to Data Science instead of Computer Science. If the less competitive major genuinely interests you, this can work. But applying to a less competitive major with the plan to **switch into a capped major** later is risky and fails far more often than it succeeds.

This also explains why you should carefully choose **alternate majors**. An alternate should never serve as a placeholder you hope to escape. The alternate should represent a major you would genuinely be willing to complete if you cannot switch. If a campus admits you only to your alternate major without the chance to switch, would you still seriously consider enrolling? If not, then your strategy depends entirely on a successful switch later. That represents exactly the kind of fragile plan this chapter warns against.

Bringing It All Together

Strategic major choice does not require predicting the rest of your life. You are reducing avoidable risk at the moment you apply. This chapter emphasizes two key points. First, picking a major represents a major decision (no pun intended). And second, information equals power.

Major choice affects not just what you study, but whether you get **admitted**, whether you can switch later, and whether you graduate on time without adding costly extra years. In California's public university systems, where majors are often highly competitive, understanding these dynamics becomes essential.

Information equals power. Successful college students usually have done their homework before they apply. They research policies, verify their academic preparation, and test their backup plans while building their college list, not after admission decisions arrive in the spring. The UC Freshman Admission by Discipline dashboard[8], campus-specific major admission data[9], Common Data Set statistics, departmental websites, and published degree requirements all contain the information you need. Students who use that **information strategically** end up with the best choices in the spring. In practice, strategically choosing a major means taking four specific steps as you finalize your college list.

Four steps for strategically choosing a major

First, research how each campus admits students to majors. Go back to your initial college list. For each school, answer these questions: How does this campus admit students to majors? Does my major face capacity constraints here? Does the major have supplemental admission criteria, GPA cutoffs, or competitive review processes? Details like 'Berkeley and UCLA review only the first-choice major' or 'Haas School of Business must be listed as the primary major' are important to know before applying.

Second, use available data to understand major-level selectivity. For UC campuses, check the interactive Freshman Admission by Discipline Dashboard to see how your intended academic area compares to the overall campus admit rate. If Engineering admits at 15 percent while the campus overall admits at 35 percent, that campus functions as a reach school for Engineering applicants. Layer this on top of the school categorization work you did earlier. A target school may need **re-categorization** as a reach

8 universityofcalifornia.edu/about-us/information-center/freshman-admission-discipline

9 admission.ucla.edu/apply/first-year/first-year-profile/2025/major (example for UCLA)

school once you factor in your intended major. For CSU campuses, check the Impaction Matrix[10] online.

Third, test your backup plans for realism. If you do not get admitted to your first-choice major, would switching later require a competitive review? Does the major sit in the same college, or would you need to cross into a capacity-limited school? If the answer depends on phrases like 'highly competitive' or 'space permitting,' treat that path as uncertain.

Fourth, match your preparation to the majors you are choosing. Review the preparation section earlier in this chapter. Can you place into the first required courses, or will remedial work delay your progress? If a major requires you to be on track by the end of freshman year, treat readiness as part of the decision, not something to figure out later.

When you do this work up front, results tend to look different in the spring. Instead of surprises, you end up with real choices. You can compare offers knowing not just where you got admitted, but what you study once you arrive. That makes the difference between a college list that looks balanced on paper and a plan that works out in real life.

Once you understand how major choice shapes your college list, the next question becomes: **how do you get admitted?** In the next chapter, we will examine how colleges evaluate applicants, breaking down the Three Pillars that form the foundation of every application: academics, extracurricular engagement, and personality traits.

---

[10] calstate.edu/attend/impaction-at-the-csu/Documents/ImpactedProgramsMatrix.pdf

4 | Three Pillars of a Strong Application

How Colleges Evaluate Applications

In the previous chapter, we examined how major choice shapes your college list and even influences whether you get admitted at all. Now we turn to a different question: once you have strategically built your college list, what makes a **strong application**?

When students talk about college admissions, they often reduce the process to a single question: 'Is my GPA good enough?' Or sometimes: 'Do my extracurriculars stand out?' In reality, most colleges do not evaluate applicants through a single lens. They use a layered system that weighs academic readiness, engagement outside the classroom, and personal traits together.

Holistic Review

Most colleges, particularly private ones, look at applications via **multiple dimensions**, not just through academic metrics. This process is referred to as holistic review. Admission teams evaluate academics, extracurriculars, and personality traits to understand who you are and what you might contribute to their campus.

There are several advantages of using a holistic review system. First, holistic review allows students to present a **more complete picture** of what they bring beyond GPA and test scores. It also recognizes that students do not all have access to the same resources and opportunities. And when colleges receive far more academically qualified applicants than they can admit, holistic review provides additional dimensions for evaluation.

The downside is opacity. Holistic review does not follow a published formula, which means the process can feel **unpredictable** or even random to families. Often decisions that seem unjustified reflect information you cannot see: what other applicants brought to the pool, what institutional needs shaped that admissions cycle, or how a reader interpreted your context differently than you hoped. And without a transparent rubric, there is no way to know for sure that every decision is based on merit alone.

Three Pillars

To make sense of holistic review, think of your application as resting on three foundations. Academics determine whether you clear the academic threshold. Extracurricular engagement shows how you use your time and take initiative. Personality and context explain who you are, what you value, and what shaped your path. **A strong application stands on all Three Pillars.** Weaknesses in one area does not automatically disqualify you, but neglecting an entire pillar often does.

Understanding how these Three Pillars work, and how colleges interpret the evidence within each one, allows you to make smarter decisions throughout high school, not just at the point of application. More importantly, it helps you build an application that allows you to put your best foot forward.

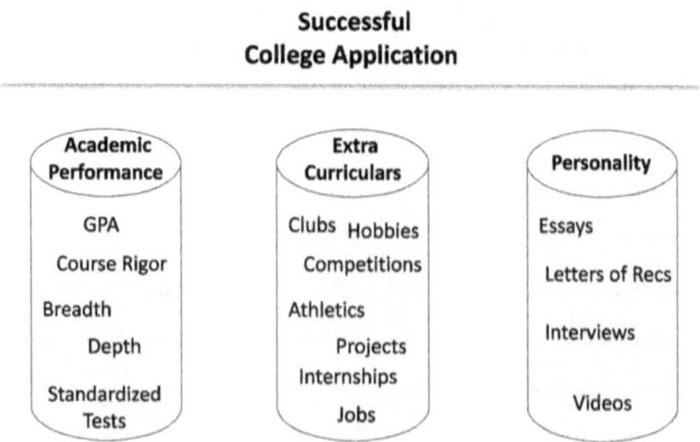

Pillar One: Academic Performance

Your academics form the foundation of your college application. Before admissions officers evaluate any other part, they usually determine whether a student is academically prepared to succeed in the classroom. This pillar functions as a **gatekeeper**. If you lack academic readiness, extracurriculars and personality traits rarely compensate. Colleges evaluate multiple academic signals together, interpreting them in the context of the opportunities available to you.

GPA: Balancing Challenge and Performance

Your high school GPA is the main academic building block but figuring out how to build the 'right' GPA is more nuanced than students often realize. Here is the fundamental tension: colleges want to see both **academic rigor** and **strong grades**. A transcript full of easy A's will not compete well, and a transcript full of challenging courses with mediocre grades raises questions about readiness. The sweet spot is challenging yourself academically while still performing well.

The right strategy depends on where you are applying and what you are trying to accomplish. For **highly selective colleges**, rigor and performance are not an either-or choice. You need **both**. These schools expect you to take the most challenging courses available and succeed in them.

For less selective colleges, especially if you are chasing merit scholarships, **protecting your GPA** becomes more important. Many merit scholarships have strict GPA cutoffs, and a 3.85 might qualify while a 3.75 might not. If you are chasing merit, take rigorous courses where you can handle them well, but do not sacrifice your GPA by overloading yourself with advanced classes you cannot manage successfully.

Academic rigor vs performance

The guiding principle is to take the highest level of rigor you can handle well.

Balancing rigor with performance requires you to be honest with yourself. If you struggled in Honors Chemistry, taking AP Chemistry might not be the smart move. If you excelled in AP Calculus AB, taking AP Calculus BC or a higher math makes sense. The goal is to push yourself without damaging your GPA.

Recalculating Your GPA

Many colleges do not simply accept the GPA on your transcript because high schools calculate GPA in wildly different ways. Some high schools give significant extra credit for honors and AP courses, while others do not add any weight at all. To account for this variety, colleges usually recalculate the high school GPA using their own formulas.

The **UC** and **CSU** are very **transparent** about how they recalculate GPA, and we will cover those formulas later. For private colleges, the process is less transparent. Given that uncertainty, the best strategy is to do the best you can and focus on performing well in core academic courses, especially those related to your intended major.

Unweighted vs. Weighted GPA

Colleges usually look at both unweighted and weighted GPA, even when only one appears on your application. Unweighted GPA (typically on a 4.0 scale) shows your raw performance across all courses. Weighted GPA accounts for the difficulty of your courses by giving extra points for honors, AP, IB, and other advanced coursework.

Admissions officers also do not just look at a single number. They look at **grade trends** over time, **consistency** across core subjects, and your performance in the most challenging courses you took. A strong upward trend is positive, as is a high plateau of continuously strong performance. Consistent performance across math, science, English, social studies, and world language is important. Taking advanced courses and doing well in them is key.

Accounting for Grading Differences

Colleges **compare** you to other students from **your high school,** which helps them account for differences in grading standards. Some high schools practice grade inflation, where A's are relatively common. Others maintain stricter grading standards, where even strong students rarely earn straight A's. By comparing applicants from the same high school, admissions officers can calibrate their expectations and evaluate you relative to the grading culture at your school.

This comparison also lets colleges assess how you **used the resources** available to you. Two students with identical GPAs may be evaluated very differently if one attended a school with extensive AP offerings while the other attended a school with limited resources. Admissions officers understand these differences and adjust their expectations accordingly.

Five Core Subjects

One of the simplest and most effective strategies is to continue taking courses in **all five core** academic areas through **all four years** of high school. That means taking math, science, English, social studies, and world language every year. And yes, this includes senior year.

Many students lighten their senior year load after college applications are submitted, dropping math or a language once they have met minimum requirements. This is sometimes referred to as **senioritis**. Colleges notice when students taper off academically, and it raises questions about motivation and readiness. Staying engaged in core academics through senior year signals that you take learning seriously, not just college admissions. It also keeps your skills sharp, which matters later in college when you need to perform at a higher level immediately.

Course Rigor, Depth, and Breadth

Course rigor is evaluated relative to what your school offers. Colleges expect you to **challenge yourself**, but they also understand that not every school provides the same opportunities. You are not penalized for lacking AP courses if your school does not offer them.

This is where the **school profile** becomes critical. Every high school sends a document called a school profile along with your transcript. This profile explains what courses the school offers, how grading works, what the student-to-counselor ratio is, what percentage of graduates attend four-year colleges, and other contextual information that helps admissions officers interpret your choices.

For example, a student at Palo Alto High School, which offers more than 20 AP courses, would be evaluated differently from a student at a small rural high school in the Central Valley with only three AP courses. If the Palo Alto student took only three AP courses when so many were available, admissions officers see underutilized opportunity. If the Central Valley student took three AP courses, that reads as maximizing available resources.

> **School profile**
> The school profile provides this context. It shows what colleges will consider when evaluating your application alongside your peers.

As part of rigor, colleges also look for depth and breadth. **Depth** refers to how far you go in a particular area. A student interested in science might take Biology, Chemistry, Physics, and then AP versions of all three. A student focused on humanities might progress from World History to AP U.S. History to AP Government and AP European History. Going deep in an area related to your intended major demonstrates serious preparation and sustained interest.

Academic **breadth** matters because colleges value exposure across multiple disciplines rather than early overspecialization. Even if you go deep in science, you still need strong preparation in English and social studies. If you concentrate in humanities, continuing math and science through senior year strengthens your application. Narrowing your focus too early can limit your competitiveness, especially at colleges that prioritize well-rounded intellectual development.

AP and IB Coursework

Both programs follow standardized curricula and assessments, which helps compare students across different high schools, states, and even countries.

The **AP program**, run by the College Board, offers individual college-level courses. Many students take AP courses primarily in junior and senior year, though some schools offer them earlier. There is no limit to how many AP courses you can take.

The **IB Diploma Program** is a two-year curriculum taken in grades eleven and twelve that includes six subjects, an extended essay, and a volunteering requirement. The IB is more structured than AP, with less flexibility in course selection but more emphasis on interdisciplinary thinking and research.

Most American high schools offer AP courses, but the number and variety of AP courses vary. Relatively few American high schools offer the IB Diploma Program, and even fewer offer both AP and IB, giving students a choice between the two. This means that for most students, the question is not 'AP or IB?' but rather 'How many AP courses should I take, and in which subjects?'. For the small number of students whose schools offer both programs, the practical considerations are straightforward. If you want to **maximize** your **weighted GPA**, AP is usually the better option. You can take more AP courses than the six courses allowed in the IB Diploma Program, which means more opportunities to earn weighted credit.

Most colleges do not prefer one program over the other. What matters is that you **challenge yourself** and **perform well**. Focus on core academic areas and subjects related to their intended major. For example, if you are interested in Engineering, consider taking AP Calculus, AP Physics, and AP Chemistry, or the IB equivalents in math and sciences. A student applying as a History major might take AP English Language, AP English Literature, AP U.S. History, and AP Government, or the IB Diploma with higher-level courses in language, literature, and history. Choosing advanced courses demonstrates both preparation and focus.

Taking the AP or IB exams has multiple benefits. Both programs increase your **weighted GPA**. During admissions, AP and IB exams provide external validation of what you learned in the course. High school grading standards vary widely. An A in the AP Calculus course at one school might represent very different mastery than at another school. AP and IB exams offer a **standardized benchmark** that helps admissions officers interpret your grades more accurately.

When you take an AP or IB course, colleges generally expect you to sit for the corresponding exam. **Taking the exam** signals follow-through and a willingness to be evaluated against a national standard. When students take AP courses but consistently skip the exams, admissions officers may wonder why. Strong exam scores confirm that your classroom grades reflect subject mastery. A score of 4 or 5 on an AP exam reinforces the credibility of an A in the course.

At many colleges, a score of 4 or 5 on an AP exam (or an IB score of 6 or 7) grants **credit** for the equivalent college course. This allows you to skip entry-level general education requirements. In practice, this can save you time and tuition. Beyond credit, AP and IB scores often determine **course placement**. A strong AP Calculus score might allow you to start in Multivariable Calculus rather than repeating material you have already mastered. Some institutions grant credit generously, whereas others are more restrictive (especially highly selective schools). Before you decide which AP or IB exams to take, check the credit and placement policies at all colleges you are considering.

Dual Enrollment

Dual enrollment (DE) allows students to take actual **college courses** while still in high school. These courses are offered by local community colleges as well as four-year universities. In California, dual enrollment has become increasingly common, and many high schools have formal partnerships with nearby community colleges.

When done thoughtfully, dual enrollment can demonstrate academic rigor, strengthen your **weighted GPA**, and provide transferable college credit that counts toward your future degree. Dual enrollment also helps students whose high schools have limited course offerings. A student at a small high school that offers only a few AP courses might use dual enrollment to access Calculus or college-level English.

Keep in mind that a single semester of a college course typically covers the same material as a full year of high school coursework. This means the pacing is faster and the workload is often heavier than what you experience in a regular high school class. Also, dual enrollment carries long-term consequences that many students are not aware of.

> **Dual enrollment**
> DE courses become part of your permanent college record.

When applying to graduate school, law or medical school, or any other professional program, you will be required to **submit transcripts** from every college you have ever attended. This includes dual enrollment courses you took in high school. A poor grade you earned at sixteen can resurface years later when you are applying to competitive graduate programs. This **permanence** makes dual enrollment fundamentally different from AP courses. If you struggle in an AP course, that grade appears on your high school transcript, but the course itself does not follow you later in college.

Another potential risk concerns **financials.** Federal financial aid is not available indefinitely. Programs such as Pell Grants and federal student loans are limited by academic progress rules. Generally, students can receive federal aid for up to 150 percent of the units required for their degree. For a typical 120-unit bachelor's degree, that means federal aid usually ends after about 180 attempted units. At many institutions, dual enrollment counts toward that total. Once you reach the credit limit, you may **no longer be eligible** for federal aid, even if you have not yet finished your degree.

Standardized Tests

Another way to evaluate a student's **academic readiness** is through standardized tests. The **SAT** and **ACT** are designed to measure academic skills closely tied to high school coursework: reading, writing, and math. They measure how well you can apply knowledge under time pressure and work accurately at speed. Colleges use test scores in several ways. Scores can support confidence in your academic readiness, help compare students across schools with very different grading standards, and identify academic strengths.

At the same time, standardized testing is one of the most confusing and **controversial** parts of college admissions. Policies have changed rapidly in recent years, and different colleges use test scores in very different ways. What worked for your older sibling or cousin might not apply to you. During the COVID-era disruptions, many colleges suspended testing requirements because access to official tests became difficult. Students could not reliably take SAT and ACT exams, so colleges stopped requiring them. Over time, many colleges extended **test-optional** policies due to concerns about equity and questions about whether scores add meaningful information. The UC and CSU went even further and adopted **test-blind** policies, meaning they do not consider SAT or ACT scores in their admissions decisions.

A comeback?

Strong SAT or ACT scores can strengthen your application at test-optional schools, and some top schools require test scores again.

Recently, Harvard, MIT, Yale, Brown, Stanford, and other highly selective schools announced that standardized test scores are **once again required**. They cite research showing that scores help identify students who will succeed academically. This trend will likely continue. Grade inflation has made it harder for admissions officers to distinguish between students with similar GPAs from different high schools.

At the same time, general concerns about **college readiness** have grown. For example, UC San Diego faculty recently raised alarms about incoming students arriving unprepared for college-level math, even when their high school transcripts suggested strong preparation. Standardized tests provide an external benchmark that can help validate (or question) what high school transcripts suggest.

Choosing between SAT and ACT

The good news is that you do not need to prepare for both the SAT and the ACT. A better strategy is to focus on the exam that is the better fit for you. If your school offers the PSAT/NMSQT, it is worth taking as it gives you early testing experience and may qualify you for National Merit recognition.

To decide between the two tests, take a full-length practice test for both the SAT and ACT. Then compare the results. In most cases, the 'better' test is the one on which you **perform more strongly**, though personal preference also matters. Some students are more comfortable with the SAT's structure, while others do better on the ACT. Once you identify the stronger fit, it usually makes more sense to prepare for that test rather than divide your effort across both.

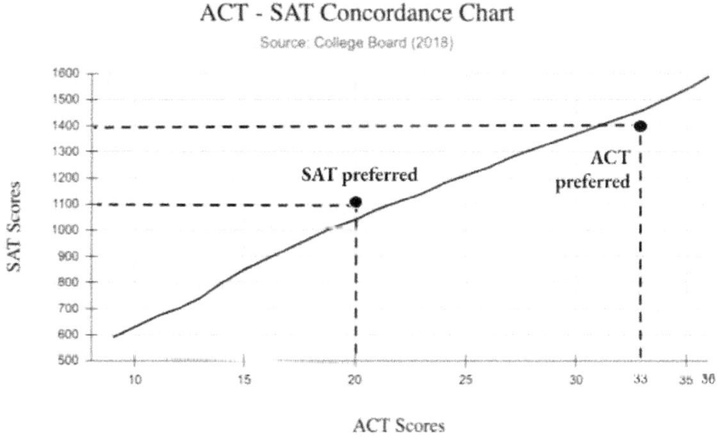

The **concordance chart**[11] can help you compare scores across the two exams. For example, an ACT score of 20 is comparable to an SAT score of 1040. If your SAT score is 1100, which is above 1040, it makes more sense to focus on the SAT. By contrast, an ACT score of 33 is equivalent to an SAT score of 1460. If your SAT score is 1400, which is below 1460, the ACT is the stronger

[11] satsuite.collegeboard.org/media/pdf/guide-2018-act-sat-concordance.pdf

result. Once you know which exam presents you more favorably, the next question is whether your final score is strong enough to submit.

When to Submit Scores

Many students struggle whether to submit their SAT or ACT at test-optional schools. The general rule is to submit scores that **strengthen your application** and withhold them when they do not. But how do you know if a score will help or hurt you?

> **To submit or not to submit**
> A useful benchmark is the college's middle 50th percentile test-score range for admitted students (in the Common Data Set). If your score falls at or above the midpoint, submitting it strengthens your application.

For example, if a college's middle 50th percentile SAT range is 1300 to 1500, the midpoint is 1400. A score of 1400 or higher generally helps, whereas a score of 1200 probably would take away from your application and should not be submitted.

However, withholding scores can leave **unanswered questions**. It may sound counterintuitive, but this is particularly true for students with a high GPA. Admissions officers are likely to wonder why a student with a 3.95 GPA chose not to submit test scores and they may suspect grade inflation or even laziness. On the other hand, very low scores will not strengthen your profile and therefore should never be submitted. Since testing policies continue to evolve, check each college's current policy rather than assuming.

In holistic review, your GPA, coursework, and testing scores do not tell the whole story. Once colleges establish that you can handle the coursework, they turn to the Second Pillar: how you spend your time outside the classroom.

Pillar Two: Extracurricular Engagement

Extracurricular activities show how you engage **outside the classroom**. Colleges do not expect applicants to have a polished résumé since ninth grade. But what they want to see is progression over time: curiosity turning into commitment, participation turning into responsibility, and interest turning into impact.

What kind of activities you do matters far less than **how you engage** in them and what the pattern of your involvement reveals about you. The type of activity, whether it is sports, community service, or family responsibilities, carries no inherent advantage. What matters is that your activities, taken together, create a coherent picture of who you are and how you engage with the world.

Natural Progression

Freshman year functions as a year of **exploration**. This is the time to try different activities, even ones that feel unfamiliar or slightly uncomfortable. Joining clubs, testing out sports, experimenting with music, or volunteering allows you to learn what holds your attention. Admissions officers do not penalize experimentation early on; in fact, they expect it.

By **tenth grade**, patterns should begin to emerge. Sophomore year is typically when students start **narrowing their commitments** and investing more time in a smaller number of activities. Instead of trying everything, you begin choosing what to keep. That choice signals self-awareness and intentionality. Colleges are already starting to see the outlines of who you are becoming.

Eleventh grade is where depth becomes important. By this point, admissions officers expect to see sustained involvement in a few core areas. This is often where **leadership** develops, whether formally through titles or informally through responsibility. This includes mentoring younger students, running rehearsals, coordinating volunteers, managing logistics, training new members, or being the person others rely on.

If you already have a sense of your intended major or career direction by eleventh grade, extracurriculars that align with that interest will strengthen your application. This does not mean every activity must match your major but at least some of your activities should **reinforce your career interest**. A student interested in Engineering might show increasing responsibility in robotics or a maker project. A student interested in social sciences might deepen involvement in community organizing, research, or advocacy. Alignment adds coherence and credibility.

Senior year still matters, even though you apply to colleges early in the school year. The best approach is to stay academically steady, keep your main commitments going, and show follow-through. It is fine to start a new activity in twelfth grade if it is genuinely important to you, but do not treat senior year as the time to add activities for college. **Last-minute résumé padding** rarely looks credible. What helps is continuity and maturity: finishing what you started, taking on real responsibility, and ending high school with the same seriousness you want colleges to believe you will bring to campus.

What Extracurriculars Signal

A strong activities section is not about how many clubs you joined. It shows a pattern of follow-through, growth, and impact. First, colleges look for **sustained commitment**. Time matters because it shows consistency. Sticking with an activity for multiple years signals that you can stay engaged even when the work becomes repetitive or challenging. One or two long-term commitments usually say more about you than a crowded list of short, random stints. Second, admissions officers look for **increasing responsibility**. Leadership is not limited to formal titles like president or captain. What matters is whether your role evolved. Responsibility is often more persuasive than hierarchy.

Finally, colleges look for **real impact**. Impact does not need to be flashy; it can be local and still meaningful like improving a tutoring program, building a useful tool, or strengthening a community effort. Whenever possible, quantify that impact. Numbers help a reader understand scope and significance: how many students you worked with, how many users relied on something you built, or how much money you helped raise. The goal is to give context for your contributions.

What Counts as EC?

Extracurriculars include any activity you do **outside of school**. This covers a wide range including sports (school teams, club sports, recreational leagues), performing arts (band, orchestra, choir, theater, dance), visual arts (studio art, photography, graphic design), academic clubs (debate, Model UN, science Olympiad, math team), community service and volunteering, student government and leadership organizations, cultural or identity-based clubs, religious youth groups, coding or maker projects, and entrepreneurial ventures.

Internships and research can be valuable learning experiences. An internship lets you test whether a career path really interests you, see how a workplace operates, and develop professional skills. Research helps you build college-level skills in inquiry, synthesis, and problem-solving. Admissions officers are not expecting graduate-level work. They look for **curiosity, initiative, and follow-through.** A self-directed project, a consistent lab assistant role, or a community-based research effort can all show process, learning, and growth.

But other experiences provide equally valuable learning. Working at a coffee shop teaches customer service, conflict resolution, and accountability. Volunteering consistently at a food bank shows commitment and service. Coding a personal project demonstrates initiative and problem-solving. What matters is authenticity and depth, not the prestige of the program name. One category of activities may even raise concerns: **pay-for-play programs** where families pay thousands of dollars for students to 'conduct research' or participate in expensive summer programs. These activities often signal privilege more than initiative. Admissions officers recognize these programs, and when an experience appears purchased rather than earned, it can work against you.

Untraditional Activities

Many students undersell their paid work or **family obligations** because they do not look like traditional extracurriculars. However, colleges usually value them. A consistent job signals time management, accountability, and interpersonal skills in a professional setting. Caregiving indicates responsibility and contribution to your family. If these responsibilities limited what else you could do, that is important context. The key is how you present it. Do not simply list 'worked at a restaurant.' Explain the scope. What did you do? Were you trusted to train others, handle closing, manage cash, deal with customers, and coordinate shifts? That makes the work visible. Let us have a look at an example.

> **Presenting an activity**
>
> **Weak presentation**: Cashier at local grocery store (10th-12th grade)
> **Strong presentation**: Cashier, Vons, Fresno, CA (10th-12th grade) 20 hours/week during school year, 35 hours/week in summer. Handled customer transactions, trained three new employees, assisted with inventory management, and regularly closed the store independently. Contributed income to family household expenses.

The second description shows responsibility, progression, and real contribution. It also contextualizes why the student may not have had time for many other activities.

Some students feel the need to fill every activity field in the application, but **quality matters more than quantity**. Admission officers recognize padded activity lists. A smaller number of meaningful commitments usually produces a clearer and more persuasive narrative than a long list of superficial involvements. Remember that the type of activity matters far less than the **story** it tells about you. Whether you spend your time playing water polo, coding personal projects, or caring for younger siblings, what colleges want to see is that you engaged deeply, contributed meaningfully, and learned something about yourself in the process.

Awards and Competitions

What you do outside of school shows up not only in your activities section but also in any awards or recognition you receive. Awards provide a different lens on the same commitments, offering **external validation** of your achievements. Academic competitions test you against a broader pool of students. For example, the American Mathematics Competition (AMC) measures problem-solving ability under time pressure. Athletic awards, such as league championships or Most Valuable Player demonstrate performance in measurable and competitive contexts.

School-level awards such as honor roll, Principal's List, or departmental recognition show consistent academic performance within your school context. These matter less than regional, state, or national-level recognition, but they still have value, especially when they reflect achievement relative to the opportunities available to you. The key is proportionality. A national-level award in a subject related to your intended major strengthens your application significantly. A collection of participation certificates does not add much.

However, many students do impressive work in contexts that do **not produce formal awards.** In this case, focus on substance and outcomes: what you built, led, improved, performed, or contributed. Admissions officers understand that not all schools, communities, or families provide equal access to competitive programs. The absence of awards does not weaken your application if your activities section demonstrates depth, growth, and impact in other ways.

Your activities and awards show what you have done and how you have spent your time. They should demonstrate initiative, commitment, and growth. But knowing what you did is not the same as understanding who you are. That requires a different kind of evidence, which brings us to the Third Pillar.

Pillar Three: Personality Traits

If the First Pillar answers, 'Can you handle the academics?' and Pillar Two illustrates how you engage with the world outside of school, the Third Pillar asks a harder question: Who is this student, and what will they add to our campus community?

This is where the process becomes a bit vague. Identity and potential contributions are qualitative and cannot be measured on a scale or counted in hours. They require **interpretation**. Admissions officers are evaluating traits like maturity, curiosity, judgment, and character, which are hard to discern and even harder to compare. Different colleges also value different qualities, and what resonates at one school may not stand out at another. This pillar is where your essays become critical, because they give you the opportunity to shape how colleges see your unique qualities.

Student Voice: Essays

Essays are key to show who you are as a person. They are the only place in the application where the admissions officer directly hears **your voice**. Your essays turn you from an applicant into a real person. They also reveal communication skills, reflection, and maturity. In a competitive pool where many students look strong on paper, essays can help a reader understand how you think and what you value.

The **personal statement** is the main essay that most colleges read as part of your application. Written in 650 words or less, it is your opportunity to speak directly to the admissions team. Personal essays generally follow one of two structures. The **narrative approach** tells a single story with a clear arc, while the **montage** weaves together several small moments or images that build toward a larger idea.

The goal is not to tell your life story. It is to do something both simpler and much harder: make a few key personal qualities unmistakable through concrete detail. A useful way to check if your essay is specific enough is to ask if another student could swap their name into this essay and still have it make sense. If yes, it is probably too generic.

> **Golden rule for essays**
> Show, don't tell.

Instead of writing 'I am passionate about helping others,' you show one specific moment where you noticed a problem, took responsibility, and stayed with it long enough to create change. Keep that principle in mind as you move into supplemental essays.

Supplemental Essays

Beyond the personal statement, many colleges ask for additional essays. Many students treat supplemental essays as annoying chores to get through after finishing the main personal statement. Do not underestimate the significance of supplemental essays. They reveal whether you did your homework, whether your goals align with what the school offers, and whether your interest is specific enough to be credible.

Supplemental prompts vary widely. The most common is the **'Why us?'** essay, which asks some version of 'Why do you want to attend this college?' or 'What will you contribute to our community?'. These prompts function as tests. Can you name specific programs, courses, professors, research opportunities, or campus resources that connect to your interests and experiences? Or will you write vague praise about campus beauty, prestige, or 'the vibrant community?'

Other supplements ask you to engage with intellectual questions or campus values. For example, Stanford invites applicants to write a note to their future roommate[12], while Caltech asks to describe a meaningful STEM-related experience[13].

> **Supplemental essays**
> A strong supplemental essay connects three points: what you care about, what you have already done, and what you bring to that particular college.

The more **specific** you are, the better. Name the professor whose research interests you. Identify the specific interdisciplinary program that combines your two passions. Explain how a particular campus resource connects to work you have already started. Essays are the place where you show who you are in your own voice. Letters of recommendation add an outside perspective. They reflect how adults who have worked with you see your character, your habits, and the way you show up in a classroom or community.

---

12 admission.stanford.edu/apply/first-year/apply.html

13 admissions.caltech.edu/apply/first-year-applicants/supplemental-application-essays

Letters of Recommendation

Many applications use two kinds of sources, teacher recommendations and counselor recommendations. **Teacher recommendations** add texture to your academic record: how you think in class, how you handle difficulty, how you contribute to discussions, and how you work in groups. The strongest teacher letters are specific and include small, real examples that only someone who knows you well could write. Ask a teacher from a core academic subject, ideally linked to your planned major.

Counselor recommendations (and the school profile that accompanies them) place you in the larger context of your high school. Counselors can explain how your course rigor compares to what your school offers, what the school's grading culture is like, and what opportunities exist. The counselor letter is a key part of understanding your environment and your individual choices within it.

> **Waive your FERPA[14] rights**
> Giving up the ability to read your recommendations signals to colleges that the letters of recommendation are candid.

A short **brag sheet** can help a teacher remember details and help the counselor position you in the school context, especially at large public schools where they support many students. Private colleges typically require two teacher recommendations and one counselor recommendation. The UC and CSU generally do not require letters of recommendation (UC Berkeley occasionally requests them).

Personal Context

Your school counselor provides your high school context, but they cannot explain your individual circumstances. That context must come from you. Personal context should focus on **extraordinary circumstances** or significant constraints, not minor inconveniences. This includes serious illness, major family hardship, sustained work that supported your household,

---

[14] FERPA = Family Educational Rights and Privacy Act

caregiving responsibilities, or disruptions that substantially limited your time or access to opportunities. These are factors a transcript or activity list cannot explain.

When circumstances like these are part of your life, colleges need to know about them to interpret your record accurately. Personal context helps an admissions reader understand why your path may look different from someone else's. If you do not provide this information, the reader may make the wrong assumptions. The appropriate place to share this information is usually the **'Additional Comments'** or 'Additional Information' section of the application. This section is optional and it is completely acceptable to leave it blank if there is nothing that needs explanation. Do not use it to list additional activities, repeat information already provided elsewhere, or write another essay! Use it only when context is necessary for understanding your choices or performance.

Interviews

College interviews can add an additional dimension to an application. They humanize the file and provide a different perspective that transcripts, essays, and activity lists cannot fully capture. While interviews **rarely make or break** an application, they can reinforce the overall narrative or raise concerns if handled poorly. Not all colleges offer interviews. Among those that do, format and weight vary significantly.

Interviews conducted by **admissions officers** are less common and carry some weight in the review process. **Alumni interviews** are far more common, especially at private colleges such as Stanford, USC, Pomona, or Claremont McKenna. The interviewers are former students who were trained to represent the institution and submit evaluative feedback. Alumni interviews provide context and perspective but usually do not influence admissions decisions in a major way. Often, alumni interview programs exist more for alumni relations than for applicant evaluation. In many cases, interviews are availability-based, and not every applicant who wants one will receive one.

Interviewers typically **evaluate** a student's communication skills, intellectual curiosity, engagement, maturity, and authenticity. They also note how well a student articulates their interests and whether those interests align plausibly with what the college offers. The UC and CSU do not offer interviews for freshman admission; interviews are primarily a feature of private colleges.

Portfolios, Auditions, Creative Supplements

For some applicants, portfolios and auditions are optional enhancements. For others, they are central to the admissions decision. **Portfolios** and **auditions** exist to answer a question that transcripts cannot: can this student **perform, create, or produce** at a level appropriate for advanced study in this field? In general, Bachelor of Fine Arts programs place heavy emphasis on auditions or portfolios. Studio Art, Graphic Design, Architecture, and Visual Communication programs may ask for an art portfolio, while Music, Theater, Dance, and Musical Theater programs often use auditions or prescreening materials. Film, Media, and Creative Writing programs may also request work samples, such as short films, scripts, storyboards, or additional writing.

Some private Engineering, Computer Science, or Design programs encourage technical portfolios showcasing coding projects, robotics work, apps, websites, or hardware builds. Unlike the rest of the application, portfolios and auditions are usually **reviewed by faculty**, not admissions officers. Optional creative supplements should only be submitted if they add new and meaningful information and are up to the expected standards.

Demonstrated Interest

Outside of the Three Pillars, some private institutions track the level of applicant interest. Demonstrated interest is primarily an **enrollment management** tool. Many private schools must manage their yield, the percentage of admitted students who actually enroll. If too many admitted students decline, the school misses their enrollment targets and tuition income. If too many accept, they run into housing and capacity problems.

When demonstrated interest is considered, the underlying question is simple. If we admit this student, how likely are they to enroll? To gauge this, some colleges track whether an applicant attended official information sessions, campus tours, virtual open houses, admissions webinars, or completed an interview when offered. Others track email engagement or whether applicants submit optional supplements. To verify if a college tracks interest, refer to Section C7 in the Common Data Set.

How Colleges Weigh the Three Pillars

Once you understand what sits inside each pillar, the real question becomes how to prioritize your effort. You cannot optimize everything, and colleges do not value everything equally. The good news is that this process is not a black box.

What Research Tells Us

While no school publishes a specific admissions formula, most share enough information to guide smart decisions. Two specific sources provide great insight: national admissions data from the National Association of College Admissions Counseling (NACAC), and each college's Common Data Set. Section C7 of the CDS lists admissions factors and categorizes them as Very Important, Important, Considered, or Not Considered. That table tells you how a particular college will evaluate your application.

When we look at the NACAC **national admissions data**[15], a clear pattern emerges. Certain factors matter more than others, and that hierarchy stays consistent across institutions.

> **Academics dominate**
> Overall GPA, grades in college-prep courses, and course rigor sit at the top at almost all colleges.

This supports the idea that academic performance functions as gatekeeper rather than tie-breaker. If your academic record does not demonstrate readiness, strength elsewhere rarely compensates.

In the middle tier, we find **extracurricular activities** and **letters of recommendation**. They do not rescue weak academics, but they add meaning

[15] nacacnet.org/factors-in-the-admission-decision/

and credibility once the academic bar is cleared. This is where colleges begin to understand how you use your time, whether you follow through, and how adults who know you describe your engagement and character.

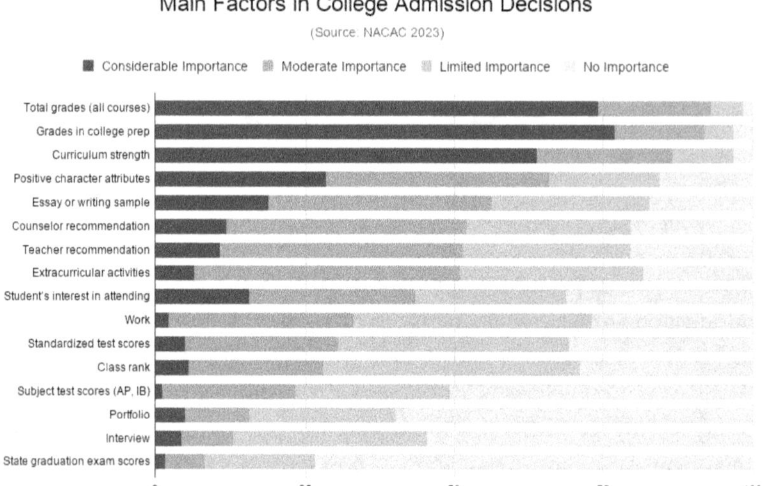

After that come the highly **variable factors**. Demonstrated interest, interviews, portfolios, and work experience may matter a great deal at one college and not at all at another. This is where many students waste time by assuming all schools value the same qualities. Some colleges track interest closely, while others explicitly mark it as not considered. Some interview widely, and others never interview. Some programs require portfolios and treat them as central, but most majors do not.

The school's **Common Data Set** helps you decide where to focus your energy. If a college lists essays as very important, invest there. If demonstrated interest is not considered, do not stress about visits or webinars (other than for learning more about the college for your own benefit). If recommendations matter, prioritize strong teacher relationships. This is also where public and private colleges often diverge. Private colleges tend to place more weight on qualitative factors like essays, recommendations, interviews, and interest. Large public universities rely more heavily on academics, partly because of scale and partly because of transparency requirements.

The individual steps in devising your strongest application are straightforward. First, use the NACAC data to understand the **overall hierarchy**. Then, research the CDS to see how that hierarchy applies at the **specific schools** on your list. Allocate your time and effort accordingly. Build the strongest academic record you can. Commit deeply to a few meaningful activities. Write essays that show how you think and what you value.

Nevertheless, even when you do all this well, outcomes can still be disappointing. Sometimes, a few admission factors are completely **outside of your control**. That is where institutional priorities come in.

Institutional Priorities

No application is evaluated in a vacuum. When the admissions team reads your file, they assess it in the context of a much larger task: **building an incoming class.** That broader context explains outcomes that often feel confusing or unfair from the outside.

This invisible layer of admissions operates most strongly at private institutions, particularly the highly selective ones. Public universities tend to be more transparent. The University of California publishes its comprehensive review factors, and the CSU campuses publish eligibility indexes and impaction thresholds. You can usually trace a decision back to published criteria. At many private colleges, that is not how decisions work.

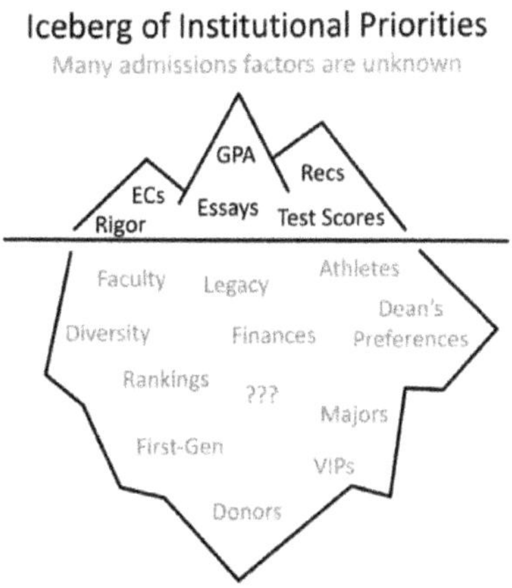

A helpful way to think about institutional priorities is the **iceberg model**. What you see above the surface are the factors colleges openly discuss: GPA, course rigor, test scores, essays, recommendations, and activities. Below the surface are their institutional priorities. Every admissions cycle, colleges begin with constraints and goals that have nothing to do with any one applicant. One of the most common is **academic balance**. Colleges do not just admit the highest performing students. They accept the right number of students for each academic area. As we have seen, a student applying to a capped major faces tougher odds than a similarly qualified student applying to an uncapped one.

Geographic diversity is another common factor. Many private colleges aim to enroll students from a wide range of regions to avoid overconcentration from any single state or city. In practice, this means two equally qualified applicants can face different odds based on where they live, simply because one region has already reached its informal target.

Enrollment management also plays a role. Some colleges track who is likely to enroll if admitted, based on application round, historical yield patterns, and financial considerations. Applying early is also known to influence admission outcomes. Athletic recruiting also shapes a portion of the class; colleges need to make sure that all their athletic rosters are filled. Legacy status matters at some institutions, and occasionally, even donor relationships can influence decisions. These factors are rarely spelled out in detail, but they operate consistently behind the scenes.

This is where many familiar stories come from. The student with a low SAT score who gets admitted while their friend with a higher one is denied from the same school. The 'perfect' applicant who is rejected by the colleges they thought were slam dunks. Often, these stories are less about the individual applicant and more about institutional priorities.

The most important thing to understand is that this admissions layer is **not personal.** A denial does not mean you were unqualified. More often than not, factors outside your control shaped the outcome. Trying to reverse-engineer or predict those factors is usually a waste of energy.

> **Focus on what you can influence**
> Build strong academics and choose meaningful activities showing initiative, personality, and impact. Write reflective essays and apply to a balanced list of best-fit colleges. Everything else is outside of your control.

International Students

International students are evaluated using the same Three Pillars as domestic applicants. In addition, there are a few requirements that determine if they are eligible for admission. Most colleges require proof of **language proficiency** if English has not been your primary language of instruction. Commonly accepted exams include the TOEFL, IELTS, and Duolingo English Test. If you do not meet a college's stated minimum score, you are ineligible for admission, regardless of how strong the rest of your application is.

International applicants must also submit **official academic records** from all secondary schools attended. When transcripts are not in English, certified translations are required so admissions officers can evaluate coursework and grading accurately. Finally, international students must demonstrate the ability to **finance their education**. Most students will apply for an **F-1 student visa**, and that process requires financial certification from the institution.[16]

What This Framework Means for You

This chapter laid out how colleges evaluate applications across the Three Pillars: academics, extracurricular engagement, and personality traits, all evaluated in the context of opportunities available. For now, the key takeaways are straightforward. First, **academics dominate**. More than 90 percent of colleges consider GPA and course rigor as the most important factors in admissions decisions. Academics is the gatekeeper. If your academic performance does not show you are ready for college, strengths in other areas rarely compensate.

Second, extracurriculars help most when they reveal **depth, growth,** and genuine **engagement** over time. The type of activity matters far less than how deeply you engage and what the pattern of your involvement reveals about you. Third, personal qualities can become a key factor when many applicants look similar on paper. **Essays and context** often determine who gets admitted and who does not.

---

[16] For more information, see: *Mission: Accepted! U.S. College Admissions for International Students*

Lastly, **institutional priorities** can shape outcomes in ways you cannot control. Rather than trying to predict hidden priorities, focus on building applications that are well-supported across all Three Pillars. The students who succeed are the ones who understand what colleges value, allocate effort realistically, and present themselves authentically. In the chapters ahead, we will show you exactly how to do that within UC, CSU, and private college application systems. Let us begin with the University of California.

The University of California[17]

5 | The UC System

California's Research Powerhouse

When people talk about the University of California, they usually think about prestige. Rankings. Famous professors. Scientific discoveries. UC Berkeley's Jennifer Doudna won the 2020 Nobel Prize in Chemistry for developing CRISPR-Cas9 gene-editing technology. That same year, UCLA's Andrea Ghez earned the Nobel Prize in Physics for discovering a supermassive black hole at the center of our galaxy.

In 2025, the UC system won the most Nobel Prizes awarded to one university system in a single year. These are not isolated achievements. UC researchers have shaped modern medicine, technology, and public policy. But understanding the UC from the student perspective requires us to look **beyond headlines and awards**. You need to understand how the UC's mission shapes everything from class sizes to acceptance rates to what a campus can (and cannot) do for you.

[17] All information is based on publicly available sources and my independent counseling experience, not on my role as a UC application reader.

Mission and Structure

The University of California was designed to do three things at once: **educate** students, produce new **research,** and **serve** the state of California. Unlike many private universities, the UC was not built primarily around undergraduate teaching. Teaching matters, but it exists alongside large-scale research and public service.

The UC system includes ten campuses. Nine of them enroll undergraduate and graduate students. One campus, UC San Francisco, focuses entirely on graduate and professional education in the health sciences. Across the system, the UC also operates hospitals, medical schools, research institutes, agricultural programs, and environmental reserves. But the scale goes beyond academics. The University of California is **one of the largest employers** in California. Hundreds of thousands of faculty, staff, clinicians, and researchers work across campuses and medical centers statewide. That workforce reflects how deeply the UC is embedded in California's economy and public infrastructure, not just its education system.

For students, this structure has **real consequences**. UC campuses often feel more like small cities than colleges. Professors balance teaching with research and clinical responsibilities. Advising and support services exist, but students are expected to take initiative and seek them out. The system is designed to function at scale, not to provide handholding.

R1 Research Culture

You read earlier that all UC campuses are classified as R1 research institutions. What does that mean for students? R1 is the highest designation for research activity in the United States. To earn this status, universities must demonstrate **high research activity** across multiple disciplines, substantial research funding, and significant doctoral program enrollment. Only about 150 universities nationwide hold this classification.

R1 research universities
UC faculty are hired and promoted largely based on research output. Professors run labs, publish research, apply for grants, and supervise graduate students in addition to teaching undergraduates.

Research is not an afterthought but a central activity. This creates both opportunity and pressure for students. The **opportunity** is significant. Undergraduates have access to research that simply does not exist at other universities. Students work in labs, contribute to published studies, and participate in projects tied to real-world problems. Even first- and second-year students can get involved if they are proactive. You can work alongside graduate students and postdoctoral researchers, and can see how knowledge is created, not just transmitted.

The **pressure** is equally real. Large lecture classes are common, especially in popular majors such as Biology, Computer Science, or Economics. Lower-division courses routinely enroll 300, 400, or even 500 students. Professors may not know your name. Success often depends on whether you attend office hours, seek research positions, and intentionally build relationships. The UC rewards independence and initiative. Students who wait to be noticed often struggle. These tradeoffs are defining features of research universities. Students who thrive at the UC are the ones who understand this early and act accordingly.

Setting Realistic Expectations

One of the biggest adjustments for new UC students is class size, especially in the first two years. Lower-division courses usually are taught in **large lecture halls**. A student taking Introduction to Biology or General Chemistry might be one of 400 students in the room. The professor lectures, and students take notes. If you have questions, you attend **office hours** or discussion sections led by graduate student teaching assistants.

This can feel impersonal, especially if you came from a small high school or expected more interaction with faculty. But large lectures are a structural reality at large research universities. They teach **foundational material** efficiently while professors focus on specialized upper-division courses and graduate seminars.

Upper-division courses are typically smaller. Once you move into specialized coursework, class sizes shrink. Small seminars of 30 to 50 students are more common. This is where you get more faculty interaction, discussion-based learning, and academic depth. Your first year may feel overwhelming and impersonal. By your third and fourth years, the experience often becomes much more engaging. Students who persist usually find the upper-division experience rewarding.

Why Residency Matters

The UC system is financially supported in part by California taxpayers. That public funding comes with certain expectations.

> **Priority for California residents**
> The UC serves California residents first, and that priority shows up in two concrete ways: admissions and tuition.

For Fall 2025, the UC admitted more than 77 percent of in-state applicants, compared to 62 percent for out-of-state students[18]. This pattern aligns with the UC's public mission and with ongoing pressure from the state legislature to prioritize access for California residents.

In tuition, the gap is even more significant. For 2026–27, California residents pay between $18,000 and $20,000 per year in tuition and fees, while out-of-state and international students pay roughly $55,000 before room and board. That gap reflects the public subsidy provided by California taxpayers.

Despite that priority, perception often tells a different story. You may have heard that the UCs are "**impossible to get into**." Everyone seems to know a student with a 4.0 who did not get into *any* UC. What this usually means is that the student did not get into any campus they applied to, not that the

[18] University of California News (2025)

system rejected them everywhere. In many cases, students only apply to the most selective campuses, such as UCLA, UC Berkeley, or UCSD. Not being admitted to the most competitive campuses does not contradict the fact that the UC prioritizes California residents. It reflects the selectivity of individual campuses and our very human tendency to overgeneralize from personal experience.

Both of those advantages, higher admission priority and lower tuition, depend on whether the UC classifies you as a California resident. **Residency** is a legal classification with specific requirements, and for some students the rules are more nuanced than expected. The full picture is covered in the next chapter.

Access and Equity

Because the UC system is both selective and publicly funded, access is a constant tension. The system has expanded enrollment of California residents in recent years, but demand still far exceeds capacity. The UC addresses this tension through financial aid and targeted support programs.

Many low-income students from California pay little tuition after financial aid. The UC provides **financial aid** packages that meet most of the demonstrated need of California residents through a combination of grants, scholarships, work-study, and loans. This makes them affordable for families across income levels. But paying for college and succeeding in college are two different challenges. This is why there are several support initiatives targeting specific types of students.

Students who are **first-generation** or from **low-income** backgrounds often arrive at the UC with academic potential but less familiarity with how universities operate. They may not know how to navigate office hours, research opportunities, or academic policies. Many do not realize that professors expect students to advocate for themselves or that opportunities rarely come looking for them. The UC attempts to close this gap through targeted support that begins before college and continues through graduation.

Educational Opportunity Program

The Educational Opportunity Program, or EOP, is one of the UC's most important support structures for students who show strong potential but have faced structural barriers to opportunity. Students typically qualify for EOP if they are first-generation college students, come from low-income households, or attended under-resourced high schools.

The program provides something many UC students lack: a clear **point of contact**. EOP students receive dedicated academic advising that goes beyond course selection. Advisors help with major planning, academic recovery, and understanding university rules. Many campuses also offer summer bridge programs or first-year seminars to ease the transition into college-level work.

EOP often acts as a **navigation hub**, connecting students to tutoring, mental health services, food pantries, and emergency grants. Just as importantly, EOP creates community. Knowing where to go and who to ask can be the difference between persistence and burnout. If you may qualify, indicate your interest in the UC application by checking the EOP option. The support is real, and the difference it makes is measurable in retention and graduation rates.

Nine Undergraduate UC Campuses

The UC system has ten campuses, but UC San Francisco is a graduate and professional campus only and does not enroll undergraduates. The nine undergraduate campuses together enroll **over 300,000 students** (237,000 undergraduates and 63,000 graduate and professional students). While they share a common mission, each campus has a distinct academic identity, regional context, and level of selectivity. Applications to the UC have reached record highs in recent cycles and competition is not softening. Students building a UC list today need to be more **deliberate** about **realistic targets** than they would have been just a few years ago.

Two Flagships

Berkeley and UCLA occupy the top tier in selectivity, reputation, and breadth. Due to their low admit rates, both campuses are reach schools for all applicants. **Berkeley** is known for intellectual intensity and exceptional depth across nearly every discipline, with a demanding academic culture that emphasizes research and independent thinking. **UCLA** combines that same academic weight with the energy of a major city and a vibrant campus environment. For students who thrive under pressure and want name recognition, these two campuses are in a category of their own.

Highly Competitive

UC San Diego and UC Irvine sit just below the two flagships and should also be considered reaches for many applicants. **UCSD** has grown dramatically in application volume and now exceeds Berkeley in total applications. It is exceptional in STEM, medicine, and the biological sciences, and its residential college system sets it apart from most large research universities. **Irvine** has followed a similar trajectory, with deep ties to Orange County's technology and healthcare industries and rising selectivity across Computer Science, Engineering, and the biological sciences. Neither campus is a safe target for students applying to competitive majors.

Strong Middle

UC Davis and UC Santa Barbara are strong research universities that remain more accessible than the tiers above. **Davis** is world-renowned for its veterinary school, agricultural programs, and viticulture program. Its location in the Sacramento Valley ties Davis directly to California's farming, food, and wine industries. **Santa Barbara** combines rigorous academics in Engineering, Physics, and the Environmental Sciences with a coastal setting and an active campus life. Both campuses are reaches for competitive majors.

Accessible and Distinctive

UC Santa Cruz, UC Riverside, and UC Merced are the most accessible UC campuses, but this category is shifting. Santa Cruz and Merced have seen significant increases in applications over the past two years. They should no longer be treated as automatic admits. **Santa Cruz** has a residential college system, strong programs in Computer Science and Environmental Studies, and a campus set on forested hills above the Monterey Bay. **Riverside** has built a strong identity around social mobility and enrolls a high proportion of first-generation students. **Merced** is the newest and smallest campus, with the kind of small class sizes, faculty access, and undergraduate research opportunities that are nearly impossible to find at the other UCs. All three campuses are worth considering on their own terms, not just as fallback options.

Putting It Together

The UC is not one university with nine locations. Each campus has a distinct academic identity, a different level of selectivity, and a different relationship to the industries and communities around it. A strong UC list takes all of that into account. Be honest about where your numbers are competitive, deliberate about fit, and balanced across tiers.

The next chapter covers what you need to be eligible to apply, how California students can guarantee themselves a place in the system, and how residency affects how much tuition you pay.

6 | Eligibility and Pathways to Admission

System-Wide Rules Behind Every UC Application

Earlier, we looked at the three main parts of every college application: academics, extracurriculars, and personal qualities. Now, let us focus on the University of California, a system so popular that 251,907 students applied to one or more UC campuses for Fall 2026 admissions. The UC has its own rules, its own vocabulary, and its own logic that rewards students who take the time to understand it.

The University of California is **not one university**. Nine universities share a name, a system, and a set of minimum requirements, but each campus makes its own admissions decisions. The individual campuses do not communicate with each other about admissions decisions. That is why one student can be accepted at UC Santa Barbara and rejected at UC San Diego in the same week.

Understanding how the UC system and the individual campuses operate leads to smarter planning and usually better outcomes. This chapter covers the requirements for eligibility, the guaranteed pathways for California students, and how the UC determines how much tuition you pay. The next chapter will look at how UC campuses evaluate applications, how the nine campuses differ in their approach, and which programs require additional materials beyond the standard application.

First-Year Applicant

UC eligibility rules vary depending on where you are in your academic life. If you apply straight out of **high school**, you are considered a first-year applicant. If you have been enrolled at another four-year institution or a community college, you must apply as a transfer student. But how about a high schooler who stretched themselves and took college classes while in high school? If you took dual enrollment classes during high school or a college course in the summer right after graduating from high school, the UC still considers you a first-year applicant. However, enrolling in a **non-summer term** at any college after graduating from high school means you must apply as a transfer student.

The UC has completely **different eligibility rules** for first-year and transfer applicants, so it is important to know which category you fall into. This chapter (and the next one) discusses freshman applications. We will look at transfer applicants separately. As a first-year applicant, your eligibility starts with your high school record.

ELIGIBILITY

Eligibility vs. Admission

Two distinct layers determine if you are admitted at a UC. The first layer is **eligibility**, which means that you meet the minimum requirements to be considered at all.

> **Eligibility**
> Students must complete the A-G subject requirements with grades of C or better and meet the minimum GPA for their residency category (3.0 for residents, 3.4 for nonresidents and international students).

The UC also expects eleven of the 15 required year-long A-G courses to be completed by the start of twelfth grade, and seven of the 15 must be taken during the last two years of high school.

The second admissions layer is **selection**, where campuses choose among a large pool of qualified applicants. Here is a number that puts that the competition in perspective. For Fall 2026, admitted students typically completed between 22.5 and 27 year-long (45 to 54 semester) college preparation courses, compared to the required minimum of 15 year-long courses. That is **seven to twelve more courses** than what it takes to be eligible to apply! These numbers are a reminder that meeting the minimum makes you eligible but not competitive.

First, let us discuss what it takes to be eligible for admission. Your college prep A-G coursework and your UC-specific GPA in those courses determine whether you can even apply to a UC.

A-G Requirements

The A-G subject requirements are the UC's definition of a **college preparatory education**, the specific subjects they expect you to have completed before you arrive on campus. The UC wants to know that you can handle university-level work from day one. A-G requirements are also one of the most common sources of **accidental ineligibility**. Students can be genuinely strong and hardworking and still discover too late that a course they assumed counted does not meet the UC criteria. The fix is simple: plan early and verify everything.

How do you know if a planned high school course is approved by the UC? If you attend a California high school, you can check your courses against the **UC A-G Course List**[19]. Every approved California high school course is listed there. If you are an out-of-state or international student, talk to your counselor early about how your coursework maps to the UC expectations. Out-of-state courses are not pre-approved the way California high school courses are, and the comparison takes time to sort out. If you take online or outside-provider courses, verify UC acceptance before you enroll.

All A-G subject requirements must be completed in 9th through 12th grade, with two exceptions: qualifying coursework in math and foreign languages

---

[19] hs-articulation.ucop.edu/agcourselist

completed in seventh or eighth grade counts, too. High school courses are not the only way to satisfy the A-G requirements. You can also meet them through qualifying AP exam scores or by completing UC-transferable college courses.

However, these options are not equivalent. A **UC-transferable college course** adds to your A-G course count, and its grade enters your UC GPA calculation. A semester-long college course earns one honors point in the weighted GPA (even though it satisfies a full year of an A-G requirement).

An **AP exam score** (without the equivalent course) can fulfill a subject requirement but does **not add** to your A-G course count or UC GPA. For example, a qualifying AP Spanish Language score can check the subject area E requirement, but if you also want the course credit and GPA boost, you need the class itself.

Here is an overview of the full A-G framework:

Area	**Subject**	**Required / Recommended**	**Notes**
A	History/ Social Science	2 years / -	1 year world history/geography + 1 year US history (or ½-year US history + ½-year civics)
B	English	4 years / -	College-preparatory composition and literature; max. 1 year of advanced ESL/ELD may count
C	Mathematics	3 years / 4 years	Must cover elementary and advanced algebra and geometry
D	Lab Science	2 years / 3 years	At least two of three disciplines: biology, chemistry, physics
E	Language other than English	2 years / 3 years	Same language throughout; ASL accepted
F	Visual & Performing Arts	1 year / -	One discipline: dance, music, theater, visual arts, or interdisciplinary arts
G	College Prep Elective	1 year / -	Additional coursework from A-F areas or other approved electives

Area A: History and Social Science

To fulfill subject area A, students need **two years** of history, including one year of world history, cultures, or historical geography, and one year of US history. Alternatively, the US history requirement can be split into half a year of US history and half a year of civics or American government.

Qualifying exams include: for US history, AP US History or AP African American Studies (score of 3+), or IB History of the Americas HL (score of 5+); for US or Comparative Government, AP Government and Politics (score of 3+, satisfies the half-year civics requirement); for world history, AP European History, AP World History, AP Modern World History, or AP Human Geography (score of 3+), or IB History HL or IB Geography HL (score of 5+). If you are relying on an exam to satisfy area A, verify the specific score requirements for each campus.

Area B: English

Four years of college-preparatory composition and literature are required. If English is not your first language, only one year of advanced ESL or ELD coursework can count toward the requirement, and your 12th-grade English course must be a non-ESL/ELD college-preparatory class. The UC is looking for four years of rigorous English **reading and writing preparation** on your transcript. Qualifying exams include AP English Language and Composition or AP English Literature and Composition (score of 3+), or IB HL English Literature (score of 5+), all of which satisfy the full four-year requirement.

Area C: Mathematics

Three years of high school math are required, and **four are recommended**. Your coursework must cover elementary and advanced algebra and two- and three-dimensional geometry. High school-level math completed in **7th or 8th** grade can count if it appears on your high school transcript and meets the UC criteria. Qualifying exams include AP Calculus AB or BC (score of 3+), AP Precalculus (score of 4+), or IB Mathematics HL Analysis and Approaches (score of 5+), all of which satisfy two years of the requirement but do **not cover geometry**. A full year-long course covering geometry content is required, period.

Area D: Laboratory Science

Two years of lab science are required, and **three are recommended**. Students must cover at least **two of the three** core disciplines: Biology, Chemistry, and Physics. While two year-long courses in Biology and Chemistry fulfill this requirement, taking two years of just Chemistry (e.g. Chemistry in grade 10 and AP Chemistry in grade 11) does not. Earth and Space Sciences can count as a third year if the course includes fundamental knowledge and appropriate lab work. Two exams from different disciplines can satisfy the two-year requirement. Qualifying AP exams (score of 3+) include AP Biology, AP Chemistry, AP Environmental Science, and AP Physics. Qualifying IB HL exams (score of 5+) include Biology, Chemistry, and Physics.

Area E: Language Other Than English (LOTE)

Two years of the same language are required, and **three are recommended**. The UC recognizes many languages, including American Sign Language. Math and LOTE are the only areas that accept coursework **completed in seventh or eighth** grade if it is documented on your high school transcript. Qualifying AP exams (score of 3+) include Chinese Language and Culture, French Language and Culture, German Language and Culture, Italian Language and Culture, Japanese Language and Culture, Spanish Language and Culture, Spanish Literature and Culture, and Latin. Any IB HL Language B exam (score of 5+) also satisfies the full two-year requirement. For international students who attended school where the language of instruction was not English, that schooling usually satisfies this area E requirement.

Area F: Visual and Performing Arts

This requirement often comes as a surprise to students. Area F covers Visual and Performing Arts. **One year-long course** is required, chosen from a single discipline: dance, music, theater, visual arts, or interdisciplinary arts. The full year does not have to be a single course. Two one-semester courses taken in different years can satisfy the requirement, if both semesters are in the same discipline. For example, a semester of dance in ninth grade and a second semester of dance in tenth grade satisfies the requirement. A semester of dance paired with a semester of theater does not; the discipline must stay consistent across both semesters.

You can repeat a course for credit, and have it count toward Area F, as long as the content is not identical to what you took before. A student who takes Folklorico Dance I and then Folklorico Dance II is a good example. Both courses fall within the dance discipline, but each covers different regional styles, choreography, and technique, so the content is distinct and both semesters count. Qualifying AP exams (score of 3+) include AP Art History, AP Art and Design, and AP Music Theory. Qualifying IB HL exams (score of 5+) include Dance, Film, Music, Theatre Arts, and Visual Arts.

Area G: College-Preparatory Elective

Area G covers the College-Preparatory Elective. **One year** is required, and it can be satisfied by two one-semester courses from different disciplines. The courses must come from the A-F subject areas or other UC-approved electives, and they cannot have been taken prior to ninth grade. Think of area G as an opportunity to show either depth in a potential major or genuine curiosity across academic fields. Not every elective offered at your high school automatically qualifies. Check the UC A-G Course List to confirm before assuming a course counts.

Qualifying AP exams (score of 3+) include AP Computer Science A, AP Computer Science Principles, AP Microeconomics, AP Macroeconomics, AP Psychology, AP US Government, and AP Comparative Government. Qualifying IB HL exams (score of 5+) include Computer Science, Economics, Philosophy, Psychology, and Social and Cultural Anthropology.

Grade Rules That Make or Break Eligibility

Two requirements determine whether your academic record clears the eligibility bar. First, you must complete 15 A-G courses with grades of C or better between ninth and twelfth grade. Second, your capped weighted UC GPA must meet the minimum threshold for your residency category: 3.0 for California residents and 3.4 for out-of-state and international students. Both requirements must be met. A strong GPA with too few qualifying courses leaves you ineligible, and so does a transcript full of A-G courses with a GPA that falls short.

UC Eligibility
Minimum of 15 A-G courses with C or higher between 9th and 12th grade and minimum capped weighted GPA: 3.0 (residents) or 3.4 (nonresidents)

For the **GPA calculation**, only grades from tenth and eleventh grade count. Ninth grade is considered a transitional year into high school, and twelfth grade grades are simply not available when students apply in fall of senior year. This means your GPA is built entirely on two years of coursework, which is why tenth and eleventh grade matter so much. There is no freshman year to average in, and no senior year to save you.

Grades of C or better are the baseline to meet UC requirements. If a D or F is in a course needed to satisfy an A-G area, the course must be repeated unless the requirement is fulfilled through another qualifying course. You have until the summer after eleventh grade to address this. Students who take more than 15 A-G courses may still be eligible with a D or F, as long as they still have 15 qualifying courses with grades of C or better covering all subject areas. For example, a student with 18 A-G courses and one D may be eligible to apply, but the failing grade is likely to hurt their competitiveness.

A few other **grade rules** are worth knowing before you finalize your course plan. Pass and credit grades (P/NP) are not acceptable for A-G requirements. If you earned a C or higher, you cannot repeat the course for a higher grade; repeats are only allowed to clear a deficiency. The replacement course must be at the same level or higher. For example, an AP course can replace a non-AP course, but a non-AP course cannot replace an AP course. A C-minus counts as a C for high school coursework, but not for transferable college courses. This is worth knowing before you enroll in dual enrollment courses.

Meeting the eligibility bar and **being competitive** are two different things. A transcript with several C grades technically clears the minimum, but a pattern of C grades will work against you in the review process, particularly at the more selective campuses. Grades usually reflect your academic profile. But what happens when there is a gap, a missed course, or a grade you regret? The UC has a specific answer for that: course validation.

Validation

The concept comes from a logical premise. If you can master advanced material, you probably understood the basics first.

> **Validation**
> Successful completion of a higher-level math or LOTE course validates a course you never took or a low grade (D or F).

Validation does **not exist** in science, history, English, or any other A-G area outside of math and language. This means a D in the first semester of biology cannot be cleared by earning a strong grade in the second semester. Even if a student passes the second semester of biology with a B, the D in the first semester still stands as an unmet requirement. The first semester must be retaken for a C or better or covered by another course. There is no workaround.

For **mathematics**, higher-level courses generally validate the sequence below them. For example, Algebra II validates Algebra I, and Math III validates Math II. Precalculus or Calculus validate the foundational algebra sequence, including Algebra I and Algebra II. The second semester of a math course can also validate a D or F in the first semester of that same course. Math courses approved under area C for Computer Science are excluded from the general validation rules, so a Computer Science course does not validate Algebra I, Algebra II, or Math I, II, or III.

Two important changes take effect in 2026. First, Statistics and 'Additional Math' no longer validate Algebra II or Math III for either omissions (missing courses) or deficiencies (D or F grades). Second, students must complete a full year of geometry content. Advanced math coursework can only clear a D or F in geometry if completed by summer 2026. After that cutoff, no coursework can clear a geometry deficiency; a **full year of geometry** is required[20].

---

[20] The only exception is a challenge exam administered by your high school that results in an official letter grade and transcript credit.

For **LOTE**, the same logic applies. A higher-level year of the same language validates all lower levels. Spanish III validates Spanish I and II. The second semester of any LOTE level validates a deficiency in the first semester of that same level.

However, validation comes with a **catch**. Unlike repeating a course, where the new grade replaces the original in the GPA calculation, validation keeps both grades in the GPA, and both grades remain visible during review. The D or F stops being a subject omission, but it **does not disappear** from either the transcript or the GPA. In addition, validating an omission satisfies the subject requirement but does not add the missing semester to your A-G course count.

Your UC GPA

This may come as a surprise, but your UC GPA may not be the same number that your high school puts on your transcript. UC admissions recalculate your GPA using its own rules. Since thousands of high schools grade differently, the UC needs a consistent way to compare applicants across all of them. Understanding how the recalculation works is important because it can significantly change your assumptions about **how competitive your profile** really is and, therefore, influence your college list.

Only A-G courses completed in **tenth and eleventh grade** count towards the GPA, including summer sessions following ninth, tenth, and eleventh grades. Courses taken in ninth grade can satisfy subject requirements, but freshman year grades do not factor into the GPA.

> **Grade point values conversion:**
> A = 4.0, B = 3.0, C = 2.0, D = 1.0, and F = 0.0
> High school plus and minus grades are not used (a B-plus and a B-minus are both worth 3.0 points), but college plus and minus affect the UC GPA.

Based on your A-G subjects and the letter-grade point conversion, the UC calculates three different GPAs, and each one serves a different purpose. Most campuses evaluate applications using all three GPAs, giving reviewers a layered view of your academic record.

The **unweighted GPA** shows your raw academic performance without considering course rigor. It averages your A-G grades on a standard 4.0 scale with no extra points for any course type.

The second calculation is the **fully weighted GPA**, which reflects course rigor. The UC system rewards students who took harder courses by adding one **extra grade point** for UC-approved honors, AP, IB, and transferable college courses. In the fully weighted GPA, there is no cap on how many semesters can earn the boost. The extra point only applies to grades of A, B, or C though. A D or F in an honors course earns nothing extra, so taking a harder course and struggling in it does not help your GPA. The UC uses this uncapped version specifically for **ELC identification**, where students are ranked within their own school. It may also factor into the campus review process.

The third variation is the **capped weighted GPA**, and it is probably the most important of the three to understand. We discussed earlier that not every high school offers the same number of AP and honors courses. A student at a well-resourced school with twenty AP options has a structural advantage over a student at a school that offers five, simply because more courses are available to boost the GPA. The capped weighted GPA aims to level the playing field. By limiting the honors boost to **eight semesters total**, with no more than four coming from tenth grade, the UC makes GPAs from very different schools more comparable to each other. It also makes the number more consistent and reliable as an eligibility measure.

In practical terms, the capped GPA affects you most directly. It determines whether you meet the **minimum GPA** threshold and whether you qualify for the **statewide admissions guarantee**. When the UC states that in-state students need a minimum GPA of 3.0 or higher, they refer to the capped weighted GPA. It is also the number behind virtually every UC admissions profile and data table you will come across. When someone mentions a UC GPA requirement or shows you an admit range, this is almost always the capped GPA. In their review process, most campuses also look at the fully weighted and unweighted versions in addition to the capped GPA.

> **Three types of GPA**
> **Unweighted GPA**: No honors points included
> **Fully weighted GPA:** All honors points included, used for ELC
> **Capped weighted GPA:** Up to eight honors points, determines UC eligibility and statewide guarantee

Which courses earn the honors boost depends on where you attend school. For **California students**, the UC 'A-G Course List' shows which school-designated honors courses have been approved for the extra point. Approved honors classes are marked with a gold star. Not every course labeled 'honors' at your high school qualifies.

For **out-of-state and international students**, the rule is more restrictive. The UC grants the honors boost only for AP and IB courses, not for school-designated honors courses.

Worked Example

The following example puts the UC GPA rules into practice. A student's tenth and eleventh grade courses are shown below with their grades, whether they are included in the GPA, and whether they receive the UC honors boost.

Most high school courses run for a full year, which counts as **two semesters** in the UC GPA calculation. Each semester is graded separately. A full-year A contributes 4.0 + 4.0 = 8.0 grade points across two semesters. The honors boost adds 1.0 bonus point per semester, so a full-year qualifying honors course adds 2.0 bonus points total.

10th Grade Courses

Area	Subject	S 1	S 2	UC GPA?	UC Honors?
A	World History	A/4.0	A/4.0	yes	no
B	English 2	A/4.0	A/4.0	yes	no
C	Geometry Honors*	A/4.0	A/4.0	yes	no
D	Biology Honors*	B/3.0	B/3.0	yes	no
E	Spanish 2	B/3.0	B/3.0	yes	no
F	AP Art History	A/4.0	A/4.0	yes	yes
-	P.E.	A/4.0	A/4.0	no	no

* School honors only, not recognized as honors course by the UC

11th Grade Courses

Area	Subject	S 1	S 2	UC GPA?	UC Honors?
A	AP US History	A/4.0	A/4.0	yes	yes
B	AP Language/ Composition	A/4.0	A/4.0	yes	yes
C	Pre-Calculus	B/3.0	B/3.0	yes	no
D	AP Chemistry	A/4.0	A/4.0	yes	yes
E	Spanish 3	B/3.0	B/3.0	yes	no
G	AP Computer Science	A/4.0	A/4.0	yes	yes
G	Psychology	B/3.0	B/3.0	yes	no

While Geometry and Biology are labeled honors courses at the student's high school, they are not UC-approved as honors course, so they receive no boost. PE is non-A-G and is excluded from the GPA calculation entirely. This student completed 13 A-G courses across 10th and 11th grade (26 A-G semesters).

Unweighted GPA

The unweighted GPA treats every A-G course the same, without boost.

10th grade points:

English 2:	4.0 + 4.0 = 8.0
Geometry:	4.0 + 4.0 = 8.0
Biology:	3.0 + 3.0 = 6.0
World History:	4.0 + 4.0 = 8.0
Spanish 2:	3.0 + 3.0 = 6.0
AP Art History:	4.0 + 4.0 = 8.0
10th grade subtotal:	**44.0**

11th grade points:

AP Language & Composition:	4.0 + 4.0 = 8.0
Pre-Calculus:	3.0 + 3.0 = 6.0
AP Chemistry:	4.0 + 4.0 = 8.0
AP US History:	4.0 + 4.0 = 8.0
Spanish 3:	3.0 + 3.0 = 6.0
AP Computer Science:	4.0 + 4.0 = 8.0
Psychology:	3.0 + 3.0 = 6.0
11th grade subtotal:	**50.0**

Total grade points: 44.0 + 50.0 = 94.0 ÷ 26 A-G semesters
= 3.62 unweighted GPA

Fully weighted GPA

The fully weighted GPA includes all bonus points for honors classes.

The qualifying honors courses include AP Art History in tenth grade and AP Language & Composition, AP Chemistry, AP US History, and AP Computer Science in grade eleven. That is a total of 5 AP courses × 2 semesters = 10 qualifying semesters. Geometry, Biology, Psychology, Pre-Calculus, Spanish 2, and Spanish 3 receive no boost.

Unweighted points:	94.0
Honors bonus:	10 semesters × 1.0 = 10.0
Fully weighted total:	104.0 ÷ 26 A-G semesters
	= 4.00 fully weighted GPA

Capped weighted GPA

The capped weighted GPA limits the honors bonus to eight semesters.

This student has ten qualifying semesters, but **only eight** bonus points apply.

Unweighted total:	94.0
Capped honors bonus:	8 semesters × 1.0 = 8.0
Capped weighted total:	102.0 ÷ 26 A-G semesters
	= 3.92 capped weighted GPA

This student's unweighted GPA is 3.62, their fully weighted GPA is 4.00, and their capped weighted GPA is 3.92.

UC **admission profiles** typically use the **capped weighted UC GPA**, so use that number when comparing yourself to published GPA ranges. A student using the fully weighted version may believe they are more competitive than they really are. In our example, the student is eligible for admissions as both a California resident (3.0 minimum) and nonresident applicant (3.4 minimum).

Dual Enrollment

College courses taken through dual enrollment or directly at a four-year college count toward the **A-G requirement** if the college is accredited, the course is UC-transferable and baccalaureate-level, it carries at least 3 semester units or 4 quarter units, fits a clear A-G subject area, and you earned a C or better. A C-minus does not qualify. Transferability can usually be checked through the ASSIST database[21]. Courses may be taken in person or online.

[21] assist.org

College courses that meet these criteria receive the honors **GPA boost**, just like AP, IB, or UC-approved honors classes (within the UC limit on honors points). Because these courses are taught at the college level, they are often viewed as strong evidence that a student is **ready for advanced academic work**. Transferable college credit earned in high school also becomes part of your UC academic record after enrollment. If you passed the course with a C or better, you generally cannot repeat that course at the UC, and the units will count toward the total units required for your degree.

Your college transcript is not optional: its grades and content become part of your **permanent academic record**. Before you sign up for a college course, understand that a grade earned at 16 will follow you. Permanently. Another rule that often surprises students is how college courses translate into high school credit.

> **How college courses translate into A-G credit**
> One semester of a college course counts as one full year of a high school A–G subject requirement but contributes only one grade to the UC GPA.

For example, a student who takes Calculus I at a community college for one semester may satisfy one full year of high school math. However, for GPA purposes, it still counts as one course grade, not two semester grades like a typical year-long high school class.

Standardized Testing

As a **test-blind** institution, the UC does not use SAT or ACT scores for admissions decisions or scholarships. If you have already tested and are wondering whether to submit scores, the answer is that they will not help you for admissions. However, once admitted, self-reported scores may be used for course placement. In May 2026, more than 600 UC faculty members have called for the return of standardized testing for STEM majors, citing too many students being unprepared for college math. My prediction is that standardized testing is likely return in some form.

The UC, however, does **consider AP** and **IB courses**. Taking an AP or IB course earns you the honors boost in the GPA calculation regardless of your exam score. The exam score itself does not affect your UC GPA, but strong scores serve two other functions. First, they demonstrate **academic readiness** in a way that adds useful context to your application. Second, they can earn you **college credit** once you enroll. Some students arrive at a UC campus with enough AP, IB, or college credits to place out of General Education courses or enter with sophomore standing. The UC encourages students who complete AP courses to also sit for the exam. Self-reported AP and predicted IB scores can be entered directly into the UC application.

For international students and those who have completed fewer than three years of high school in the United States, the UC requires **proof of English** language proficiency through tests such as TOEFL, IELTS, or Duolingo. Unlike its paper predecessor, the English section of the digital SAT has not been approved. Campuses may have specific score minimums and tests they accept, so check each campus admissions page for details.

Residency

Many students assume that because they live in California, they are automatically considered California residents. The reality is more nuanced than that. The UC uses residency in two separate ways, and one does not guarantee the other.

Residency for admission purposes determines which GPA minimum applies to you. You qualify as a California resident if you attended a California high school for at least three years and graduated from one, or if you have lived in California for at least 12 months before enrollment. California residents need a minimum 3.0 capped weighted UC GPA to be eligible, and out-of-state and international students must have at least a 3.4 GPA.

Residency for tuition purposes is a separate issue. The financial difference between resident and nonresident tuition is tens of thousands of dollars per year. We will discuss the details of how the UC defines residency and what it means for both admissions and tuition later. If there is any ambiguity in your situation, such as a recent move, time spent out of state, or a non-traditional family setup, contact the admissions office before you submit your application.

Nonresident Applicants

International and out-of-state students bring academic backgrounds that do not always map neatly onto California's A-G framework. The GPA calculation uses the same tenth and eleventh-grade A-G courses, weighted and capped, but the minimum GPA is 3.4. In addition, the UC grants the honors GPA boost **only for AP and IB** courses. School-designated honors courses do not earn the extra point in the GPA calculation, though they may still be considered during the selection process as an indicator of course rigor. International transcripts are evaluated on their content, not matched against a pre-approved list. If your transcript format is non-traditional in any way, confirm how the UC will handle it well before senior year.

Special Diplomas, Home-Schooling, Admissions by Exception

Not every student applying to the UC has a traditional high school diploma. The UC allows certain alternatives. For California students, the main option is the Certificate of Proficiency upon successful completion of the High School Equivalency Test **(HiSET)**. The UC also accepts the General Education Diploma **(GED)** and proficiency examinations from other states. Students with one of these credentials still apply through the regular UC application as first-year applicants. The alternative credential can satisfy the diploma requirement, but the academic expectations stay the same: students still need to meet UC's subject requirements and minimum GPA requirements for eligibility.

For **home-schooled students**, the critical question is whether your coursework can be verified through a recognized program. Students with an approved district record apply as standard applicants and go through the same review process as any other student. If your transcript is competency-based, mastery-based, or cannot be verified through a recognized program, the UC has no reliable way to evaluate your academic record through the standard process. In this case, admission by exception becomes the only available pathway.

Admission by exception (AbE) exists because the UC recognizes that real life does not always follow a standard path. AbE is a discretionary pathway for students who fall short of standard eligibility but show meaningful evidence of potential. There is no separate application and no box to check. Homeschooled students apply through the standard UC application and explain their circumstances in the Personal Insight Questions and the 'Additional Information' section. The admissions office **identifies candidates** for AbE during the review process itself. Each campus sets its own criteria, and the number of students admitted this way is very small. If your path has been non-standard, make sure to **explain your circumstances** fully.

GUARANTEED ADMISSION

Meeting the eligibility requirements puts you in the pool. But for California students, the UC has built in something more: two pathways that guarantee access to the system regardless of how competitive individual campuses have become. Let us now have a look at those access pathways and what they mean in practice.

Eligibility in the Local Context

Imagine two students with the same GPA attending different high schools. One school offers twenty AP courses, strong college counseling, and every resource available. The other has limited AP offerings, fewer resources, and harder circumstances. A 3.8 GPA at the second school may represent a more impressive accomplishment than a 3.8 at the first. The Eligibility in the Local Context (ELC) program is designed to account for that.

Top 9% of the class
ELC identifies students who rank in the top nine percent of their graduating class at a participating California high school.

The program guarantees that, if you are not admitted to any of the campuses you applied to, the UC will offer you admission at a campus where space is available. In practice, this typically means UC Merced.

To identify students for ELC, the UC uses the **fully weighted GPA**, with no cap on honors semesters, calculated from tenth and eleventh grade coursework. Since students are ranked within their own high school, the cap does not apply. The goal is to identify the top nine percent relative to their peers at that same school, so the uncapped version gives a more precise ranking.

To qualify, you must also have completed eleven yearlong A-G courses by the end of junior year (the visual and performing arts course is not required at that point). Beyond the safety net of guaranteed admissions, the ELC status signals that **you have outperformed** many of your peers at your high school. This is precisely the kind of contextual achievement that comprehensive review is designed to recognize.

Statewide Guarantee

The Statewide Admission Guarantee is the UC's commitment that its strongest California students have a place somewhere in the system.

> **Top 9% in California**
> California students who rank in the top nine percent of all high school graduates statewide (based on capped UC GPA and A-G course totals) are guaranteed admission through the UC Statewide Index.

The **capped GPA** is used because the statewide guarantee is a cross-school comparison. Students are being ranked against applicants from every California high school, not just their own. Using the capped weighted GPA creates a more consistent and equitable comparison across schools with very different resources.

If you qualify but none of the campuses you applied to admits you through the regular review, you will be **offered admission** at a campus where **space** is available. You are not promised your first choice or any specific campus, but you are promised a seat somewhere in the system. In the past, that seat has typically been at UC Merced and, occasionally, UC Riverside. To enroll under the guarantee, you must complete all 15 A-G courses by the end of senior year and maintain the minimum 3.0 GPA.

Now that we understand the eligibility requirements and the pathways that guarantee California students access, let us look at the other side of the equation: how much you will pay, and the rules and nuances that determine it.

UC TUITION

At most UC campuses, in-state tuition and mandatory fees come out to roughly **$18,000 to $20,000 a year**. This does not include health insurance, since many students can waive that charge by staying on a parent's plan. UC Merced and UC Riverside are usually the least expensive campuses, while UC Irvine is at the top of the range, at about $20,000.

Residency Classification

Every UC applicant must complete a Statement of Legal Residency, which is how the university determines what tuition rate they will pay: in-state or out-of-state. A shortened version is included directly in the **UC application**, and for most California students who have lived and attended high school here, residency is confirmed right there without any further steps.

But for students whose residency cannot be confirmed at the application stage, the UC will send a separate request to complete the full Systemwide Statement of Legal Residence. That **longer form** must be submitted no later than when you file your Statement of Intent to Register (but ideally before that). Missing the deadline means being classified as a nonresident by default and billed accordingly.

Generally, establishing California residency for tuition purposes requires **physical presence** for at least **366 consecutive days** before the first day of classes, demonstrated intent to make California your permanent home, and financial independence from out-of-state parents. Moving to California in tenth grade may be enough to qualify for the resident GPA threshold for admission, but the 366-day physical presence requirement for tuition is a separate clock. It does not start until you have established California as your permanent home, which means having a California driver's license or ID, registering to vote in California, and demonstrating financial ties to the state.

Financial dependence is the other key variable that catches families off guard: if out-of-state parents still claim you as a tax dependent, your **parents' residency** usually **overrides yours** for tuition purposes. And for students on a non-immigrant visa, no amount of time spent in California schools changes the tuition classification. This covers a wide range of visa types including student, exchange visitor, business, and temporary work visas. If your visa requires you to return to your home country, you are classified as a nonresident for tuition purposes, regardless of how many years you attended school in California. Permanent residents with a green card are eligible to establish California residency for tuition through the same 366-day process as US citizens and can qualify for in-state tuition, once that requirement is met.

Not every student has a straightforward immigration story, and for those who are undocumented or lived in California without ever establishing legal residency, AB 540 becomes critical.

AB 540

This California law allows eligible students to pay in-state tuition, regardless of immigration status.

You may have heard that you need **three years at a California high school** to obtain in-state tuition via AB 540, but that is just one way to qualify. The attendance requirement can also be satisfied through three years at a California adult school or a California community college, or any combination of the three. There is also a second path: three years of California high school coursework combined with three years of total attendance at any California elementary or secondary school. The high school **completion requirement** is equally flexible. A high school diploma or its equivalent counts. A California community college associate degree also qualifies, as does meeting the minimum transfer requirements to UC or CSU.

If you meet both the attendance and completion requirements, you are potentially eligible for AB 540 regardless of your immigration status. Keep in mind that AB 540 affects **tuition classification only**. It has no bearing on whether you are admitted. AB 540 does not apply to students holding a non-immigrant visa.

Statement of Legal Residence

Students who are **not U.S. citizens** or permanent residents have one additional step after submitting their UC application. If your residency status cannot be determined automatically, you will receive an email invitation to complete the full **Systemwide Statement of Legal Residence**. Do not ignore that email. It is the gateway to your AB 540 classification, and the difference between in-state and out-of-state tuition is almost $40,000 per year.

In the AB 540 section, you confirm your California school attendance, select all the qualifying criteria that apply to you, and upload transcripts from every California school you attended. If you are undocumented, you also attest that you have filed or will file an application to legalize your immigration status as soon as you are eligible. Filling out this section does not automatically classify you as a California resident. The UC proactively asks students to complete it, in case the full residency review does not result in resident classification. If you have already completed your California Dream Act Application (CADAA) and answered the AB 540 questions there, the affidavit transfers automatically, and usually no separate filing is required.

Tuition Stability Plan

College is a significant financial commitment, and families often worry whether tuition will increase unpredictably after their student enrolls. The UC's Tuition Stability Plan locks in your tuition at the rate set for your entering class and keeps it flat for **up to six years**. You know what you are committing to financially before you enroll. The plan also covers nonresident supplemental tuition, so out-of-state and international students have the same financial predictability. For families comparing the UC against private universities where costs can be more variable year to year, that stability is a meaningful factor.

Application Fees

The UC application fee is **$80 per campus** for domestic applicants and $95 per campus for international and non-immigrant applicants. Fee waivers are available for domestic applicants (US citizens, permanent residents, and students eligible for AB 540 benefits) who demonstrate financial need.

Eligible students can receive **up to four waivers** covering four campuses at no cost. Eligibility is determined automatically within the application based on family size and income, which you enter in the 'About You' section. If you qualify, the application will tell you about the waiver before you select the campuses you want to apply to. International and non-immigrant applicants are not eligible for fee waivers regardless of financial circumstances.

Moving Forward

We now understand what the University of California requires before it will even consider you, the special pathways that give California students guaranteed access to the system, and how you qualify for in-state tuition. Yet, being eligible only gets you to the door. The harder question is how the UC campuses decide who they let go through that door.

The next chapter explains how the UC reads and evaluates applications, how the nine campuses differ in their approach, and which programs require supplemental materials beyond the standard application.

7 | How UC Admissions Works

Comprehensive Review, Campus Differences, Supplementals

In the previous chapter, we discussed what it takes to be eligible for admissions to the University of California. This chapter covers how the nine campuses read and evaluate first-year applications. We will also look at the supplemental materials that some programs require beyond the standard application. UC admission decisions happen through a process called comprehensive review. Students who understand this process build better campus lists, make smarter course choices, and write better answers for the Personal Insight Questions.

How the UC Reads Applications

Each year, the UC system receives over **one million applications**. For Fall 2026, 251,907 students applied to an average of 4.5 campuses each. With this many applications, the UC does not simply admit the top applicants based on their grades. Instead, each campus uses a **comprehensive review process** that looks at each application holistically. Each application is evaluated by multiple readers to limit potential bias and keep the process consistent.

> **Comprehensive review**
> The UC evaluates your entire application in the context of your personal and academic background.

Two students with the same GPA might be assessed very differently if one attended a school with limited resources and the other had every advantage.

The comprehensive review process reflects the belief that academic potential and life context cannot be separated, and that including context produces better decisions.

Independent review

Each campus conducts its own review independently and simultaneously. Campuses do not know where else you applied within the UC system.

Applying to five campuses does not make any one campus more or less likely to admit you. Every campus reads your application as if it were the only one. With hundreds of thousands of applications to read, the UCs would not even have the time to coordinate. This is why results can vary so much across the system. A student who is on the edge at UCLA might be a comfortable admit at UC Santa Cruz. Each campus has its own separate pool with its own levels of competition.

In essence, UC admissions teams frame the review process around two questions: Can you handle UC academics? And how will you engage with the opportunities and intellectual life of this campus? This is both an academic screen and a contribution question.

13 Review Factors

The 13 Review Factors are the UC's formal framework for evaluating every application. If you recall the Three Pillars from Chapter 4, academics, extracurriculars, and personal qualities, you will recognize them here. What the 13 Factors add is structure and, more importantly, a fourth dimension that runs through all of them: **context.**

Nothing in your application is read in isolation. Every factor is interpreted considering what was available to you and what was happening in your life. The 13 Factors are reflected across the entire application. They show up through your self-reported coursework, your school's profile information, your activities list, your PIQs, and in the 'Additional Comments' section. Together, they form a comprehensive picture.

Academic Pillar: Factors 1 through 9

Nine of the thirteen factors are academic, and that number alone tells you something important. At its core, the UC is admitting students it believes can succeed in a demanding university environment. Everything else in the review matters, but the **academic foundation** comes first. Students who are surprised by a rejection often focus on what they did outside the classroom without fully reckoning with whether their academic record made a convincing case that they were ready for UC-level work. It usually starts there.

Factors 1 through 3 assess your **UC GPA**, the courses you completed **beyond the 15-course minimum**, and how you performed in **honors, AP, IB, and college coursework**. Together, they answer one question: Did you challenge yourself, and did you rise to that challenge? Both the choices you made and the results you produced are in view at the same time.

ELC status (Factor 4) identifies students who rank in the top nine percent of their graduating class at a participating California high school. It is a meaningful data point that goes beyond GPA. How did you perform relative to peers who shared the same school environment, the same course offerings, and the same circumstances? Rising to the top of that group says something a GPA alone cannot. If your school does not participate in ELC, this factor does not apply.

Your **senior year** program (Factor 5), meaning the type and number of A-G courses you have listed as in progress or planned, is evaluated as part of the review. By the time you apply in the fall of twelfth grade, your course schedule is already set, so this reflects the cumulative result of how you planned your high school years. A rigorous senior year signals sustained commitment. A noticeably lighter one after a strong junior year may invite questions. The UC holds you accountable for the courses you listed after admission. Dropping courses or letting your senior grades fall significantly below what you applied with can put your admissions offer at risk.

How your performance compares to what was available at your high school (Factor 6) considers your **academic environment** and context. A 3.8 GPA at a school that offers three AP courses is not the same as a 3.8 at a school that offers twenty. The UC has access to key data through the school profile, so they know what resources were available to you. While the UC does not publish specifics, they make it clear that your file is interpreted in the context of your environment.

Factors 7 and 8 shift the focus from breadth to depth, rewarding outstanding **achievement** in a specific subject and exceptional **project work** in any academic field. A special project can be something like a sustained research effort, an engineering build, or a programming project. The fact that two separate factors are dedicated to academic depth is an important signal. The UC is not just looking for students who are well-rounded. They are actively looking for students who **went unusually far** in something, whether through research, independent study, competition, or a sustained project. A student who spent three years pursuing a single question in biology is telling a different story than one with ten superficial activities.

An **upward trend in performance** over time (Factor 9) is an encouraging signal in an application. Weaker grades in ninth or tenth grade followed by a noticeably stronger eleventh grade tell a story of growth and readiness. If your record shows that arc, address it in your PIQs. A trend without a story behind it is much harder for a reader to interpret.

Extracurricular Pillar: Factors 10 and 11

Factors 10 and 11 evaluate your life outside the classroom. The UC asks whether you have demonstrated genuine **commitment, impact, or leadership** in any area. That area can be anything. A sport, a job, a creative pursuit, a family responsibility, a community role. What matters is depth and authenticity.

The broadest factor on the list, Factor 10, covers **talents, awards, leadership, community service,** and **extracurricular involvement**, but also **work** and **family responsibilities**. A student who spent their high school years working to help support their family, or caring for a younger sibling, is demonstrating exactly the kind of character this factor is looking for. If your activity list looks sparse because you were carrying real responsibilities outside of school, say so. The UC framework is built to account for it.

Factor 11 covers **projects** completed within the school curriculum or through **school programs**, and it is separate from outside activities. A student who led a research project through their science class, organized a school-wide initiative, or produced the school play has done meaningful work, and this factor recognizes it.

Taken together, Factors 10 and 11 reward **intention and depth** over volume. The student who spent three years going deeper and deeper into robotics, who can trace a clear line from their first club meeting to leading a team to a regional competition, is telling a more compelling story than the student who filled every available slot with unconnected activities. The UC is looking for evidence that you found something that genuinely mattered to you and pursued it with seriousness. That kind of focus, whether it shows up in a field of study, a creative practice, a community role, or a personal responsibility, is what these two factors evaluate.

Context Through Factors 12 and 13

Factors 12 and 13 assess the **context, circumstances and environment** that shaped everything else in your application. Factor 12 looks at your academic accomplishments considering your life experiences and special circumstances. Low family income, first generation college status, the need to work, a disadvantaged educational environment, personal or family hardship, and veteran status are all explicitly named in the framework. They are a formal part of the evaluation because the UC recognizes that identical outcomes achieved under different conditions represent different levels of accomplishment. Factor 13 adds **location**, where you live and where you went to school, as a final layer of that same context.

Personal qualities

Your personal qualities are layered across all 13 Factors and expressed through every part of what you submit.

Your determination might show up in your essay about pushing through a difficult year or through long-term commitment to an activity. Your resilience might be visible in an upward grade trend and explained in the 'Additional

Comments' section. Your intellectual curiosity might come through in a deep, independent project and in how you write about it. No single part of the application carries your personal story alone. The strongest applications are the ones where the same qualities show up consistently across multiple places, reinforcing each other.

This all comes together in the **Personal Insight Questions**. They are your opportunity to give perspective allowing admissions to interpret your application in context. Earning a 3.5 GPA while working 20 hours a week or managing real family responsibilities tells a different story than the same GPA without any of that context. Your transcript cannot provide that context; only your PIQs can. The next chapter covers strategies and tips for writing strong PIQs in more detail.

Taken together, the 13 Factors demonstrate that UC admissions decisions are not based on GPA alone. Academic rigor, growth, achievement, contribution, and context are all built into the review process. The UCs reward students who challenge themselves, make the most of what is available to them, and can articulate who they are and what they value. The 13 Factors also provide a common framework to assess a huge number of applications efficiently and holistically.

13 Comprehensive Review Factors

1. Academic grade point average in all completed A-G courses, including additional points for completed UC-certified honors courses
2. Number of, content of and performance in all A-G subject areas beyond the minimum requirements
3. Number of and performance in UC-approved honors and Advanced Placement courses
4. Identification by UC as being ranked in the top 9 percent of their high school class ('eligible in the local context,' or ELC)
5. Quality of a student's senior-year program, as measured by the type and number of academic courses in any A-G subject area in progress or planned

6 Quality of their academic performance relative to the educational opportunities available in their high school

7 Outstanding performance in one or more academic subject areas

8 Outstanding work in one or more special projects in any academic field of study

9 Recent, marked improvement in academic performance, as demonstrated by academic GPA and the quality of coursework completed or in progress

10 Special talents, achievements and awards in a particular field, such as visual and performing arts, communication or athletic endeavors, special skills, such as demonstrated written and oral proficiency in other languages; special interests, such as intensive study and exploration of other cultures; experiences that demonstrate unusual promise for leadership, such as significant community service or significant participation in student government; or other significant experiences or achievements that demonstrate the student's promise for contributing to the intellectual vitality of a campus

11 Completion of special projects undertaken in the context of a student's high school curriculum or in conjunction with special school events, projects or programs

12 Academic accomplishments in light of a student's life experiences and special circumstances

13 Location of a student's secondary school and residence

Source: University of California Office of the President

Holistic vs. Fixed-Weight Review

Most UC campuses use holistic review, meaning no single factor carries a predetermined weight, and every application is evaluated in the context of everything else. Berkeley, Davis, Irvine, UCLA, San Diego, Santa Barbara, and Santa Cruz all use this approach. But two campuses are more structured in their evaluation process.

Fixed-weight review

UC Merced assigns 70 percent of the review weight to academic factors and 30 percent to non-academic factors. UC Riverside calculates an Academic Index Score for each applicant using fixed criteria.

Both methods still evaluate the same range of information, but they apply it more formulaically. Academic achievement is the highest priority across all nine campuses, regardless of the method used.

Nine Campuses, Nine Approaches

Every UC campus operates with significant autonomy. They share the same eligibility rules and the same 13 review factors, but each school applies them differently, runs its own review process, and has its own policies around majors, alternates, and supplemental materials.

Let us now look at how each **campus applies comprehensive review**. For more context, we also look at their specific admissions statistics for Fall 2025: the middle 50th percentile of admitted California residents with their capped weighted GPA range, total A-G course semesters, and honors course semesters. The 'middle 50th percentile' means that half of all admitted California residents fell within that range, with 25 percent above it and 25 percent below. This data is drawn from the 2025 UC Office of the President admissions summary[22].

These numbers are not cutoffs, and falling outside the range does not mean you will not be admitted. They also say nothing about the strength of a student's PIQs, the depth of their extracurricular involvement, their life circumstances, or any of the other factors that go into a comprehensive review decision. A student admitted with a GPA at the lower end of the range likely **brought something else** to the file that made the difference.

Nevertheless, the data shows how **competitive** the admitted pool is at each campus and how much the approach **varies** across the system. Use the ranges

[22] universityofcalifornia.edu/about-us/information-center/admissions-residency-and-ethnicity

as rough pointers to calibrate your list and combine them with other list-building inputs like your school's historical outcomes in Naviance, major selectivity, and your own fit factors. Here is how each campus approaches review, major selection, and any program-specific requirements.

UC Berkeley

Fall 2025 CA resident admit rate: 14 %. Middle 50 %: GPA 4.16–4.29.
A-G courses 48–57 semesters. Honors courses 18–28 semesters

UC Berkeley uses **comprehensive review**. Unlike many other campuses, Berkeley guarantees review of your primary major only; alternate majors are generally not reviewed. In highly selective colleges, such as Engineering, applying to the correct major from the start is critical.

Several Berkeley programs require **supplemental applications** with December or January deadlines. UC Berkeley may request letters of recommendation from first-year applicants. Finally, a side note on the academic calendar. Berkeley and UC Merced are the only two UC campuses on the semester system (the others use the quarter system). Students at either campus should expect a different academic rhythm than they would experience at the other seven.

UC Davis

Fall 2025 CA resident admit rate: 37 %. Middle 50 %: GPA 4.07–4.28.
A-G courses 47–56 semesters. Honors courses 14–25 semesters

UC Davis uses **comprehensive review** and takes a flexible approach to major selection. Applying undeclared or exploratory is actively encouraged. Davis also considers alternate majors. When choosing an alternate, pick something outside the area of your first-choice major.

Major choice is a selection factor for three colleges: Engineering, Agricultural and Environmental Sciences, and Letters and Science. Students interested in Landscape Architecture apply as a Pre-Landscape Architecture and submit a separate application to the Landscape Architecture department in February of their first year. Admissions to Pre-Landscape Architecture does not guarantee a spot in the major itself.

UC Irvine
Fall 2025 CA resident admit rate: 22 %. Middle 50 %: GPA 4.10–4.29.
A-G courses 47–55 semesters. Honors courses 15–26 semesters

UC Irvine uses **comprehensive review.** Every application is evaluated for a **specific major**, and the campus admits you to either your first or alternate choice based on availability and qualifications.

Two programs cannot be listed as alternate majors: Nursing Science and Business Administration. If either is your target, your first-choice application needs to stand entirely on its own. A few programs require supplemental materials: Dance B.A. and B.Mus. require an audition and Art B.A. a portfolio. Drama B.A. applicants have the option to submit an audition or portfolio.

UCLA
Fall 2025 CA resident admit rate: 10 %. Middle 50 %: GPA 4.21–4.32.
A-G courses 48–57 semesters. Honors courses 20–30 semesters

UCLA is the most applied-to university in the United States. It uses **comprehensive review**, with every aspect of an application being considered in context. Like Berkeley, UCLA does **not consider alternate majors**. Only your first-choice major is reviewed. In 2025, over half of all admitted students had a GPA of 4.0 (58.8%).

Applying undeclared within the College of Letters and Science does not affect your chances and is a legitimate option for students still exploring. However, undeclared is not available in Engineering, and selecting Undeclared-Engineering specifically does impact admission due to space limitations. Nursing and the School of Music do not offer an undeclared path. Major choice is a direct factor in admission to five professional schools: Arts and Architecture, Engineering, the School of Music, Nursing, and Theater, Film and Television. All five require supplemental materials beyond the standard UC application, covered later.

UC Merced

Fall 2025 CA resident admit rate: 97 %. Middle 50 %: GPA 3.54–4.16. A-G courses 44–53 semesters. Honors courses 8–21 semesters

UC Merced is the newest campus and operates differently from the other campuses. It uses a **fixed-weight review** system, with academic factors weighted at 70 percent and non-academic factors at 30 percent. This review is more formulaic than the holistic approach but allows UC Merced to send out acceptances before any other UC, sometimes as early as December. Major choice is not a factor in first-year admission, applying undeclared does not affect your chances, and the campus considers alternate majors if you are not selected for your first choice. Merced is the only campus offering a second **admission cycle for the spring semester**. The application filing period for spring admission runs July 1–31.

Merced also offers something no other UC campus has: **SJV PRIME+**, an eight-year **BS to MD program**. Students with ties to the Central Valley can earn a Bachelor of Science at UC Merced and complete their MD at the UCSF School of Medicine through UCSF Fresno. SJV PRIME+ requires its own supplemental application.

In addition, Merced is the only UC campus with an early admission program: the **Merced Automatic Admission Program.** This program gives eligible California students an early admission path to UC Merced before the standard UC application even opens. The application takes less than 10 minutes to fill out. The 2025 deadline to apply was **October 15**, so students accepted to MAAP know very early that they have a place at Merced. You still need to submit the standard UC application and select Merced as a campus.

To qualify, you need a weighted UC GPA of 3.0 or higher with no grade below a C, and you need to be on track to complete all 15 A-G courses by graduation. Accepted students receive a renewable MAAP **scholarship of $3,000** per year for up to four years. Check UC Merced's website to see whether your school district participates.

UC Riverside

Fall 2025 CA resident admit rate: 87 %. Middle 50 %: GPA 3.66–4.18. A-G courses 45–53 semesters. Honors courses 10–22 semesters

UC Riverside uses a **fixed-weight system** to evaluate applicants, applying a consistent formula across all applications to calculate an Academic Index Score. Every applicant is measured against the same criteria at the same weights, making the process more formulaic and less subjective than comprehensive review. Applying as undeclared is permitted, but not available for the Bourns College of Engineering, School of Business, School of Education, and School of Public Policy. Students interested in any of those programs must apply directly to a specific major.

UC San Diego

Fall 2025 CA resident admit rate: 25 %. Middle 50 %: GPA 4.15–4.30. A-G courses 47–56 semesters. Honors courses 17–27 semesters

UC San Diego uses **comprehensive review**, considering every achievement in the context of the opportunities available to the applicant. Students are reviewed for their first-choice major. Applying undeclared is permitted, but students interested in selective majors are strongly encouraged to apply directly to that major. If you are not admitted to your first-choice major, the campus may consider you for an **alternate major** or undeclared status if space is available.

Every student belongs to one of eight **residential colleges**, each with its own general education requirements, advising, and traditions. Your college assignment shapes your academic experience but has nothing to do with your major or how your application is evaluated. As part of the UC application, you can **rank your top four** colleges. The ranking is optional but highly recommended. You can update it until January through your applicant portal.

UC Santa Barbara

Fall 2025 CA resident admit rate: 32 %. Middle 50 %: GPA 4.16–4.30. A-G courses 46–55 semesters. Honors courses 16–26 semesters

UC Santa Barbara uses **comprehensive review.** Applying undeclared is permitted within the College of Letters and Science, but not in the College of Engineering or the College of Creative Studies. Students intending to apply to either college should apply directly to their preferred major, as movement between colleges later may not be allowed.

Alternate majors are available, with one exception: Engineering majors can only be listed as a first choice. Students applying to Creative Studies are encouraged to choose an alternate major in the College of Letters and Science. Within Letters and Science, the Dance B.A. and Music B.M. require an audition. The **College of Creative Studies** involves faculty review and requires a supplemental application. Art, Music Composition, and Writing and Literature majors within Creative Studies must also submit supplemental materials and evidence of talent in the discipline.

UC Santa Cruz

Fall 2025 CA resident admit rate: 71 %. Middle 50 %: GPA 3.86–4.22. A-G courses 46–54 semesters. Honors courses 12–22 semesters

UC Santa Cruz uses **comprehensive review** with a genuine emphasis on exploration. Applying undeclared is actively encouraged, and the campus considers alternate majors if you do not qualify for your first choice. Computer Science is the exception: both the B.A. and B.S. are selective, and students applying to either are strongly encouraged to list an alternate major outside of Computer Science. No programs require supplemental materials or auditions at the application stage.

The Baskin School of Engineering, the Division of Social Sciences, and the Division of Physical and Biological Sciences all have high-demand majors that may be **limited in capacity**. Students applying to any of those areas are encouraged to indicate their primary major of interest and list an alternate outside their primary area.

Every UC campus reviews their applicants in different ways, but they all use the same application. Where things diverge is in what some campuses ask you to submit on top of it.

Supplemental Materials: Three Separate Processes

The standard UC application is clean and efficient: one application, one activity list, and four short essays are submitted between October 1 and November 30. Unlike many private universities, the UC does not accept letters of recommendation as part of the standard application.

For many applicants, submitting the application is the end. Yet three processes go **beyond the standard application**. They are independent from each other and missing any one of them can have serious consequences (including automatic removal from consideration). Because rules can shift, always confirm supplemental requirements on the official admissions pages.

Performing and Fine Arts

The first category requiring extra material covers performing arts, fine arts, music, dance, theater, and other creative programs. These disciplines have always assessed candidates through work samples and live performance rather than transcripts alone. An **audition** tells a music program far more than a GPA can, and a **portfolio** shows an art program what you can do. If you are applying to any of these programs, expect an audition, a portfolio, a talent submission, or some combination. This is not UC-specific but standard practice in these fields. If you are applying to any of these programs, check your target campus admissions page, as the requirements vary by school and may change from year to year.

Direct Entry Programs

The second category covers **selective academic programs**. They require additional essays, videos, or separate applications due to their competitiveness and specific focus. Let us have a closer look at a few examples.

At UC Berkeley, the **Haas School of Business** offers direct entry for first-year applicants through two programs: the Spieker Undergraduate Business Program and the Global Management Program (GMP). In addition to the UC application, applicants must complete a Haas supplemental application, typically due in **early January**. The supplement includes written responses and a video component. If the Haas supplemental is not submitted by the deadline, the applicant is not considered for admission to Haas. Applicants not admitted to GMP may be considered for admission to the College of Letters and Science. Applicants not admitted to Spieker are not automatically reviewed for an alternate major.

The **M.E.T. Program** (Management, Entrepreneurship & Technology) is jointly offered by the College of Engineering and the Haas School of Business and leads to two bachelor's degrees. Applicants must submit a separate M.E.T. supplemental application, typically due in **mid-December**. This includes written responses and a video component. If the M.E.T. supplemental is not submitted, the application is withdrawn from M.E.T. consideration but remains under review for the College of Engineering major selected. If an applicant submits the supplemental but is not admitted to M.E.T., the application continues to be reviewed for the corresponding engineering major.

At UC Merced, **SJV PRIME+** is an eight-year B.S. to M.D. pathway in partnership with UCSF and UCSF Fresno. It requires a separate application that includes additional essays focused on commitment to medicine and service in the San Joaquin Valley.

At UC Santa Barbara, the **College of Creative Studies** is a small, selective college designed for highly self-directed students. It emphasizes independent study and close faculty mentorship. Applicants must complete a separate supplemental application with additional written responses, and in certain majors, submit evidence of talent in the discipline.

Whether it is a performing arts program or a highly competitive academic initiative, the principle is the same. If supplemental materials are required, missing the deadline almost always removes you from consideration for that specific program. Many **deadlines** fall in **December or January**, only weeks after the UC application closes. Always confirm the exact requirements for your intended major at every campus on your list.

Augmented Review

In addition to special programs, augmented review extends the application process beyond the standard UC application. You **do not apply** for it, instead, the admissions office selects you. Some UC campuses use this process for applicants who look promising, but whose original application does not provide enough information to make an admissions decision. If you are selected, the campus **emails you**. These messages typically arrive between December and February and often come with short response windows. Check your inbox regularly during that period, including your spam folder.

Augmented review can include a written **questionnaire** with paragraph-length responses about your accomplishments, circumstances, school environment, or academic history. It may also include a fall semester grade update and up to two **letters of recommendation** from teachers, counselors, or coaches. When you write your augmented review responses, go back to your original application and think about what may have prompted the request. Focus on adding context to what is already there, like for example, explaining a grade trend, describing a challenge in more detail, or clarifying an accomplishment. Be specific and make it easy for the reviewer to connect what you are saying to what they have already seen.

Random Verification

Each year, the UC selects a **random sample** of applicants for pre-admission verification. Selected students are usually notified in **December** and will be asked to submit **documentation** to confirm specific parts of their application. This can include transcripts, proof of honors or awards, confirmation of activities or work experience, and other details you listed. If you are selected for random verification, you must respond and submit the requested documents by the stated deadline to remain under consideration.

Random application verification

Selected students who fail to provide the required documentation will *not* be considered for admission.

In other words, ignoring the request can result in your application being canceled. This is why you should treat the UC application as an official record from the beginning. Keep copies of transcripts. Save award certificates. Hold onto emails confirming programs, competitions, or leadership roles. Do not rely on memory months later.

Speaking of honesty. All campuses screen the Personal Insight Questions for **plagiarism** including AI. Draft and revise your answers in a word processor, not inside the UC application portal. Save versions as proof that the work is yours. This way, if you are ever asked to verify something, you will be prepared. Most students will never hear about verification at all. But if you do, respond promptly and carefully.

UC Scholarships

After you submit your UC application, scholarships require a separate look. The most prestigious award in the UC system is the **Regents Scholarship**, which every campus offers. Each campus runs its own process, sets its own award amount, and defines its own criteria. Some campuses package top merit awards under related names like Regents' and Chancellor's, Chancellor's Excellence, or Fiat Lux. Do not assume the names or structures are the same across campuses.

Regents Scholarship

Consideration for the Regents Scholarship is automatic. Submitting your application is usually enough for initial consideration.

Berkeley is the exception: finalists get a **faculty interview** in early March, and scholarship decisions are sent out at the end of that month. At some campuses, Regents finalists hear back before general admission decisions go out. Beyond the Regents Scholarship, many campuses offer additional merit and donor-funded awards that do require a **separate application** after November 30. Some campuses use the UC application, others ask admitted students to complete a separate scholarship application, and some use a platform called **Scholarship Universe**, where students build a profile to match with awards throughout the year.

The safest approach is to treat scholarship research as its **own task**, separate from the admissions process. After you submit your UC application, log into each campus portal, check the financial aid and scholarship pages, and confirm whether any additional steps apply to you.

Provisional Admission

All acceptance offers to a UC campus are provisional and based on the assumption that you will complete all planned senior-year coursework and maintain appropriate academic standing through graduation. Significant drops in senior-year grades, failure to complete the A-G courses listed on your application, or unauthorized schedule changes that reduce rigor can all result in a **rescinded offer**. The UC monitors senior-year performance, and campuses follow up when a student's record changes significantly after admission.

Integrity matters just as much as grades. The UC screens the PIQs for plagiarism and AI, and any misrepresentation or falsified information in the application can jeopardize admission, even after an offer has been made.

UC Application Timeline

Now that we understand how UC admission works, let us put it on a calendar. UC Merced is the only campus offering two application windows, for fall and spring admissions. The filing period for spring admission runs from July 1 to July 31, before the fall application opens. All other UC campuses admit first-year students only for the fall term.

Timeline
The UC application opens on August 1 for data entry. Applications may be submitted between October 1 and November 30.

After submitting your application, each campus gives you access to an **applicant portal**. In these campus-specific portals, you see requests such as residency verification steps, missing documents, supplemental instructions, or financial aid related tasks. Even if you rarely check email, check your inbox and campus portals regularly during winter and early spring.

As discussed, the process may continue with any supplemental material with deadlines in December and January. A small number of applicants may be invited to provide additional information through the augmented review process, typically between January and February.

UC **admissions decisions** are released by each campus individually in the spring (usually around March). The deadline to commit to a college is on **May 1**. This is done by submitting a Statement of Intent to Register through the campus portal. Missing this deadline usually means forfeiting your offer of admission. After committing to a campus, final transcripts must be submitted by July 1, and AP and IB exam scores are due on July 15.

	Overview of Key Dates
July 1 - 31	Spring admission application filing period (UC Merced only)
August 1	UC application opens for review
October 1 – November 30	Official filing period
December - January	Supplemental applications, auditions, augmented review, application verification requests
March	Acceptance decisions released
May 1	Deadline to submit Statement of Intend to Enroll
July 1	Final high school transcripts are due
July 15	Official AP/IB exam scores are due

We now understand how the UC evaluates applications, what each campus prioritizes, and what supplemental requirements exist. What remains is how to present yourself best when filling out the application.

The next chapter walks us through the UC application from start to finish. We will discuss how to calculate your UC GPA, how to approach your Personal Insight Questions, and how to build an activities list that reflects your full picture. That is what the next chapter is for.

8 | Filling Out the UC Application

Step-by-Step Guide

By the time you start filling out the UC application, most of your college preparation is already done. Your transcript shows your courses and grades, and your activities highlight what you have done outside the classroom. Ideally, you have started drafting your answers to the PIQs the summer before senior year.

The UC application makes all this available to reviewers and admission officers who do not know you and have limited time to review your information. This chapter guides you through the application itself, so you can put your best foot forward.

Before You Start

Do not wait until October 1 to look at the UC application[23]. It opens every year on August 1, and creating your account early gives you the advantage of time. You can explore the different sections, understand the requirements, gather materials, and work in stages over several weeks. Students who do this tend to submit stronger applications than those who rush the application over a single weekend. The filing period is from **October 1 through November 30**. If you miss that deadline, you cannot apply to the UC as a freshman for that cycle.

---

[23] admission.universityofcalifornia.edu/apply-now.html

Have the following material ready

- Unofficial transcripts for every high school you attended
- Your full senior year course list
- A list of your activities, jobs, volunteer work, and awards
- Dual enrollment courses, including the college name, course titles, units, and grades
- Your California State Student ID (California public schools)
- Your Social Security number, if you have one
- Any AP or IB scores already received, as well as planned exams
- Household income information for fee waiver purposes
- A credit card or check for the application fee

Since the UC application has many small fields, detailed drop-downs, and important explanatory text throughout, I recommend to not complete it on your phone. Use a **laptop or desktop** to avoid any mistakes. And last but certainly not least, draft your PIQ responses in a separate document, not the application itself.

Use a personal email address that you can still access after graduation (not a school-issued account). When filling out the application, **save your progress** regularly as the application times out after 20 minutes of inactivity. Although the application sections can technically be completed in different orders, it is best to start with the 'About You' section, as it affects what appears later in the application.

Section 1: About You

Most of the 'About You' section is routine data collection: legal name, date of birth, address, phone number, email, and a few optional demographics questions covering ethnicity, race, gender identity, and sexual orientation that have no bearing on admission. The parts worth slowing down for are the SSID authorization, the household income questions, the 'Your Background' subsection, and the residency questions.

California State Student ID

If you attend a California public school, you can **import your transcript** data directly into the UC application rather than entering it manually. This is a real time saver! Enter your California State Student ID (SSID) and approve the auto-upload. The import can take up to twelve hours to become available in the UC app. If the import does not auto-populate, or if your school does not participate, you enter all coursework manually. Either way, compare every course against your actual transcript before submitting. You are responsible for the accuracy of what gets submitted, regardless of how it was entered.

Citizenship, Residency, Statement of Legal Residence

The questions in this section determine two things: how much your tuition is going to be and whether you qualify for AB 540. This California law allows certain students who are not California residents to pay in-state tuition anyway. The difference between in-state and out-of-state tuition is almost $40,000 per year, so you want to get these questions right.

Residency
Because most students are financially dependent on their parents, the UC determines residency based on where the parents live.

Families must generally establish California residency for at least one year before the start of the term to qualify for in-state tuition. A family that recently relocated to California is therefore unlikely to qualify for in-state tuition right away. The same applies to a student attending a California boarding school while their parents live in another state or country.

The **AB 540** questions check if you qualify for in-state tuition, even if you do not fulfill the residency requirements. The application asks whether you have attended a California school for three or more years during grades K through 12 and whether you will graduate from a California high school. A student whose parents are not California residents, but who grew up here, attended school here, and will graduate in California may still qualify for in-state tuition through AB 540. This pathway was designed primarily for **undocumented students** and mixed-status families. The UC application itself only asks screening questions about AB 540 eligibility. If admitted, students who qualify will complete the required exemption paperwork with the campus they enroll in.

The 'About You' section asks for your Social Security Number to match your application with financial aid records such as the Free Application for Federal Student Aid (FAFSA) or the California Dream Act Application (CADAA). Students who do not have a SSN should select 'no.' It has no bearing on how the application itself is reviewed. If you are unsure about any of these questions, talk to your school counselor before submitting the application. Misrepresenting your residency is considered a serious integrity violation and can result in rescinded admission.

Household, Fee Waivers, Parents' Education

The UC application automatically calculates **fee waiver** eligibility from the household size and income figures you provide. If you qualify, the waiver covers the application fee for up to four campuses. Beyond four, the standard fee applies for every additional campus. Even if you qualify for the fee waiver, you still need to accept the waiver in the billing screen before submitting the application. If you make an error in the income figures, you can go back and edit them, and the waiver eligibility will recalculate automatically. If you have already submitted and believe the waiver was not applied, contact the UC Application Center directly[24].

The questions about your **parents' education level** provide important context and determine eligibility for the Educational Opportunity Program. Being the first in your family to attend college is meaningful context.

Section 2: Campuses and Majors

In this section, you decide which UC campuses you apply to, and which major you want to pursue at each one. If you have worked through the major selection guidance in Chapter 3, most of the research and consideration is already done. This section is where you record those decisions for the UC.

---

[24] ucop.edu/application

Add all the UC campuses you plan to apply to. Fee waiver info appears on this screen if you qualify. After selecting the campuses, you will choose your intended major. You can select **different majors** for each campus. For example, a student interested in computing might apply to Computer Science at UCSB, Data Science at UCLA, and Statistics at UCD.

Each campus provides its own **list of majors**. The list is typically sorted alphabetically, not grouped by field. Related programs may appear far apart, so scroll carefully rather than selecting the first option. Most campuses also allow you to select an alternate major in addition to your first choice. If you list an alternate major, it should be a field you would genuinely be happy to study. Switching into a different major after enrolling is not always possible, especially in highly impacted programs. At UC Berkeley and UCLA, applicants are reviewed for their first-choice major only.

UC San Diego residential colleges

UCSD applicants are also asked to rank their top four residential colleges. The ranking is optional but skipping it means the campus assigns you without any input from you.

Each UCSD college has its own living community and GE requirements, and the differences are big enough that it is worth researching and ranking them based on your actual preferences. The UCSD college ranking does not affect admission decisions.

If you submit your application and later decide to **add another campus**, you can log back into the UC application and apply to additional campuses if the filing period is still open (before November 30). This section moves quickly if you have already built your campus list and major plan. The real work is making sure the choices you enter are the ones you actually want to pursue.

Section 3: Academic History

Unlike many other colleges, the UC does not ask your high school to send official transcripts. You **self-report** every course and grade, and your high school only sends official transcripts to the UC campus you actually enroll in.

Have your unofficial transcripts in front of you and work through them systematically. Do not enter anything from memory. Report every high school attended and every course and grade, including repeated courses. The UC verifies self-reported coursework against official transcripts, and significant discrepancies can result in rescinded offers.

Verifying your A-G courses

Before entering their coursework, California students should confirm that each course appears on the **UC-approved A-G List**[25] for their high school. Not every course offered at a California high school automatically qualifies. The same is true for honors credits. The UC application uses four honors codes: AP for Advanced Placement, HL for UC-approved honors level, IB for International Baccalaureate, and NH for no honors. Out-of-state and international students receive the honors boost only for AP and IB courses.

High schools

List **every high school** you attended, regardless of how long you were there or what grades you received. If your school does not appear in the search, enter it manually. Report everything exactly as it appears on your transcript. If a school is missing or a grade is wrong, it can create problems later.

Online courses from accredited providers such as UC Scout or Apex Learning should be reported under the school that issued the grade. If the course appears on your high school transcript, enter it under the high school. If it appears only on a separate transcript from the online provider, add that provider as another high school and enter the course there.

Some outside coursework that is not A-G certified is accepted through **principal certification**, meaning the home high school has reviewed it to meet A–G requirements. This can include coursework from online publishers, language schools, or university extension programs. In those cases, the course should be entered under the home high school and briefly clarified in the 'Additional Comments' section.

[25] hs-articulation.ucop.edu/agcourselist

Summer coursework

Report summer courses under the school that **issued the grade**. If the course appears on your main high school transcript, enter it there. If it appears only on a separate transcript from the summer program, list that institution separately in 'Academic History' and enter the course under it.

Summer courses can count toward A-G requirements and GPA if they meet A-G standards and are equivalent to courses offered during the regular school year. Only courses taken the summers after 9th, 10th, and 11th grade count toward the UC GPA. Courses taken the summer after graduation do not count toward fulfilling A-G requirements or the GPA calculation.

Entering Courses Grade by Grade

The application prompts you to enter all coursework from ninth grade to twelfth grade. Ninth grade courses count toward A-G subject requirements but do not factor into the UC GPA calculation. For every grade level, enter the course names **exactly as they appear** on your transcript; do not rewrite or 'improve' course titles. Once you are enrolled, the UC staff compares the application directly to the transcript during verification, and mismatched course titles can create unnecessary problems.

Only enter courses that appear on your school's UC-approved A-G List. If an approved A-G course does not appear in the dropdown menu, you can enter it manually. P.E., sports, driver's education, test preparation, and similar non-A-G courses do not belong in the 'Academic History.' You can enter these courses in the 'Other coursework' section under 'Activities and Awards.'

Senior year coursework

In twelfth grade, enter first-semester courses as 'in progress' and second-semester courses as 'planned.'

If your school used more than one grading or term system, report that accurately. This can happen with block schedules or schools that have changed from semesters to quarters. If none of the listed grading systems fit your record, choose 'Other' and explain it briefly in the 'Additional Comments.'

> **Repeated coursework**
> Report all repeated courses. The passing grade (A, B, or C) replaces the original (D or F) in the GPA calculation, but you must still enter the original course and grade.

The UC requires full transparency. A student who earned a D in Algebra 1 in ninth grade and retook it the following year for a B needs to **report both attempts**. Omitting a repeated course can become a real issue once you are admitted. The UC has **specific rules** about how repeated courses are evaluated and counted.

First, you can only repeat a course in which you earned a D or F; you cannot repeat a passed course with a grade of C or higher. A course can be repeated multiple times until a passing grade (C) is earned, but the repeat course must have a similar curriculum to the original. A non-honors course cannot replace an honors course, but a transferable college course may replace a non-honors, honors, AP, or IB course. The passing and non-passing grades are not averaged; the **passing grade replaces** the D or F for the GPA calculations. To count toward the GPA, the repeat course must be completed by the summer following 11th grade.

If your transcript has a grade that you are worried about or a semester that went badly, do not leave it unexplained. If there is a genuine reason like a family crisis, an illness, or a school transition, address it in the 'Additional Comments' section. Give as much context as possible, but do not make excuses or blame your teachers.

7th and 8th grade

High school-level math or a language other than English taken in seventh or eighth grade can count toward A-G subject requirements, but do not factor into the UC GPA calculation. Only report courses where you received a C or better.

Dual Enrollment and College Coursework

College courses taken while in high school must be entered as college coursework, not with the grade-level high school classes. A course taken at a community college during tenth grade is not treated as a tenth-grade course in the UC's framework. Even if you took the class during the school year, it should not appear in the ninth through twelfth grade high school courses.

List every college where you took coursework, even if you took only one class or if the course also appears on your high school transcript. First, add the college as a separate institution under 'Colleges attended in high school,' and then enter the individual courses under 'College courses taken in high school,' including the grade received. You must enter it as college coursework with the college, units, and correct grade for the UC to evaluate it correctly.

Dual-enrollment courses should **appear only once** in the application. If the college issued the grade, report the course under 'College courses taken in high school,' not as a high school course. Even if a college course appears on your high school transcript through a dual enrollment program, it should still be **reported as a college course** with the college listed as a separate institution.

Report all grades exactly as they appear on the college transcript, including withdrawals and incompletes. Common **transcript codes** include CR (credit), EW (excused withdrawal), IN (incomplete), NC (no credit), NP (no pass), PS (pass), WF (withdraw failure), WI (withdraw), and WU (withdraw unauthorized). The UC routinely requests college transcripts after enrollment, so omitted courses or grades can create serious problems.

For colleges other than California community colleges, students need to enter the course manually, including the department and course number, course title, number of units, honors designation as college-level (CL), and the correct A-G subject area. If you attended a college program that did not grant units or grades, such as a summer enrichment or pre-college program, report it in 'Activities and Awards' instead.

Mixed Records

Students with both **international and U.S. records** need to report the full ninth through twelfth grade academic history from both systems, even if ninth grade is considered middle school in the country where the coursework was taken. Course titles may be translated into English if needed, but grades should be reported using the original grading system. Do not convert grades informally into U.S. letter grades. Use the 'Additional Comments' to clarify the grading system.

Additional Comments in Academic History

This optional section has a 550-character limit and is your opportunity to provide **academic context** that is not captured elsewhere in your application. Address any of the following if relevant: declining grades tied to a specific circumstance, limited access to courses or programs at your school, restrictions on AP/honors offerings, repeated courses, gaps in education or early graduation, or a non-traditional school environment. You may also include notes provided by your counselor or principal certification details. Be concise and factual; this section is for academic context only.

Section 4: Test Scores

By the time you reach this section, the heaviest data entry is behind you. As the University of California is **test-blind**, they do not consider standardized tests like the SAT and ACT for admission decisions or scholarships. However, the UC does consider AP and IB exams.

AP Exams

Taking AP courses and sitting for the official AP exam has multiple benefits. First, taking AP courses in high school gives you the UC honors **GPA boost**. Second, reporting official AP exam scores adds another piece of academic information to your record. Because the AP exam is the same nationwide, it provides a **standardized measure** of how well you mastered the material covered in the course. A score of 3 or higher is considered a passing score.

Third, AP exam scores can also help readers **interpret your transcript**. A strong exam score alongside a strong course grade reinforces that you understood the material at a high level. In some cases, a high exam score paired with a slightly lower course grade can show mastery that is not fully reflected in the transcript alone. The general recommendation is to **report scores of 3** or higher. Some campuses also award college credit for qualifying AP scores, so check the individual campus policies.

If you **self-studied** for an AP exam without taking the course in your high school, the coursework does not appear on your transcript and does not contribute to your GPA. The benefit of self-studying for an AP exam is that it demonstrates your initiative and academic interest in a specific field.

IB Exams

If you are pursuing the full International Baccalaureate diploma, check the corresponding box in this section of the application. The UC recognizes the full diploma as a distinct achievement, separate from individual course and exam scores. IB Higher Level courses give you the honors GPA boost. Higher Level exams with scores of 5, 6, or 7 can also earn college credit at UC campuses (Standard Level exams generally do not). **Report** all exam scores, including **predicted scores** for planned exams.

English Language Proficiency

International applicants whose primary language of instruction was not English report TOEFL iBT, IELTS, or Duolingo English Test scores here. Unlike the paper version, the digital SAT does not satisfy the English proficiency requirement. If you took the test more than once, report all sittings or your highest overall score. Scores must be no more than two years old. Check individual campus policies before submitting; some campuses request higher exam scores than others.

International Exams

International exams such as IGCSE, GCSE, A-Level, AS-Level, and similar international exams belong here, including projected scores for exams not yet taken. Do not leave this section blank if you have international credentials.

Section 5: Activities and Awards

This section reports what you did with your time **outside the classroom**. The UC is asking for substance: what you did, how long, what you were responsible for, and what it produced or changed. Each description has a **350-character** limit. The six categories are award or honor, educational preparation program, extracurricular activity, other coursework, volunteer or community service, and work experience. You can enter **up to 20 entries** across all six categories. Focus on quality over quantity.

Awards and honors can be academic, athletic, community, or arts recognition. Educational preparation programs include AVID, EAOP, TRIO, Upward Bound, and MESA, among others. Other coursework is for academic work that does not appear in your A-G history, such as language schools, religious studies, career and vocational courses, and non-transferable college courses.

Volunteer and community service explicitly includes family responsibilities and unpaid internships. For work experience, the application asks whether the position was paid and how the income was used. If you worked to contribute to household expenses, support your family, or cover personal costs, say so. It is important context that helps reviewers understand your responsibilities.

Making Descriptions Count

A strong activity description has three ingredients: what you did, what you were responsible for, and what the outcome was. The difference between a weak entry and a strong one almost always comes down to specificity and ownership. Consider this example:

Activity description
Weak: Member of robotics team. Competed at regional level.
Better: Led software subteam of 6; designed and programmed autonomous navigation and drive systems; identified and resolved critical sensor failures under competition deadlines; presented technical solutions to full team; qualified for regional competition two consecutive years, advancing to state finals.

Quantify as much as you can. For awards and honors, especially, numbers do the work that adjectives cannot. Be mindful not to exaggerate or fabricate entries because the information is subject to verification. The Appendix includes a word bank of action verbs organized by activity type.

Section 6: Scholarships and Support Programs

This section takes only a few minutes but can have a meaningful financial and academic impact. Select every scholarship category that applies to you. Failing to check a relevant category can mean missing consideration for an award you would have qualified for. Some scholarship consideration is triggered **automatically** through this section, so take a few minutes to read each option carefully.

The UC support programs include the **Educational Opportunity Program** for first-generation and low-income students, as well as foster youth support programs. EOP is not just financial aid; it connects students to academic support, advising, priority registration at some campuses, and a community of peers navigating similar experiences. If you are a first-generation student, a low-income student, or both, this is one of the most important boxes you will check in the entire application.

If you have ever been in **foster care**, check this section. All UC campuses offer dedicated Guardian or Hope Scholars programs providing academic advising, housing support, financial aid, counseling, priority registration, and career planning. None of these resources reach you unless you identify yourself in the application.

Section 7: Personal Insight Questions

The Personal Insight Questions are the only place in the UC application where your voice comes through directly; everything else is data: grades, courses, test scores, and activity descriptions. The PIQs turn your record into a real person.

Do not wait until senior fall to write your PIQ answers. The eight prompts usually stay the same every year. Ideally, you begin the writing process the **summer before senior year**. Draft your responses in a word processor and save the versions as you revise. Paste the final text into the application once you are done. The UC application has no autosave and drafting inside the application itself risks losing your work. The PIQs must be your own writing in your own voice. All responses are checked for plagiarism, including content generated by AI.

You choose **four out of eight prompts**. Each response is capped at **350 words**. Since all eight prompts carry equal weight, the goal is to find the four that let you say something genuine, specific, and true about who you are.

Choosing Your PIQs

Before you get started, take time to **brainstorm**. Write down the experiences that shaped you, the values you live by, and the challenges that changed how you think. Then **map those stories** to the prompts rather than reading the prompts and trying to construct a story from scratch. Students who start with their own experiences usually write stronger responses than students who start directly from the prompt.

Once you have your material, look for **range**. Think of your four PIQs as puzzle pieces that together form a single picture. If three responses revolve around the same activity or theme, the application feels narrow even if the individual responses are strong. The reader should finish your four PIQs feeling like they know you from multiple angles, not just one. **Prompt 8** is worth approaching with particular care. Because it places no constraints on what you can say, students frequently digress and produce responses that feel unfocused or repeat what they have already said elsewhere.

The Eight Prompts

1. **Leadership:** Describe an example of your leadership experience in which you have positively influenced others, helped resolve disputes, or contributed to group efforts over time.
2. **Creativity:** Every person has a creative side, and it can be expressed in many ways: problem solving, original and innovative thinking, and artistically, to name a few. Describe how you express your creative side.
3. **Talent or Skill:** What would you say is your greatest talent or skill? How have you developed and demonstrated that talent over time?
4. **Educational Opportunity or Barrier:** Describe how you have taken advantage of a significant educational opportunity or worked to overcome an educational barrier you have faced.
5. **Significant Challenge:** Describe the most significant challenge you have faced and the steps you have taken to overcome this challenge. How has this challenge affected your academic achievement?
6. **Academic Subject:** Think about an academic subject that inspires you. Describe how you have furthered this interest inside and/or outside of the classroom.
7. **Community:** What have you done to make your school or your community a better place?
8. **Strong Candidate:** Beyond what has already been shared in your application, what do you believe makes you a strong candidate for admissions to the University of California?

Common PIQ Mistakes

One of the most frequent problems is **burying the topic**. Some responses do not reveal what they are actually about until several paragraphs in, or sometimes not until the very last sentence. By that point, the reader has been trying to follow an unclear thread through the entire essay. State what the response is right in the beginning, then use the rest of the space by delivering on it.

Another common mistake is writing to **sound impressive**. Some students reach for elevated language, grand themes, or dramatic framings that feel performative rather than personal. A related issue is using the response to **lecture the reader** on a topic or field of research. The admissions team is not reading your PIQ to learn about quantum physics or economic theory. They are reading it to learn more about you. If the response could have been written by anyone who has read the same books or taken the same courses, it is not personal enough.

Making the response **about someone else** is another common issue. Some PIQs spend so much time describing a parent, a teacher, or a coach that the applicant nearly disappears. Those people may have been genuinely influential, and that influence can be part of the story. But the response needs to be about what you did, what you thought, what you learned, and how you changed.

The biggest mistake, however, is to write a PIQ **without reflection**. Many times, students describe what happened in detail but skip any insights they have gained. A PIQ without the why behind the what is a missed opportunity.

Helpful Framework

There is no single correct way to write a PIQ response, and the best essays often find their own shape. But if you are staring at a blank page or a draft that is not working, it helps to have some structure to get started. I developed the six-step S.S.T.E.P.S. method to provide a framework for a strong PIQ response.

S.S.T.E.P.S. Method

State Your Point	At the very beginning, state your main idea so the reader knows what the PIQ is about. Do not make them guess.
Story	Present a specific personal experience or scene that pulls the reader in and makes it personal.

Take Action	Explain what steps you took. Not what happened around you or what your team accomplished. What did you do?
Effect	Show what changed because of your actions. This can be external (something you built, changed, or contributed to) or internal (a shift in how you think or who you are). The best responses show both.
Perspective	Articulate what you have learned and what you understand now that you did not before. This is the most important part and the one most students rush or skip entirely.
So What?	Why does it matter? Connect the experience to the future. How does what you learned shape how you act now, and how will it influence your time in college?

Most students spend too much space on what happened and not enough on what it meant. As a rough guide, aim for about 30 percent story and 70 percent reflection. Most drafts get this backwards, rushing the ending with a sentence or two about what the student learned. That is usually where the most important writing lives, and it deserves more than an afterthought.

Reading about a framework is one thing; seeing it in action is another. The following is an annotated sample PIQ response with each element of S.S.T.E.P.S. identified so you can see how the method works inside a real piece of writing.

Annotated Sample PIQ

I learned what leadership really means when my robotics team's robot kept failing, and I realized the real problem was not the robot but how we handled pressure.

> **State your point:** The main idea is stated in the first sentence. The reader knows immediately what this PIQ is about.

During a scrimmage, the robot ran for about thirty seconds, drifted sideways, froze, and stopped responding. Everyone immediately started guessing. Maybe the battery was dying. A loose wire. Corrupted code? I was the captain of the software subteam, and suddenly everyone was looking at me for an answer I did not have.

> **Story:** A specific scene with a real problem and real pressure. The student's individual role is established immediately.

That night, I realized the real issue was that we had no reliable way to diagnose problems. At the next practice, I proposed a simple testing system. Instead of trying random fixes, we ran the same routine repeatedly and logged the sensor data each time. I added debugging outputs so we could see exactly when the robot stopped reading inputs. I also worked with the mechanical lead to inspect wiring while I tested smaller sections of the code.

> **Take action:** Every verb belongs to the student. Proposed, added, tested. Lots of 'I'-statements. The reader never has to wonder what this person did.

Eventually, we noticed the failure always happened at the same point in the routine. The problem was a filter in my code: bright gym lights caused sensor spikes, the filter overcorrected, and the navigation loop froze. Once I adjusted it, the robot stopped failing. But the bigger change was how our team approached problems. Instead of arguing over guesses, people started trusting the testing. When something failed, we ran the routine again, checked the logs, and looked for patterns. At first, it felt tedious, but over time, everyone saw that careful testing solved problems faster than frantic guessing.

> **Effect:** Two things changed, the robot and the team's behavior. The reader can see the before and after.

I used to believe a leader needed the answer or at least needed to look like they had one. Now I think leadership is creating a process that helps people find the answer together. I also learned that panic spreads quickly, but structure can spread just as fast. More personally, I learned that not knowing something is not the same as failing. What matters is whether you can stay steady enough to keep moving.

Perspective: The reflection moves in two directions, outward toward leadership and inward toward personal learning.

In college, I want to build environments where uncertainty becomes a problem to solve rather than a reason to panic.

So what? One sentence connects the experience to what comes next.

What makes this response strong is not the problem the student solved but the thinking they did afterwards. The reader learns what happened, how this student thinks under pressure, what they value, and what kind of person they are becoming.

Sometimes, though, the four PIQ responses are not enough to capture the full picture. If there is context that would help a reader understand your application more completely, there is a dedicated section for it.

Additional Comments

This is your second opportunity to provide more context, this time personal rather than academic. The field allows up to **550 words**; significantly more space than the 550-character limit in the 'Academic History.' If you have nothing that genuinely needs explanation, leave it blank.

Good uses include **extenuating circumstances** that affected your academic or extracurricular performance, such as an illness, a family situation, or a special education need. Use it to clarify anomalies in your transcript or activities like a gap in your education, a school change, or an unusual grading system. However, this section is not the space for a fifth PIQ or commenting on circumstances in a way that reads as a complaint rather than context.

Section 8: Review and Submit

This is your last opportunity to **catch mistakes** before the application is submitted. Review every section carefully. Pay special attention to the

'Academic History.' Compare your course entries against your transcript one more time. Confirm that in-progress and planned courses are correctly marked. Check that dual enrollment courses are entered as college coursework. **Generate a PDF** of your application and read it to catch any errors.

Once you submit, consider the application as locked. If you discover an error after submitting, contact the UC Application Center. Limited corrections may be possible in specific circumstances, but do not count on it. The fee is $80 per campus for domestic applicants and $95 for international and non-immigrant applicants and can be paid by check or with credit card. Submitting the application means signing your name to the accuracy of everything in the application. In the **Statement of Integrity**, you confirm that the PIQs are your own writing and that the information you provided is accurate. Withholding information, including poor grades, or submitting falsified content can result in cancellation of your application.

After You Submit

Submitting the application is not the finish line. It is the start of a months-long period during which staying organized matters as much as anything you put in the application itself. After submitting, create an account for the **applicant portal** for each campus and create a folder in your email for UC correspondence. Check both the portal and your email account regularly. Time-sensitive requests, including augmented review invitations, verification notices, and supplemental deadlines, come through both channels. Missing a deadline because you were not checking is one of the most avoidable mistakes.

If you are applying to programs with **supplemental applications**, such as Haas, MET, SJV PRIME+, UCLA professional schools, or performing arts programs, keep in mind that those deadlines arrive quickly after November 30. Between December and February, a limited number of applicants are contacted for augmented review or random verification. Make sure to provide the requested documentation by the stated deadline, or your application may be withdrawn from consideration at that campus.

If you decide not to proceed with a UC application before decisions are released, you should withdraw it through the applicant portal for each campus. Most campuses provide a '**Withdraw application**' or 'Cancel application' button within the portal. Because applications are reviewed separately by each campus, you must withdraw the application individually at every UC to which you applied.

Accepting an Offer

Admissions decisions come out in spring, typically in March. All offers are provisional pending your senior year grades and graduation. If you are admitted to more than one UC campus, you can accept only one offer. To hold your place, submit your **Statement of Intent to Register** and pay the required $250 deposit by May 1. That deposit is applied to your first term's tuition but is nonrefundable and non-transferable. Some students who received a UC application fee waiver may qualify to defer the SIR deposit until financial aid is disbursed.

After You Commit

Several deadlines follow quickly after submitting your SIR, and missing them can affect your housing, enrollment, and financial aid. Check your **residency status** in your portal. Most California students had their legal residency confirmed during the application process. If yours was not, you will have received an email with a questionnaire to complete, or you will see it listed as a task in your portal. Complete it immediately. The UC charges nonresident students significantly more in tuition than California residents, and if the classification is wrong, it only gets corrected going forward. You will not be reimbursed for what you already paid.

Apply for **housing** as soon as the portal opens. Most campuses guarantee housing for first-year students but only if you meet the deadline. Register for **orientation** at the same time. Spots fill fast, and orientation is usually where you receive your class registration window. As a freshman, you will already have one of the last registration windows on campus, so you cannot afford to fall behind before you even start.

Complete any required **placement exams** before orientation. Most UC campuses require incoming students to complete writing, math, chemistry, or language placements depending on their intended courses and major. Missing a placement exam can result in a registration hold or being dropped from a course you need in your first term.

Submit your official final **transcripts by July 1** and have official **AP and IB** scores sent directly from the testing agency **by July 15**. Do not request these at the last minute. High school registrars and testing agencies get backed up in summer. Also review your **health insurance** options. All UC students are automatically enrolled in the UC Student Health Insurance Plan (UC SHIP). If you are staying on a parent's plan, submit a waiver before the deadline, which typically falls in late summer. Missing it means paying for coverage you do not need.

Check your **financial aid** portal and confirm everything is in order. If your family's financial situation has changed since you submitted the FAFSA or CADAA, contact the financial aid office now. Finally, finish your **senior year**. Admission is provisional until the UC receives your final transcript and confirms you completed your coursework. Poor grades or dropped classes can result in rescinded offers.

Waitlist Management

If you are invited to a UC waitlist, you must **actively opt in**. The deadline to accept the waitlist offer is usually **April 15**. You can opt in to multiple UC waitlists at the same time. Keep in mind that waitlists may or may not have much movement, depending on the campus, program and year. Even if you accept the waitlist offer, you should still **commit to another school** that admitted you.

Waitlist decisions usually arrive after May 1 and can stretch from May into July. If you are admitted from the waitlist, campuses usually give you only about three to seven days to respond.

Most UC campuses do not allow extra letters or updates, and calling admissions does not help. Only **UCLA** allows an optional **waitlist response**, similar to a letter of continued interest. Keep your answer brief and concrete.

Focus on meaningful updates since you applied, such as improved grades, new awards, leadership, or completed projects. You can also briefly explain why UCLA is a strong fit. Show how you would contribute to the campus community, avoid repeating your original application, and do not send extra materials outside the official portal.

Do not rely on the waitlist

Commit to another school you would be happy to attend. Relying on getting accepted from the waitlist is not a viable strategy.

Putting It All Together

The last four chapters covered the University of California from every angle. A few things are worth carrying forward. Being eligible is not the same as being competitive. The UC is a research university system, and it selects students who show they are willing to challenge themselves, not just meet the minimum bar. Admissions is comprehensive, built around 13 factors that look at the full picture of who you are.

The Three Pillars, academics, extracurriculars, and personal qualities, are still the foundation of the application review process. What the UC adds is context. Everything is evaluated considering what was available to you and the circumstances you navigated. When everything else is comparable, the PIQs can make the difference. They are called personal and insight for a reason. Reviewers are looking for the authentic you.

Next, we turn to the California State University system. The CSU is the largest four-year public university system in the country, and for many students, it is the right fit. Where the UC is built around research, the CSU focuses on workforce readiness and preparing students for careers and professional life. It works differently than the UC, and understanding those differences matters. The next chapters break down how admission works, what the CSU is looking for, and how to apply.

The California State University

9 | The CSU System

Broad Access and Workforce Alignment

California's public higher education system has three main parts. The University of California centers around research. The California Community Colleges provide open access, job training, and transfer pathways. The California State University sits between them. The CSU was built to provide an affordable four-year education to large numbers of Californians.

Mission and System Design

Today, the California State University is the largest four-year public university system in the United States. 22 campuses are distributed across California. The mission centers on undergraduate education, applied master's programs, and preparation for the workforce.

The CSU's defining feature is **broad accessibility**. The system was designed to open doors to a four-year degree. Undergraduate learning is the core academic function across disciplines: professors focus on teaching, develop curriculum, and work directly with students. Research happens, but it supports instruction rather than being the main driving force.

Programs at the CSU are designed for completion, with clear requirements and centralized advising. The classroom experience reflects this practical approach. Instead of writing research papers and sitting for theoretical exams, assessments often include applied work like projects, labs, or other experiences tied to professional practice. If you want your academic work to translate into job-ready skills, the CSU delivers.

Workforce Alignment and Program Availability

One of the clearest ways the CSU differs from the UC lies in the offered majors. Many career-oriented fields are concentrated almost entirely within the CSU. Business is the most prominent example. Most UCs do not offer undergraduate Business majors and focus instead on graduate MBA programs. If you want to **study Business** at the undergraduate level, the CSU is where that happens. Programs emphasize accounting, finance, management, marketing, operations, and entrepreneurship, with direct application to the workforce.

The same pattern exists in other career-oriented fields: Hospitality and tourism management, supply chain and logistics, construction management, public administration, and recreation and parks management are all found in the CSU system, not the UC. These programs are designed around professional standards, licensure pathways, and industry expectations rather than academic research specialization.

Location as Opportunity

The CSU campuses are closely tied to the regions around them, and that context influences the student experience. In many cases, **opportunities outside the classroom** become part of how students learn and prepare for work. San José State University is a good example. Located in the heart of Silicon Valley, SJSU provides students in engineering, computer science, and business with easy access to internships, part-time work, and professional networks. Proximity to potential employers becomes part of the college education itself.

This pattern repeats in other industries. For example, Sacramento State sits blocks from the state capitol, allowing students interested in public policy to intern at state agencies. At San Diego State, the biotechnology corridor, international border, and military installations create unique work opportunities. Long Beach State students have access to one of the nation's busiest ports and a major aerospace hub. CSU campus location shapes career opportunities just as much as curriculum.

Selectivity and Impaction

At a system level, the CSU is designed to be accessible. Most campuses admit the majority of students who meet eligibility requirements. Acceptance rates generally are far higher than at the UC. At less selective campuses, admission rates often fall in the 60 to 90 percent range, particularly for non-impacted majors. For example, campuses such as Cal State East Bay, Bakersfield, and Stanislaus are **broadly accessible**.

However, accessibility is not uniform across the system. At high-demand campuses, selectivity looks very different. San Diego State typically admits 30 to 40 percent of applicants, and Cal Poly SLO is even more selective, depending on the year and major. Popular majors such as Engineering, Computer Science, Nursing, and Business can be significantly more selective than the campus average.

> **CSU Admissions**
> Admission is based almost entirely on academics, no essays required.

However, when more qualified students apply than a campus or program can accommodate, enrollment limits are triggered. In the CSU, this is called impaction. **Impaction** does not mean students are unqualified; it means there are only so many seats, professors, and labs available. This leads to higher admission standards. For example, applicants may need higher GPAs or extra math courses than the baseline CSU requirements to be competitive.

Impaction comes in two forms. The first is **campus wide impaction**, which happens when demand exceeds capacity across nearly all majors. Campuses such as San Diego State University, Cal Poly SLO, and San José State University are impacted campus wide. At these schools, admission is highly competitive regardless of major.

The second form is **program-level impaction**, which affects specific high-demand majors. Many CSU campuses remain broadly accessible but restrict entry to their most popular majors. For example, Sacramento State is not impacted campus-wide, but Business Administration, Nursing, Graphic Design, and Psychology are all impacted programs.

The CSU is very transparent about its admissions limitations and publishes annual information showing which campuses and majors are impacted. For students building a realistic college list, the CSU **impaction matrix** is one of the most important planning tools. Many impacted CSUs give preference to local applicants, which can make a meaningful difference in competitive majors. For example, SJSU gives local applicants a 0.25 GPA boost.

Cost, Outcomes, and Return on Investment

Cost is one of the CSU's biggest advantages. For the 2026 27 academic year[26], systemwide undergraduate tuition and mandatory fees are between **$9,000 to $10,000** per year for California residents, excluding housing and other living expenses. Cal Poly San Luis Obispo is an exception: tuition and fees run about $16,000 per year, roughly the same as a UC.

For out-of-state and international students, CSU tuition and fees typically fall between $22,000 and $24,000. This is significantly lower than the UC's nonresident tuition. Even for out-of-state and international students, the CSU often is the most affordable way to earn a four-year degree in California.

But the CSU offers more than affordability alone. Its campuses consistently graduate students into stable **employment**. Because many programs are designed around professional standards, licensure requirements, and applied

[26] calstate.edu/apply/paying-for-college/Documents/cost-of-attendance.pdf

skills, CSU graduates enter the workforce with credentials and experiences that translate directly into earnings. These strengths also show up in outcome-based evaluations. In Money.com's 2025[27] rankings, nine CSU campuses earned perfect **five-star ratings**, reflecting strong results in areas such as affordability, graduation outcomes, and post-college earnings.

First-Generation Students

The CSU enrolls a large share of first-generation college students, and the system structures reflect that reality. Clear degree pathways, centralized advising, and predictable requirements reduce reliance on informal knowledge that many students do not arrive with. Programs such as the **Educational Opportunity Program** provide targeted advising, academic support, and community for students from low-income or educationally disadvantaged backgrounds. These support systems are designed to improve persistence and degree completion.

The Cal Polys: Learn by Doing

Within the CSU system, the three Cal Poly campuses in San Luis Obispo, Pomona, and Humboldt are known for their applied learning approach that prioritizes **hands-on work** alongside theory. Generally, the term 'polytechnic' refers to an educational focus on technical and applied fields, with instruction centered on hands-on learning. This approach prioritizes labs, design studios, fieldwork, and applied projects over purely theoretical coursework.

Cal Poly SLO and Cal Poly Pomona represent the most established version of this model. Their programs are tightly structured and **project-heavy**, with sequential curricula that leave less room for unrelated electives. In exchange, students graduate with deep technical skills, extensive project experience, and strong preparation for industry or applied graduate programs. Due to their popularity, these campuses are also among the most competitive in the CSU system. Cal Poly SLO, in particular, is more competitive than several UC campuses.

---

[27] money.com/best-colleges/

Cal Poly Humboldt is the newest polytechnic campus and remains in active development. Its hands-on approach is oriented toward Northern California challenges, with applied learning tied to environmental science, forestry, renewable energy, and watershed management. Programs emphasize field-based work, community partnerships, and sustainability-focused problem solving.

Cal Poly Maritime Academy

Cal Poly Maritime Academy is a specialized campus within the Cal Poly system focused entirely on maritime careers, offering unique degrees in Marine Transportation, Engineering, Logistics, and Oceanography, many with U.S. Coast Guard licensure. The training is hands on and centered on the **training ship** 'Golden Bear,' where students gain real at-sea experience.

The campus follows a **Corps of Cadets** model with uniforms, structure, and leadership built into daily life. It is not a military academy, but the environment is regimented and best suited for students who want that structure. Admission places meaningful weight on activities and leadership, with experiences like JROTC, Sea Cadets, maritime work, and other structured leadership roles carrying real weight. Strong preparation in math and physics matters more than broad coursework.

Campus Life

Some CSU campuses have a reputation as **commuter schools.** This term describes colleges where many students live off campus or return home on weekends. However, this label **oversimplifies** a much more varied reality. Urban campuses, such as those in San José and Los Angeles, serve many students who commute to minimize housing costs or remain connected to work and family. Nevertheless, these campuses still offer robust student life that includes athletics, student organizations, and campus events. Other CSUs, such as Chico State and Cal Poly SLO, have large residential populations. San Diego State, in particular, is often associated with a strong social scene alongside its academic programs.

CSU Campuses

The CSU campuses share a common mission, but they differ in selectivity, campus environment, and how closely the school connects to your intended field. Some campuses draw the most attention because they are highly competitive or closely **tied to major industries**.

> **Most competitive campuses**
> Cal Poly SLO, San José State, San Diego State, Cal Poly Pomona, Cal State Long Beach, and Cal State Fullerton

These campuses receive high application volumes and are selective for impacted majors like Engineering, Computer Science, Business, and Nursing. At these schools, your major often matters just as much as your GPA, and admission thresholds can be significantly higher than the CSU minimum.

Several large **urban campuses** offer broad program options and strong connections to their surrounding industries. San Francisco State brings a wide liberal arts and professional curriculum in one of the country's most diverse cities, with strengths in Cinema, Creative Writing, and the social sciences. Cal State Northridge, one of the system's largest campuses, covers Business, Engineering, health sciences, and Media, and is known for its deaf studies programs. Cal State Los Angeles has deep strengths in Nursing, health sciences, Education, and Public Administration, and is recognized for its commitment to social mobility. Cal State San Bernardino serves a large and diverse student population with programs in health sciences, Business, Education, and STEM.

Some campuses offer a more **traditional college experience** with strong academics and less extreme competition. Chico State stands out for one of the most residential, community-oriented campuses in the system. Sacramento State is a major pathway into government and public sector careers given its location blocks from the state capitol. Cal State San Marcos, Sonoma State, and Cal State Channel Islands offer solid academics, growing programs, and more accessible admissions.

Other campuses are defined by their setting or **regional focus**. Cal State Monterey Bay, built on a former military base, emphasizes Environmental Science, Marine Science, computing, and service learning. Cal State East Bay serves San Francisco's East Bay region with strong applied programs in Business, health sciences, and public administration. Cal Poly Humboldt and Sonoma State attract students drawn to smaller campuses with strong environmental programs and a close connection to the natural landscape of Northern California.

Several campuses are defined by **access and value**. Cal State Bakersfield, Cal State Stanislaus, Cal State Dominguez Hills, and Cal State San Bernardino admit a broader range of students and play a major role in social mobility. These campuses have strong programs in Education, Health, Business, and Public Service and are well suited for students focused on affordability and entering the workforce.

The CSU system includes a wide range of colleges, majors, and student experiences. One campus may be a great fit because of its location, programs, or ties to local industries, while another may stand out because your GPA is more competitive there. Building a strong CSU list means looking at both:

where you are likely to be admitted and where you would want to spend four years.

> **Most common mistake**
> Some students treat the CSU as just a backup.

That can mean overlooking some real advantages, including lower cost, practical career preparation, and strong employment outcomes. The next step for us is to understand how CSU admission works. Even though campuses differ in selectivity and academic focus, they all use the same application platform. The next two chapters explain how the CSU reviews applicants, what shapes admission decisions, and how to apply.

10 | Applying to the CSU System

Coursework Over Stories

The CSU application is built almost entirely around your academic record. There are no personal essays and no detailed descriptions of your activities. Instead, the system calculates a new GPA that drives most admission decisions. That is why it is important to understand exactly how to enter your coursework correctly, since admission decisions depend on this information.

One Application, Twenty-Two Campuses

The CSU utilizes a single portal called **Cal State Apply**[28]. Each campus requires a separate $70 fee, paid by credit card, debit card, or PayPal at the time of submission. Your academic history, coursework, and personal information are entered once and shared across all campuses you apply to. Starting with the 2027–28 application cycle, Cal State Apply is expected to be more mobile-friendly, but I still recommend using a laptop or computer. Like the UC application, Cal State Apply contains many small fields, detailed dropdown menus, and important explanatory text throughout. Doing it on a phone is genuinely not practical.

The application times out after a period of inactivity, so **save your progress** regularly, especially when working through the coursework sections.

---

[28] calstate.edu/apply

Application timeline

The application opens on August 1, and the filing period runs from October 1 through November 30.

You can use the August to September window to fill in your personal information and other non-academic information but the sections covering your coursework are hidden until October 1. Impacted programs fill quickly, and most campuses stop accepting applications after the November 30 deadline. However, a small number of less competitive campuses may still accept applications after that deadline has passed.

Several CSU campuses also accept freshman applications for **spring admission.** The spring filing period for Spring 2027 runs from July 1 through August 31. Not every campus participates, and not every program is available.

Freshman vs. Transfer Applicant

Like the UC, the CSU defines a freshman applicant as someone who graduated from or is still in high school and has not earned any college grades beyond the summer immediately following graduation. Taking a course at a community college during that summer after graduating from high school is fine. But any college credit earned after that summer, for example, during a gap year in the fall or spring term, turns you into a transfer applicant. Even one course triggers this. If you are planning a gap year, enrolling in college coursework during that time permanently turns you into a transfer student.

Eligibility and Competitiveness

Meeting the CSU's **minimum GPA threshold** makes you eligible to apply. At non-impacted programs, being eligible and being admitted are often the same. However, at impacted campuses or majors, admission is competitive and depends on how you compare to other applicants. Some campuses use their own point-based systems (like SJSU's impaction points) to rank applicants within each major.

Minimum GPA
The minimum A-G GPA is 2.5 for residents and 3.0 for nonresidents.

California students with a GPA between 2.00 and 2.49 may be considered using supplemental factors, but this is not a reliable pathway. Similarly, nonresidents students with a GPA between 2.47 and 2.99 may be evaluated. 'Supplemental factors' can include things like local admission area, first-generation status, work experience, extracurricular involvement, and participation in college-preparation programs. Campuses use these when they need to distinguish between applicants with similar GPAs.

Often, the GPA minimums are only the floor. Moderately impacted programs usually expect grades well **above the minimum**, and highly impacted programs and competitive campuses expect very strong GPAs. Majors like Engineering and Computer Science are especially competitive. One example is San José State University, which uses a published impaction point system. As shown earlier in Chapter 3, a student with a 3.75 GPA can fall short of the computer science cutoff while easily qualifying for sociology. Impaction, whether at the campus or major level, determines the standard you need to meet.

A-G: Same Framework, a Few Differences

The CSU generally uses the same A-G subject requirements as the UC[29].

A-G requirements
2 years of history and social science, 4 years of English, 3 years of mathematics, 2 years of laboratory science, 2 years of languages other than English, 1 year of visual and performing arts, and 1 year of college-preparatory elective.

[29] Beginning with the 2027–2028 application cycle, CSU applicants may satisfy Area E with either two years of the same language or two yearlong introductory courses in different languages. The two semesters for Area F no longer need to be in the same artistic discipline.

All courses used to satisfy the A-G requirements must be completed with a grade of **C or higher**. For full explanations of what qualifies in each subject area, see the section on the UC A-G subject requirements in Chapter 6.

Higher Requirements at Cal Poly SLO

Cal Poly SLO has **higher requirements** than the rest of the system in both English and mathematics. For English, four years are required, and five are recommended. For math, three years are required (Algebra 1, Geometry, and Algebra 2), and five years are recommended, with the two additional years coming from advanced courses such as Trigonometry, Precalculus, or Calculus. At a campus as competitive as Cal Poly SLO, the recommended levels function as practical thresholds. Students arriving with only the CSU minimums are at a real disadvantage. The additional years of math and English can come from dual enrollment at a community college, doubling up on classes during high school, or qualifying middle school coursework (math only).

Senior Year Recommendations

The CSU strongly recommends continued academic coursework in senior year, especially **English and math.** Strong options for senior English include AP English Language and Composition, AP English Literature and Composition, IB English, and Expository Reading and Writing Course. For senior math, recommended options include AP Calculus A/B or B/C, AP Statistics, and IB HL Mathematics. Senior year courses affect two things: they matter for conditional admission, and they directly determine your math and English placement level when you arrive on campus.

Repeated Courses

The UC and CSU systems handle repeated coursework differently. While the UC only accepts repeat coursework for grades of D or F, the CSU allows you to **repeat any course**, as long as the curriculum is the same. The second difference lies in how your report the repeat in the application. In the UC application, all attempts must be reported. At the CSU, you enter a repeated course only once, **using the highest grade**. The earlier grade does not appear in the application at all, if the course title is the same and was taken at the same school district. If the repeated course has a different title, such as English versus Honors English, both entries remain in the record. Courses designed to be taken multiple times for credit, like Band or Journalism, are entered multiple times if they are A-G approved.

Course Validation

The concept of validation is explained fully in Chapter 6. At the CSU, the same principle applies; strong performance in a higher-level course can validate a gap or a weak grade in a lower-level course. The CSU applies validation to **Mathematics, LOTE, and Chemistry** (the UC does not include Chemistry). To validate a course manually, enter the course with the actual grades from your transcript. Then enter the same course a second time, putting 'Pass' in the semester being validated and 'No Course' in the other semester. Without that second entry, the validation does not register.

Online and Outside-Provider Courses

A-G courses from **accredited online providers** count toward your coursework. Enter the course under the school that issued the grade. If it appears on your high school transcript, enter it there. If it appears only on a separate provider transcript, add that provider as an additional school. Coursework that is not A-G certified but has been reviewed and granted equivalency by your home high school through principal certification is entered under the home high school. This works the same as at the UC.

Foreign Coursework

Students who attend foreign high schools report their coursework without matching it to A-G. Because foreign schools are not part of California's A–G course system, your courses will not go through the standard A–G matching process. Instead, campuses review this coursework more individually and follow up if they need clarification.

If you attended both U.S. and international high schools (also known as **mixed records**), include all your coursework. For any U.S. coursework, complete the A–G matching as usual. If your U.S. high school granted credit or equivalency for courses taken abroad, enter them using the U.S. course titles shown on your transcript. After you are admitted, you will be required to send official transcripts directly to each campus for verification. Make sure everything you reported matches your final records, since campuses will confirm your eligibility before enrollment.

Your CSU GPA

You never enter a GPA in the CSU application. The system builds one from the courses and grades you report, which means the GPA on your school transcript is irrelevant to the process. The GPA that matters for CSU admission is the one that the application generates. Small differences in GPA can matter significantly at impacted campuses, where admission decisions are often made at very tight cutoff thresholds. That is why you want to enter all coursework accurately.

> **Which courses count?**
> The CSU GPA is calculated from A-G courses completed in tenth and eleventh grade (like the UC).

Courses not assigned to an A-G category and Pass or No Pass grades are not included in the GPA calculation. Ninth-grade courses do not count toward the GPA, but they can still satisfy subject requirements. Cal Poly SLO is the only CSU campus that includes ninth grade in its GPA calculation.

Grade Point Values

The scale follows the standard rules: A equals 4.0, B equals 3.0, C equals 2.0, D equals 1.0, and F equals 0.0. Plus and minus grades are dropped and converted to the base letter grade (same as at the UC). B-plus and B-minus are both worth 3.0 points. D and F grades do not count toward your years in a subject area, but stay in the GPA calculation, so they pull your GPA down.

Honors Weighting

AP, IB, and UC-approved honors courses receive one bonus grade point. For California students, the boost applies to courses that appear on the UC A-G approved honors list[30] (marked with a gold star). For out-of-state students, the boost applies only to AP and IB courses.

Capped weighted GPA

The CSU limits the honors boost to eight semesters total, with no more than four coming from tenth-grade courses.

Including more weighted courses beyond the eight-semester cap does **not increase** your CSU GPA further. This is a major difference from the UC, which uses both the capped and an uncapped weighted GPA for its review. Students with many AP or honors courses may have a higher UC GPA than CSU GPA. Check your GPA before you submit the application. The CSU provides a **free GPA calculator**[31]. Students who run their numbers may catch misclassified courses, missing A-G categories, and entry errors while there is still time to fix them. Once you submit the first program application, most of the application locks. The CSU explicitly states that failing to report all completed A-G coursework can adversely affect your eligibility and result in denial.

Ways to Fulfill A-G Requirements

Many students discover a problem when they start mapping their transcript to the A-G requirements: a D or F in a required course, a missing subject area, or a deficiency that went unnoticed. Finding this early enough gives you real options for addressing it. The most straightforward fix is to **retake the deficient course** and earn a C or better. Summer school, an approved online provider, an adult school, or a community college course can all work, as long as the course is on the UC A-G approved list. Because the CSU counts only the highest grade for repeated courses, a retake **directly improves** the CSU GPA.

A **missing subject area** can often be addressed through a single community college course. One semester of a transferable, baccalaureate-level college course in the missing subject satisfies one full year of the A-G requirement.

---

30 hs-articulation.ucop.edu/agcourselist

31 calstate.edu/apply/gpa-calculator

The grade must be a C; a C-minus in a college course does not qualify for either the UC or the CSU.

Languages Other Than English have several additional pathways. A qualifying score on an AP or IB language exam satisfies the requirement. The California Seal of Biliteracy or documented language proficiency on your high school transcript can also work. Students who completed at least three years of schooling in a language other than English are generally considered to have met the requirement through demonstrated proficiency. AP exam scores can fill gaps in **other subject areas** as well. A score of 3 or higher on a qualifying AP exam can satisfy A-G requirements in mathematics, history, English, science, and visual and performing arts.

Application Strategy

Building a CSU list does not happen in isolation. For most California students, CSU campuses are part of a broader college list that also includes UC campuses and potentially private colleges. The CSU's lower tuition means that for many students, the financial case for a CSU is strong, even when a UC offer is available. Strong students often put CSU campuses in the 'likely' category and the UCs as target and reach schools. Private colleges fall anywhere, depending on the school and your profile.

But this is **not a universal formula**. A student applying to Engineering at Cal Poly SLO or Computer Science at SJSU may find that those programs function as reaches, not likely schools. A strong student may find UC Merced or UC Riverside sitting comfortably in their likely category. Major choice, GPA, local preference, and impaction status all influence where any given school falls for you.

What every list needs, regardless of student profile, is at least one to three likely schools, campuses and programs where admission is realistically within reach. If a CSU campus serves that role, you must do the homework and check the impaction matrix, look at historical GPA cutoffs for your specific program, and be honest about where your numbers realistically land. The goal is a solid, **balanced college** list built around your profile, your intended major, and your goals, with real options at every level. Every school on your list should be one you would genuinely enroll in if it were your only offer. Local admission priority can also shift your odds. At some campuses, being in the local area can make a meaningful difference in competitive majors.

Major Choice Determines Odds

Chapter 3 introduced you to how impaction, program caps, and entry models work across the UC, CSU, and private colleges. The examples there, including the SJSU point system, explain how major choice works and what it means for your specific application decisions.

Direct admission by major
You apply to a specific major at each CSU campus. Your admission odds usually depend on that campus-major combination and your GPA.

Unlike the UC, where most campuses consider alternate majors as part of the same review process, at the CSU, **most campuses** give you **only one major** choice. The exact system varies by campus, but the result is the same: your major determines which applicant pool you are in and what level of competition you face.

Some students try to game the system by applying to a less competitive program, hoping to switch later. Changing into an impacted major after enrollment is difficult at most CSU campuses and effectively impossible at some. Programs that have formal change-of-major processes typically require minimum GPAs and have enrollment capacity limits. Applying to a less competitive major, with the **plan to switch later,** is a very risky strategy.

Alternate and Undeclared Majors

A few CSU campuses allow you to designate an **alternate major**, but this works more narrowly than students often assume. Consideration only happens when space exists in that program and you meet its criteria. Some campuses do not use alternate majors at all. Only list an alternate you would genuinely pursue if you could not switch into your intended major later.

Undeclared admission is not a pathway into impacted programs. Students admitted without a declared major who later want to enter an impacted program must compete through the same change-of-major process as any enrolled student. If you have a specific impacted program in mind, declare it and apply directly.

CSU Direct Admission Program

If you attend a public high school in California and your district shares transcript data through CaliforniaColleges.edu, you may receive something unexpected in the mail early in your senior year: a letter telling you that you have **already been admitted** to multiple CSU campuses before you even applied. That is the new CSU Direct Admission Program. Eligible students in participating districts may receive direct admission offers to **up to 16 CSU** campuses if they meet CSU eligibility requirements, including completion of A-G coursework with at least a 2.5 GPA. To enroll, they still need to submit their application.

> **Excluded campuses**
> The most competitive campuses, SDSU, SJSU, Cal Poly SLO, Cal Poly Pomona, Cal State Fullerton, and Cal State Long Beach, do not participate in Direct Admissions.

In addition, there is another important catch to Direct Admissions: **not all majors** are eligible. Being admitted to a campus through direct admission does not automatically get you into every program there. Competitive programs like Nursing or certain Engineering tracks may still have their own prerequisites or selection criteria on top of campus admission. If you have a specific major in mind, look up whether that program has additional requirements before assuming you are in.

Private high schools are currently not included, but full statewide participation for public school students is expected in the coming years. You can and should still apply through Cal State Apply to any campus on your CSU list, including the six competitive ones not covered by this program.

Moving Forward

The CSU rewards accuracy and preparation. By this point, you understand how your GPA, major choice, and impaction shape your admissions results. What comes next is execution. The next chapter walks you through the CSU application, Cal State Apply, section by section. We will cover how to enter your coursework accurately, what the common mistakes are and how to avoid them, and what happens after you have submitted your application.

11 | Filling Out 'Cal State Apply'

Step-by-Step Guide

The previous chapter explained how CSU admission works and why the CSU is not 'UC-lite.' But when you sit down to apply, 'Cal State Apply' can feel quite familiar because, like the UC application, it asks you to self-report your coursework in detail. The main difference is that the CSU strips away almost everything else. There are no essays to write and very limited activity reporting.

This chapter covers the practical side, how the application is structured, how to enter your coursework accurately, and what happens after submission. The application itself is organized into four main areas, and you must complete all four before you can submit.

Section 1: Personal Information

This section covers biographical details, contact information, citizenship, residency, parent or guardian information, and household and financial data. The process is quite similar to the UC application, with a few specifics worth pointing out.

US citizens, permanent residents, and DACA students with an SSN should enter their number. Undocumented students and AB 540-eligible students without an SSN select 'No.' California public school students have a Statewide Student Identifier (SSID) printed on their high school transcripts. The SSID is a unique 10-digit number, separate from the SSN, that helps match records across systems.

The financial and household section includes a list of independence criteria. If any apply to you, such as being married, having dependents, being a veteran, having been in foster care, or not having had contact or financial support from your parents for the past twelve months, you are considered independent. However, **most students** are considered **dependent** and must enter at least one parent or guardian. This classification also affects the fee waivers and EOP consideration. Eligible applicants can receive up to **four fee waivers** based on the financial information entered. The waivers are calculated only after the full application is complete and must be actively accepted at the payment screen. International and nonresident applicants are not eligible for waivers.

The **'Extended Profile'** controls which questions and sections appear throughout the application. If you took any dual enrollment courses, select 'Yes' when asked about college credits. This selection unlocks the 'Colleges Attended' and 'College Coursework' sections. For the international applicant question, select 'Yes' only if you require an F-1 or J-1 visa. US citizens, permanent residents, DACA recipients, AB 540 students, and undocumented students all select 'No.'

Section 2: Academic History

This is the **most important** part of the application. The three most common mistakes are entering incorrect course information, misclassifying courses in A-G matching, and submitting before checking entries against your transcript. None can be corrected afterward, which makes the coursework section the most consequential part of the process. California students with a CaliforniaColleges.edu account can link it to Cal State Apply to **import transcript data** automatically, which significantly reduces the risk of entry errors.

High Schools

Add **up to five** high schools from grades nine through twelve. Middle schools and colleges do not belong in this section. For each school, select the term type that matches how grades were issued: one grade per course per year is full year, two is semester, three is trimester, and four is quarter. If your school uses multiple term types, enter your school multiple times, once per term type. Attendance dates must be accurate, since incorrect dates block you from entering coursework for that school.

High School Coursework

Report **only A-G courses** in this section. Non-A-G courses like CTE courses, physical education, driver's education, and similar non-college-prep classes do not belong here. When entering courses, California students will find a prepopulated dropdown as they type. Select from that list whenever possible, because those courses are already linked to the A-G database and validation rules. Students from non-California high schools must enter all courses manually and complete the A-G matching themselves.

Manual A-G matching
Manual course entries must be matched to an A-G category by hand.

Each course also requires a **course type** selection. For regular courses without GPA boost, pick 'Standard,' AP for Advanced Placement, IB for International Baccalaureate, and 'UC-approved Honors' for CSU-approved honors courses. Only AP, IB, and UC-approved Honors courses receive the extra grade point weighting. Do not mark a course as honors unless it is officially approved on the UC A-G list and are marked with a gold star.

Course titles, credits, and grades must all match your transcript. After admission, campuses compare your application entries against official transcripts, and discrepancies can result in rescinded offers. You can abbreviate a course title if it does not fit in the field, but accuracy is your top priority. **Senior year courses** are entered as 'in progress' (first semester) and 'planned' (second semester). Because CSU admission is conditional on completing exactly what you reported, dropping a required course or making significant schedule changes after receiving an offer may put that offer at risk. If anything changes in your senior year schedule, notify the admissions office at each campus proactively.

Summer Courses

Enter summer coursework under the grade level you were entering after that summer, not the grade you just completed. A course taken between ninth and tenth grade is entered under tenth grade. Each summer attended must be entered separately using the 'Add a Summer Grade Level' option.

Middle School Courses

Math and LOTE courses from middle school can count toward A-G requirements if the grade was a C or better, the course met the level required for A-G credit, and the student continued the sequence in high school without repeating it in ninth grade. Enter these courses within the high school coursework section under seventh or eighth grade.

Partial Credit Courses

Sometimes your transcript includes a course that counts for **less than a full semester**. In those cases, the goal is to enter it in a way that matches the smaller amount of credit shown on your record, rather than making it look like a standard full-term class. One way Cal State Apply handles this is by letting you create a second entry for the same high school using a quarter term type (instead of semester), which gives you a way to report fractional credit.

For example, if you completed only half of a semester-long English class and earned 2.5 credits instead of 5, you add a second copy of your high school with a quarter term type, enter the English course there, put the grade in Quarter 1, and mark the remaining quarters as 'No Course.' This tells the system to award only the partial credit you actually earned.

Dual Enrollment

College courses belong in the college section of the application, not with the high school coursework. This is the same workflow as the UC application.

Add the college in the 'Colleges Attended' section, enter the courses in 'College Coursework,' then go to 'A-G Matching' and manually assign each college course to its subject area. One semester of college coursework counts as one full year of high school credit in the A-G calculation, and UC-transferable courses also receive the honors GPA boost.

For dual enrollment to count correctly, the course must be transferable, baccalaureate-level, assigned to the correct A-G subject area, and marked with the **transferable toggle** in 'College Coursework.' That toggle does not turn on automatically, so you need to check it yourself for each class. If you skip that step, enter the course in the wrong place, or never match it to A-G, the course may not count.

Reporting college courses

Report every college and match the course codes, titles, credits, and grades exactly to your transcript, including pluses and minuses.

Enter the grade earned in the first semester in the 'Semester 1' field and the second semester grade in the 'Semester 2' field. Some colleges print two-semester grades on a single transcript line in a **reversed code format**, so the two grades do not appear in semester order. In that special case, a code like BA means the student earned an A in the first semester and a B in the second semester, even though the transcript prints BA. Because Cal State Apply reads grades in semester order, you should enter it as AB, so the grades match the correct term. Always remember to click 'Save Your Transcript.'

A-G Matching

After entering all courses, the application displays running totals for each subject area. For any course that is not yet matched, you must manually assign the A-G category by clicking **'Update A-G Course'** and selecting the subject area from the dropdown.

If Area G is short but another subject area has more years than required, the system automatically reassigns a surplus course to cover the **Area G deficit**. That automatic correction applies only to Area G. Missing years in any other required subject area, such as English, science, or history, will not be auto-corrected. Those gaps remain exactly as you entered them. Check every subject area total individually before submitting. If you try to manually override an automatic Area G reassignment, the system will revert your change.

Standardized Tests

Like the UC, the CSU system **is test-blind.** ACT and SAT scores are not used for CSU admission decisions. After admission, they may optionally be submitted and used only for **math and English placement**. AP scores of 3 or higher should be self-reported in the application, since a qualifying score may automatically satisfy an A-G subject requirement. However, self-reporting in the application is not sufficient for college credit. After enrollment, official scores must be sent directly from the College Board to your campus. CSU campuses set their own score submission deadlines, so check your campus's requirements after receiving your admissions offer.

Section 3: Supporting Information

This section covers educational programs, work, extracurriculars, and the EOP application. At some campuses and in impacted programs, this information **may be used** as a supplemental factor when applicants are otherwise similarly qualified.

Educational Programs

This section asks whether you participated in college-preparation programs during high school, such as AVID, Upward Bound, Puente, MESA, GEAR UP, TRIO, or similar programs. Select any that apply. Having nothing to report does not hurt your application.

Work and Extracurricular Experience

This is the CSU's version of the 'Activities and Awards' section in the UC application. Unlike the UC, there are **no activity descriptions** to write. You report only your hours, years of participation, leadership roles, and program involvement. Both work experience and extracurricular activities are entered through dropdown selections and are reported over the past 36 months. At campuses that use supplemental factors, sustained work experience, extracurricular involvement, and leadership can strengthen your application.

Educational Opportunity Program (EOP)

Applying for EOP at a CSU campus is fundamentally different from the UC, where EOP is a single checkbox. At the CSU, EOP is a **separate application embedded** in Cal State Apply. It includes autobiographical questions, detailed family and financial background information, and asks for two recommendations. It is one of the few places in the application process where CSU campuses consider your circumstances and potential holistically.

EOP can admit students on an **exceptional basis** who fall below standard CSU eligibility requirements but demonstrate the potential to succeed with support (but do not count on this!). The program provides meaningful support like a dedicated advisor, priority registration at many campuses, a summer bridge program, emergency financial assistance, and a peer community of students from similar backgrounds. EOP is open to California residents and AB 540-eligible students who are both **first-generation** (neither parent earned a four-year college degree) **and low-income**. To qualify, you must file your FAFSA or CADAA by March 2 and enroll as a full-time student.

EOP Deadlines and Logistics

Most campus deadlines fall in **mid-January**, with the systemwide deadline being January 31. Some campuses also require an interview. Two letters of recommendation are required from a teacher, counselor, or community member who knows you well. When you request a recommendation through the application, the system sends the recommender a link that expires after two weeks, so inform your recommenders early enough that they have adequate time before that window closes.

The Five EOP Essays

The EOP application has five different prompts. Each response is capped at **2,500 characters** (not words). Draft in a separate document first, write in complete sentences, and include specific details rather than general statements. Answer all five prompts.

EOP prompts

'Briefly describe your family's economic background. Include information about your financial challenges.'

Name what happened: job loss, unstable income, housing instability, reliance on public assistance, working to support your household. Focus on specific details that show how you meet the EOP criteria.

'Why would you like to attend college? Discuss your career and personal goals. Are there any particular circumstances, school experiences, or persons that influenced your preparation or motivation to attend college?'

Connect your motivation to real people, experiences, or moments in your life. You do not need a fully formed plan. What matters is that your goals feel grounded and genuine.

'Briefly discuss your academic background. Did you utilize any additional support at your high school, such as tutoring? Do your grades in high school and/or college reflect your academic ability or potential?'

If your grades do not fully reflect your ability, explain the specific causes: work responsibilities, caregiving, under-resourced schools, disruptions, or limited access to support. If you used programs like AVID or Upward Bound, mention them. If your grades improved over time, say so.

'List any volunteer, extracurricular activities, or work experience in which you are or have been involved.'

Include any responsibilities at home, community involvement, and consistent commitments of any kind, including paid work that helped support your family.

'Is there any additional information you would like EOP to consider in determining your admission to the program?'

Do not leave this blank. Use it to include anything important not covered in the first four responses, whether a major life circumstance, a disruption in your education, or additional context about your background. If everything has already been covered, use the space to reinforce your situation and explain why the EOP support would help you succeed.

A strong EOP application is consistent across all five responses, your financial information, and your recommendations. EOP is the one place in the CSU process where you can **provide context** and deserves your time and attention.

Section 4: Program Materials

Some academic programs and majors may also include **additional steps**, such as supplemental questions, document uploads, or instructions you need to follow after submitting your application. You will only see them once you click into the program, which is why it is important to **check this section early** and not leave it for the last minute. Missing something here can leave your application incomplete and may prevent it from being reviewed.

You will also see a **housing-related question** in the application. This is used for financial aid planning and does not affect your admission decision. The most important takeaway is simple: open every 'Program Materials' tile early, read everything carefully, and complete it as soon as you add a campus.

Residency

Residency classification for tuition purposes at the CSU follows the same framework as the UC. The full explanation in Chapter 8 also applies to the CSU. In most cases, if you are applying straight from high school, the CSU will base your residency on your **parent's residency**, not yours. Only older students who meet specific requirements can establish residency on their own.

Tuition and Housing

> **Tuition and fees**
> All CSU campuses charge the same tuition. For 2026–2027, systemwide tuition is $6,838 per year. However, mandatory campus **fees vary widely**.

These fees add about an additional $2,000 on average, although the exact amount varies by campus. That means total tuition and mandatory fees for California residents at most CSU campuses usually are **$9,000 to $10,000**.

The exception to the rule is Cal Poly SLO, with tuition and fees being roughly $16,000 per year for California residents. If cost is a major factor in your decision, Cal Poly SLO belongs in a separate financial category.

After tuition and fees, **housing** is the other big variable. Living with family can easily save about $10,000 per year compared with living on campus or renting off campus. At some campuses, the gap is even larger. In practice, campuses in higher-cost regions such as Los Angeles and San José tend to have higher total costs than campuses in lower-cost regions such as Stanislaus, Bakersfield, or Chico.

Check the financials
Use the financial aid website to check the cost of attendance and run that campus's Net Price Calculator.

International Students

International students complete the **same application** as domestic students. Additional requirements include official academic records with certified English translations, proof of **English language proficiency** (the systemwide TOEFL iBT minimum is 61, but many campuses require higher scores), and financial documentation sufficient to cover at least the first year of study. F-1 and J-1 visa holders must maintain a minimum of twelve units per term. Timelines and exact requirements vary by campus. Check each campus's international admissions page early, as some offer later deadlines or request documents shortly after submission.

Before You Hit Submit

Before submitting, **generate a PDF** of your full application and use the transcript preview and summary page to **check your A-G totals**, calculated GPA, and any warnings. Submitting means certifying that everything you entered is accurate. Errors can lead to rescinded offers, and there are no refunds for incorrect submissions, including applying to a campus by mistake.

After You Submit

Campus Portals

After submitting, you should set up your **applicant portal** at every campus where you applied. Each campus communicates with you through their portal, including document requests, residency verification tasks, financial aid instructions, housing applications, and eventually your admission decision. Regularly **check all portals** and your spam folder. A time-sensitive request that goes unnoticed because you were not monitoring the portal is an entirely avoidable problem.

You can still **add another CSU campus** after you submit, as long as that campus's application is still open. Log back into Cal State Apply, add the new program, complete any required 'Program Materials,' and submit that application.

> **Applying after November**
> A few campuses accept applications after the November 30 deadline.

Once a campus's filing period closes, you can no longer add it. If you later decide not to move forward with a campus you already applied to, withdraw that application through the campus portal.

7th Semester Transcript

Some campuses, particularly those processing **EOP applications**, request a seventh semester transcript in February, covering your senior year fall grades. This request is separate from the final transcript due after graduation. If your campus requests one, submit it by the stated deadline.

Decisions

Unlike the UC, which releases decisions in a semi-coordinated window, all CSU campuses move on their own schedules. Non-impacted programs at some campuses notify applicants as early as **December or January**, while competitive programs at selective campuses communicate closer to **spring.**

Some campuses also release different types of decisions in waves rather than all at once, so it is normal for applicants to see acceptances, waitlist decisions, and denials arrive on different dates. Unlike the UC system, most CSU campuses do **not rely on waitlists**. If you are not admitted, your main options are appeal, redirection, or applying elsewhere.

Conditional Offers

Every CSU admission offer is conditional. The campus admitted you based on the courses and grades you reported, with the expectation that you will complete your senior year as described. Earning a D or F in a required course, dropping a required course, or making unauthorized schedule changes can all trigger rescission. Senior year grades are not part of the GPA that the application calculates, but they are reviewed for conditional admission purposes. Contact the admissions office proactively if anything in your senior year changes unexpectedly.

Non-Admission Appeals

If you are not admitted and believe the decision involved a procedural or factual **error**, some campuses offer a formal appeal process with a window of roughly 15 days from the notice of non-admission. This is not a reconsideration process or an opportunity to submit new information. Contact the specific campus admissions office immediately if you think an error was made.

Post-Admission Timeline

May 1 is the national deadline to submit your intent to enroll in the campus portal. If you receive an offer after **May 1**, you typically have two weeks from the offer date to respond. Missing the deadline forfeits the offer. If circumstances change after you commit, some campuses allow a **deferral** for extenuating reasons, but you cannot defer to attend another institution. A fall-to-spring deferral at most campuses must be requested by mid-August, and not every campus offers this option.

The deadline for **final official transcripts** to be sent directly from your high school varies by campus but is typically July 1 or July 15. These must include your spring grades and graduation date. Any meaningful discrepancy between what you reported and what the transcript shows can result in a rescinded offer, even at this late stage.

After enrollment, send your official **AP scores** via the College Board, using CSU's system-wide code 3594, which covers all CSU campuses in one submission. IB scores go directly from IB to each campus. AP scores of three or higher and IB scores of five and higher can earn college credit and satisfy general education requirements, though each campus determines how they apply toward your specific major. SAT and ACT scores are used only for English or math course placement. After enrollment, check your campus portal for additional scholarship opportunities.

Redirection

If you applied to one or more CSU campuses, were not admitted anywhere, and are a CSU-eligible California resident, you may be eligible for redirection. This means the CSU is locating a place for you **elsewhere in the system**. For fall admission, redirection emails go out in mid-April. You log back into Cal State Apply, select a first-choice and second-choice campus from the campuses that have capacity, and submit your preferences. If you do not make a selection, the CSU assigns you to a campus with room.

Putting It Together

The CSU application rewards planning and precision. Every course entered, every grade reported, every A-G category assigned feeds directly into the number that determines your eligibility and competitiveness. Choose programs and campuses based on **honest GPA comparisons** against impaction thresholds, enter your academic record accurately, and submit before November 30. The one exception to this purely numbers-based admissions process is EOP.

We have now covered two of the three major tracks of California's public university system. The third option are the 116 California community colleges.

They offer a direct transfer pathway into both the UC and CSU systems. For students who did not land in their target programs coming out of high school, community college is frequently the most direct, least expensive, and most strategic route.

The next three chapters cover how that pathway works. We start with an overview of the California community college system, followed by dedicated chapters on transferring to the University of California and the CSU systems.

California Community Colleges

12 | The CCC System

Open Access and Transfer Opportunities

Community colleges are the quiet engine of California's higher education. They do not make headlines through rankings or selective admissions. Instead, they do their work through access and outcomes. Every year, more than **two million students** enroll across California's 116 community colleges, making this the largest system of higher education in the country and a primary entry point into public college education in California.

Despite this central role, community colleges are often **misunderstood**. They are frequently described as a backup option or a place students end up when their four-year plan falls apart. This framing ignores how the system was designed. California's Master Plan for Higher Education did not position community colleges below the UC or CSU. It positioned them at the beginning. Open access was not an afterthought; it was the starting point.

Mission and Structure

California's community colleges exist to do three things. They provide **open access** to college-level education. They prepare students to **transfer** to four-year universities. And they offer **career and technical education** aligned with regional workforce needs. Admission to the community colleges is open. Students are not selected based on GPA or test scores. Any student with a high school diploma or equivalent may enroll. This allows the system to serve students who would otherwise be excluded from higher education.

Community colleges enroll a more **complex student population** than the UC or CSU. Some students arrive directly from high school with strong academic records and a clear plan to transfer. Others attend part-time while working a job. Some are returning students seeking retraining. And some students need time to rebuild academic confidence after a difficult high school experience. The community college system was built to offer multiple career and entry points into higher education for all kinds of students.

Strategic Choice, Not Backup Plan

Let us address the elephant in the room. Community college still carries a **stigma.** Students hear it being called the '13th grade' or 'junior college.' Parents worry about what neighbors will think. High school counselors treat it as a last resort for students who could not get in anywhere else. Social media makes it worse, with students posting four-year acceptance letters while community college students remain quiet.

This stigma is not based on facts. It is based on outdated assumptions and social pressures that have nothing to do with educational outcomes or career success. Here is what the **data** shows. Community college transfer students graduate from UCs and CSUs at rates comparable to students who started as freshmen. They earn the same degrees. Employers do not ask where you took your first two years of coursework. Your diploma says University of California or California State University, not 'transferred from community college.'

The **cost difference** is enormous. Saving thousands of dollars over two years is not settling but smart financial planning. Graduating debt-free or with minimal debt gives you options that students with large student loans may not have. You can take the job you want instead of the job you need to make loan payments.

For many students, starting at a community college is an excellent strategic choice. Smaller classes mean better preparation in foundational courses. Transfer admission rates to competitive UCs are higher than for first-year applicants. Students who struggled in high school get a genuine fresh start. Working students can attend part-time.

The Classroom Experience

Community colleges are **teaching institutions**. Professors are hired primarily to teach, not to publish research or secure grants. Many instructors work at a community college because they love teaching and interacting with students more than doing research. **Class sizes are small** by public university standards. Introductory courses often enroll 25 to 40 students rather than hundreds. Professors know students' names. Questions are answered during class, and office hours are accessible.

Assessment tends to be **continuous** rather than concentrated in a few high-stakes exams. Students encounter regular writing assignments, problem sets, labs, quizzes, and revisions. Learning is incremental, and mistakes are expected and corrected. For students who struggled in large academic environments, this structure often makes college-level work manageable. For strong students, it allows deeper mastery of foundational material.

Community colleges do not offer large research labs, advanced graduate seminars, or extensive undergraduate research infrastructure. That **tradeoff** is real. But for lower-division coursework in writing, mathematics, sciences, economics, and other core subjects, the teaching-first model is often a strength.

Transfer Centers

Most California community colleges operate dedicated transfer centers staffed by counselors who specialize in **UC and CSU articulation**, application procedures, and major planning. These centers also provide workshops on transfer applications, or host campus visits from UC and CSU representatives. Students planning to transfer should meet with their transfer counselor regularly. They help students develop education plans that align with transfer requirements, track progress toward eligibility, and identify gaps before they become problems.

'CCC Apply' Account

If you are considering community college you should create a CCC Apply[32] account early. This is the statewide **application portal** for California's 116 community colleges. Even if you are still deciding which college you may attend, setting up the account makes it easier to move quickly once you are ready to apply.

Applying early also helps with **class registration**. At community colleges, registration priority is generally tied to completing required onboarding steps such as orientation, placement, and an education plan. Creating a CCC Apply account it is the first step that allows you to begin that process. Students who apply late may not get into high-demand courses for that term.

General Education and Major Preparation

Community college coursework serves two distinct functions for transfer students. First, **GE courses** fulfill lower-division breadth requirements at four-year universities. California has standardized these requirements through Cal-GETC. When completed correctly, these course patterns satisfy most lower-division general education requirements at the transfer institution. The next chapters explain how Cal GETC and major preparation planning work together, and which approach makes sense depending on your target campus and major.

Second, **major preparation** matters just as much as general education, and for the most competitive majors, it matters even more. Transfer admission often depends on finishing the right sequence of courses in areas like Calculus, Chemistry, Physics, Biology, Statistics, Economics, or Programming. At a community college, those classes are usually smaller and more structured than they are at a large university. For many students, this creates a better learning

---

[32] home.cccapply.org/us/

environment and a better chance of earning strong grades in the courses that matter most.

Costs, California College Promise

Community colleges are the **lowest-cost option** in California public higher education. Enrollment fees are charged per unit. For a full-time student taking about 30 units, tuition is roughly $1,400 per year. Over two years, that totals about $2,800. Many students pay even less. Under the California College Promise Grant, enrollment fees are fully waived for eligible low-income students, bringing **tuition to zero**. While additional campus fees may still apply, the core cost of enrollment is removed.

Two years of UC tuition costs between $36,000 and $40,000, not including housing or living expenses. At the CSU, in-state tuition and fees vary by campus, typically falling between $9,000 and $10,000 per year, or roughly $18,000 to $20,000 over two years. A student who completes two years at a community college before transferring **saves significantly** compared to starting at a UC or CSU right away. And students who also live at home during their community college years save even more.

How Long Does a Transfer Take?

The community college transfer pathway is often described as a two-year process. For some students, this timeline is realistic. Students who arrive at community college academically prepared, enroll full-time, and follow a clear transfer plan can complete 60 transferable semester units (90 quarter units) in two years. These students typically **transfer as juniors** after only two years.

However, many community college students do not fit this profile. They may attend part-time while working. Some need additional semesters to complete competitive major prerequisites like Calculus, Organic Chemistry, or Physics. Realistically, the average time-to-transfer is probably **closer to three years**.

The right timeline is the one that is realistic for your situation. Meet with a counselor early, map out required coursework, identify prerequisites that must be completed in order, and be honest about how many units you can reasonably carry each semester. A three-year path that gets you into a UC is far better than a two-year rush that leaves gaps in your preparation.

Higher Admissions Chances

Transfer admissions operates under different assumptions than first-year admissions. At highly selective UC campuses, first-year acceptance rates are extremely low. UCLA and UC Berkeley admit about ten percent of all first-year applicants. Transfer acceptance rates at almost all UC campuses are significantly higher than for freshmen applicants. Let us have a look at the most recent statistics.

UC Acceptance Rates Fall 2026

(Source: University of California, Transfer Admit Data 2026; Freshman Admit Data 2026)

Campus	Freshman Admit Rate	Transfer Admit Rate
UC Berkeley	10.5 percent	20.0 percent
UC Davis	45.8 percent	58.2 percent
UC Irvine	30.3 percent	36.4 percent
UC Los Angeles	10.8 percent	22.2 percent
UC Merced	96.5 percent	79.5 percent
UC Riverside	88.5 percent	70.4 percent
UC San Diego	27.2 percent	47.4 percent
UC Santa Barbara	44.0 percent	61.6 percent
UC Santa Cruz	82.3 percent	67.7 percent

Why is there such a difference between first-year and transfer admissions? First, California's public education system is built with **multiple entry points**. Not getting in as a freshman is not supposed to be the end of the road. Community colleges exist as a second on-ramp, and the UC is expected to keep that path open. The UC's goal of enrolling **one transfer student for every two freshmen** ensures that junior-level seats are always available.

Second, transfer students arrive as juniors, not freshmen. By that stage, some students have changed majors, taken time off, or even left the university. Those internal shifts create additional **openings in upper-division** programs. UC campuses often have more flexibility to admit students at the junior level than at the freshman level, where space is fixed by housing and introductory course capacity.

Third, transfer students are **easier to evaluate**. First-year applicants are judged largely on potential. Transfer applicants are assessed based on two years of college performance. The admissions office can see how you did in actual college courses, not just high school classes. That reduces uncertainty and admit rates rise as a result.

Finally, **transfer applicants** tend to be more **targeted**. Most community college students apply after they have completed the right courses and earned competitive GPAs. There are fewer speculative applications. That self-selection raises the admit rate even when campuses remain selective. The result is not a shortcut; it is a parallel pathway.

> **Second entry point**
> Over 90 percent of all UC transfer students come from a CCC.

In 2025, the top five community colleges sending transfer students to the UC system were Santa Monica College, Irvine Valley College, Pasadena City College, De Anza College, and Diablo Valley College.

UC Transfer Programs: Guarantee vs. Readiness

How can transfer students prepare for a successful transfer? The University of California offers two types of programs to increase your acceptance chances. One offers a guaranteed admission pathway (yes, guaranteed!). The other focuses on preparation for the most selective campuses.

The **Transfer Admission Guarantee** lets eligible students secure admission to one UC campus by meeting a defined set of requirements. Alongside this, **Transfer Alliance Programs** and honors pathways help strengthen your academic preparation and, at some campuses, how your application is evaluated. Most successful transfer students use both. They secure one guaranteed option while continuing to build a strong academic record for more selective campuses. The next chapter explains how to use these programs effectively.

CSU Transfer Program: ADT

The California State University uses a different transfer structure than the UC. Instead of TAG or TAP, the CSU transfer is organized around the Associate Degree for Transfer, commonly called the **ADT**.

The ADT is offered in both arts and science tracks depending on your field of study: the Associate in Arts for Transfer (AA-T) and the Associate in Science for Transfer (AS-T). These degrees are designed to bundle CSU GE with a defined set of lower-division major preparation courses into a single structured package. The degree requires 60 semester or 90 quarter transferable units.

> **Guaranteed admission**
> ADT students are guaranteed CSU admission in their selected major, enter with junior standing, and receive priority over non-ADT applicants.

However, the guarantee applies to the **CSU system**, not to a specific campus. Highly impacted campuses such as San Diego State, San José State, and Cal Poly SLO may still deny admission if space is limited. For students targeting less selective CSU campuses, the ADT functions much like a UC TAG: a structured plan with reliable outcomes. For students aiming at impacted campuses, the ADT still provides an advantage, but admission remains competitive.

Online Courses

Community colleges offer more **flexibility** than any other part of California's higher education system. Most CCCs provide a wide range of online courses, including GE classes, major preparation, and even fully online associate degree programs. The format of course delivery does not affect transferability.

Community colleges also support students who are already enrolled at four-year universities. Many **UC and CSU students** take online community college courses, especially during the summer, to complete high-demand classes when enrollment is limited on their home campus.

Transfer Outcomes and Degree Completion

Transfer students perform well once they arrive at four-year colleges. At the UC, many transfer students **graduate within three years**, and nearly nine in ten students graduate within four years after their transfer[33]. At the CSU, transfer students also graduate at high rates once they enroll with junior standing.

> **Undergraduate degree**
> The final degree is issued by the college you graduate from, not the CCC.

A student who transfers to a UC earns a University of California degree. A student who transfers to a CSU earns a California State University degree. Your diploma does not indicate that you began your journey at a community college.

Transfer Beyond UC and CSU

While most CCC transfers go to the UC or CSU, some students also transfer to private and out-of-state institutions. These pathways exist, but they operate differently and carry **more risk**. Within California, private universities such as the University of Southern California, Loyola Marymount University, Santa Clara University, Chapman University, and the University of San Diego regularly enroll community college transfers. Out-of-state public universities

33 accountability.universityofcalifornia.edu/2024/chapters/chapter-3.html

such as the University of Washington, University of Colorado Boulder, and Arizona State University also accept California community college transfers.

However, these pathways **lack standardized articulation**. Unlike UC and CSU transfers, private and out-of-state transfers evaluate courses individually, often after admission. A course that transfers cleanly to the UC or CSU may not apply toward a major at another institution. This creates a real risk. If courses do not transfer, students may need additional semesters to graduate, reducing any expected cost savings. Students who take this route should verify articulation carefully and early.

Dual Enrollment for High School Students

High school students can enroll in community college courses while still in high school. This is called concurrent or dual enrollment. Students who complete community college courses during high school **earn college credit** that can apply toward associate degrees or transfer requirements. Even without an associate degree, dual enrollment courses strengthen an applicant's profile.

However, you should consider concurrent enrollment carefully. Courses taken at community colleges become part of your **permanent college transcript**. Poor grades earned in community college courses taken during high school follow you permanently. When you apply to graduate school later in life, all academic transcripts, including those from community colleges, must be included. If you are not ready for college-level coursework, it may be better to wait until after high school graduation.

Bachelor's Degrees

Historically, community colleges did not offer four-year degrees. Recently, California has authorized a limited number of community colleges to offer applied bachelor's degrees in fields not widely available at UC or CSU campuses. These programs are intentionally narrow and **workforce focused**. Examples include Bachelor's degrees in Dental Hygiene at Cerritos College and Respiratory Care at East Los Angeles College. Other programs exist in health information management, building performance, and automotive technology.

These degrees serve students who want Bachelor's-level credentials in technical fields without transferring to a four-year university. They are not designed to compete with UC or CSU bachelor's degrees but to fill gaps in workforce preparation.

Career and Technical Education

While transfer pathways receive a lot of attention, community colleges also serve many students who are not planning to transfer to a four-year university. Career and Technical Education programs lead to **certificates** or **associate degrees** in fields such as Nursing, Dental Hygiene, Automotive Technology, Welding, Culinary Arts, Paralegal Studies, Graphic Design, and Early Childhood Education. These programs are aligned with regional workforce needs and often include hands-on training, internships, and industry partnerships.

Who Benefits Most

For the right student, starting at a community college and transferring to a UC or CSU is not just a reasonable path. It can be the best path. Here is a look at the **advantages**.

Same Degree for Less

This is the most straightforward benefit. A student who spends two years at a CCC and two years at a UC ends up with the **same degree** as a student who spent all four years at that UC. The diploma says University of California. It does not say when you arrived, where you started, or that you transferred. Nobody knows unless you tell them. **The cost difference** over the full four years is significant. And that difference does not disappear after graduation. It shows up in lower debt, more financial flexibility, and more freedom to take the career path you want rather than the one that covers your loan payments.

A Second Chance

The minimum GPA requirement for UC freshman admission is 3.0 and 2.5 for the CSU. Students who graduated below either threshold, or who did not complete the required A-G courses, are not permanently locked out. Community college is specifically designed to be the path back in.

Clean slate
UC transfer applicants are evaluated on their college record only.

A student's high school grades, GPA, and course history are not part of the transfer review. That means a student who struggled in high school has a genuine opportunity to rebuild their record from scratch. Two years of strong academic work at a CCC can open doors to UC campuses that were completely out of reach at 18. This is not a loophole. It is exactly what the system was designed to do.

Higher Acceptance Rates

Transfer acceptance rates at UC campuses are **significantly higher** than freshman rates. UCLA admits roughly 23 percent of transfer applicants compared to about nine percent of freshmen. Berkeley admits about 24 percent of transfer applicants compared to just over eleven percent of freshmen. At Davis, Santa Barbara, Riverside, and Merced, transfer admit rates climb well above 50 percent. For students aiming at campuses that felt out of reach as a high school senior, the transfer route is not just a second chance; it is a **statistically better path** to the same destination.

More Time to Mature

Not everyone is ready for a competitive four-year university at 17 or 18. The transition from high school to university is a big one, and some students need more time to develop their study habits, focus, and self-direction. Community college gives students room to grow without the high financial and academic stakes of a UC. Smaller classes, more accessible professors, and a lower-pressure setting allow students to **build the skills** and confidence they need before stepping into a more demanding environment.

Time and Space to Figure Out Your Direction

Committing to a major and a career at 17 is a lot to ask. Many students declare one because it sounded good, because their parents suggested it, or because they did not know what else to write. At a four-year university, changing direction is expensive. Every semester spent redirecting is a semester of full UC or CSU tuition. Community college is a much lower-cost place to figure out what you want to study. You can sample fields, talk to professors, and make a more informed decision before committing to upper-division coursework. Transfer students have already worked through that process and tend to arrive more focused for it.

Smaller Class Size

The courses that matter most for transfer admission (like Calculus, Chemistry, Biology, Physics, Statistics, or Economics) are exactly the courses where community colleges often **outperform** large research universities in terms of instructional quality and student outcomes. At a UC, Introductory Chemistry might mean 300 students in a lecture hall with a graduate student running discussion sections. At a community college, you may find yourself with 40 other students and a professor who answers questions during class. For students who need to build a strong foundation before moving to upper-division work, the community college classroom environment is a real advantage.

Flexibility for Working Students

Many students cannot attend college full time. They are working to support themselves or contribute to the family income. They may have caregiving responsibilities or may be dealing with circumstances that make a full residential college experience financially or logistically impossible.

Community colleges were built for this reality. **Part-time enrollment** is standard, evening classes are available, and online courses cover most GE and many major preparation requirements. Students can move at the pace that their lives allow, without paying full UC or CSU tuition. This flexibility does not come at the cost of the destination. The transfer pathway to a UC or CSU is just as open to a part-time student who takes three years as to a full-time student who takes two.

When Community College May Not Be the Best Choice

Community college works well for many students, but it is not the best starting point for everyone. The tradeoffs should be considered carefully. Cost is a nuanced factor. For California residents with **high financial need**, a UC may be more affordable than many families assume because the UC offers strong need-based aid that may include room and board. In some cases, the net cost at a UC can be competitive with a community college. The only way to know is to compare the net cost side by side, not just tuition.

Some majors are designed as **four-year sequences**, particularly in Engineering, certain sciences, and music performance. Entering these programs at the junior level can extend the time to your degree if key coursework is expected in the first two years. Students considering these paths should verify transfer feasibility early and understand the required course sequence.

Students who need early **access to research** may also prefer a four-year university. Community colleges rarely offer faculty-mentored research or the lab infrastructure that the UCs provide. Students planning for research-heavy graduate programs later may benefit from starting at a UC where research involvement begins earlier.

The **campus experience** is another consideration. Most community colleges do not offer on-campus housing, and many students live at home. That can limit the residential experience and campus involvement. The range of extracurriculars, leadership roles, and organized student life is smaller than at four-year universities. For students who are counting on the residential college experience as part of their education, this tradeoff is real.

The **transition** after transfer can be challenging. Upper-division courses are more rigorous, class sizes may increase, and expectations for independent work rise sharply. Many transfer students experience a temporary drop in grades during their first term, sometimes called **transfer shock**. Social adjustment can take time as well, since transfer students often join communities where many friendships and routines are already established.

Nevertheless, the case for starting at a community college is strong and comes down to **access, affordability,** and a genuinely competitive path to the **same degree**. But knowing why the pathway makes sense is only the beginning. The next step is understanding exactly what it takes to get there.

The next chapter walks you through the UC transfer process from start to finish. It covers eligibility, GPA, major preparation, planning tools, the application itself, how campuses review transfer applicants, and what happens after you apply. If you are thinking about transferring to a UC, the next chapter is where your real planning begins.

13 | Transferring to the UC

Major Preparation is Key

The University of California has built an entire infrastructure around the transfer pathway. Every CCC has agreements with the UC, spelling out which courses count toward UC requirements. On top of that, the system offers guaranteed admission programs, priority consideration policies, and planning tools designed specifically for the CCC-to-UC route. This chapter explains how that pathway works, what makes you eligible, how to use the available tools, and how each campus reviews transfer applicants.

A Real Second Chance

The basic idea behind the transfer pathway is straightforward. Spend two years at a California community college, complete most of your general education and lower-division coursework and **transfer to a UC as a junior**. What makes this pathway particularly powerful is that your high school record does not follow you. The UC evaluates transfer applicants only based on their college coursework, not their high school grades.

This is a real game changer for students who were not eligible for the UC immediately after high school. UC freshman admission requires a minimum 3.0 GPA in A-G coursework for California residents. Students who graduated below that threshold, or who did not complete the required courses, are not permanently locked out of the UC system. Two years of strong academic work at a CCC can **open doors to UC** campuses that were completely out of reach before.

What makes you a transfer applicant
If you enrolled in any fall, winter, or spring term at any college after graduating from high school, the UC considers you a transfer applicant.

You are no longer eligible to apply as a first-year applicant, regardless of how many units you completed. The two exceptions are college courses taken while still in high school through dual enrollment and courses taken in the summer immediately after high school graduation. Those do not trigger transfer status. But the moment you begin a **regular non-summer term** at any college after graduating, you must apply as a transfer applicant.

Junior-Level Transfer

There are several ways to transfer to a UC, but one path is the most common: the junior-level transfer from a California community college. CCC students receive **priority consideration** in UC transfer admission. As a result, most UC transfer students come from the California community college system. Students on this route complete roughly two years of college coursework before transferring, arriving at UC with 60 to 89 semester units (or 90 to 134 quarter units).

Two **more transfer levels** exist, but both come with some caveats. Sophomore-level transfer is available at only a handful of UC campuses and programs. Senior-level transfer triggers high-unit restrictions at multiple campuses and accumulating too many units before applying can close doors rather than open them. Check the specific unit ceilings for your target campuses early. Unless otherwise stated, all references in this chapter apply to junior-level transfers.

Eligibility for Admissions

Unlike first-year applicants, who are evaluated partly on their potential, transfer applicants are **evaluated** on their **college performance**. By the time you apply, the UC can see not just whether you completed the coursework, but exactly how well you handled it. That changes everything about how you should approach the next two years.

However, transfer applications do have something in common with freshman applications. Meeting the minimum requirements gets you into the applicant pool, but it does not get you admitted. In transfers, admission comes down to two things: first, how well you **prepared for your major** and second, how your **GPA stacks up** against everyone else applying to the same major at the same campus. To be eligible for junior-level transfer, you must complete all of the following by the end of the spring term before you transfer:

Eligibility

- At least 60 transferable semester units, or 90 quarter units
- A minimum overall transfer GPA of 2.4 (2.8 for nonresidents)
- The seven-course breadth pattern
- Max. 14 semester units (21 quarter units) taken Pass/No Pass

Each of these requirements is worth understanding in more detail.

Minimum Units

Not every course you take at a community college automatically counts toward the 60/90-unit minimum. To count, units must be **UC-transferable**, meaning the course has been approved for transfer credit by the University of California. Remedial or below-college-level courses, physical education, and some vocational courses typically do not count. Check the **ASSIST**[34] **database** to confirm which of your courses are UC-transferable.

Minimum GPA

To be eligible to apply, you need a minimum overall UC-transferable **GPA of 2.4, or 2.8** if you are a non-California resident. Keep in mind that this is only the starting point. The next question is whether your GPA is strong enough for your specific major at your specific campus.

---

[34] www.assist.org

Every campus publishes **minimum GPA** thresholds for major preparation. The minimum GPA tells you when a campus may begin considering you for that major. This is why transfer planning must be **major-specific**. A 3.2 may be more than enough for one program and far too low for another. At UC San Diego, for example, the published range runs from 2.8 to 4.0 depending on the program. Berkeley Engineering starts at 3.5, and UCLA Communication starts at 3.7. The UC transfer campus-by-campus section in the Appendix summarizes the most recent thresholds. That leads us to the next question: how is your transfer GPA calculated?

How Your GPA Is Calculated

Your UC transfer GPA is not just your current community college GPA. It reaches back further than that. Every UC-transferable course you have ever taken counts, including **dual enrollment** courses from high school, courses at other colleges, online and summer college courses. High school courses themselves are excluded, but **every grade from every college** you have attended goes into the calculation. Every letter grade converts to a numerical value.

A	B	C	D	F
A: 4.0	B+: 3.3	C+: 2.3	D+: 1.3	F: 0.0
A-: 3.7	B: 3.0	C: 2.0	D: 1.0	
	B-: 2.7	C-: 1.7	D-: 0.7	

To calculate your **transfer GPA**, multiply each grade's point value by the course units to get the grade points earned. Add up all grade points across every UC-transferable course you have taken, divide by the total units attempted, and you have your transfer GPA. Pass/No Pass courses, Academic Renewal notations, Excused Withdrawals, and plain Withdrawals carry no grade point value and do not count toward your unit total. Here is a simplified example:

Worked Example: Transfer GPA

Course	Units	Grade	Grade Points / Unit	Grade Points Earned
English Composition	3	A	4.0	3 x 4.0 = 12.0
Calculus I	4	B +	3.3	4 x 3.3. = 13.2
General Chemistry	4	B	3.0	4 x 3.0 = 12.0
Psychology 101	3	B -	2.7	3 x 2.7 = 8.1
Total	14			45.3
GPA: 45.3 / 14	**= 3.24**			

Based on this simplified example, this student's transfer GPA is 3.24.

Repeated Courses

Sometimes a course does not go the way you planned, and you need to repeat it. Before you do, make sure you understand how the UC handles repeats, because the rules are different from what your community college may use.

UC rule for repeated coursework

If you earned a C-minus (or below) and repeat the course, only the new grade counts. Repeating a course with a C (or above) keeps both grades on your record

Your community college's own repeat policy may differ. The UC calculates your transfer GPA its own way, and a C in a college course is on your record for good.

Seven-Course Breadth Pattern

The University of California requires students to complete seven specific lower-division courses before transferring.

Seven-course breadth pattern

Two English composition courses, one math course, and four courses drawn from at least two of these three areas: Arts and Humanities, Social and Behavioral Sciences, and Physical and Biological Sciences.

All seven courses must be completed with a grade of **C or better** by the end of the spring term before enrollment. Courses may be in progress at the time you apply, but they must be finished before you arrive. Without them, your application cannot be considered, regardless of your GPA or how strong your major preparation is.

Complete the English and math requirements as early as possible. Most campuses recommend finishing both by the end of the fall term, one year before you enroll, because they are prerequisites for many major preparation sequences. AP and IB scores can satisfy parts of this pattern, but only one of the two required English courses can be met with an AP score. The seven-course pattern is the **minimum** required for eligibility. It is not the same as completing your full GE requirement, which is broader.

GE Certification via Cal-GETC

Many California community colleges offer Cal-GETC, the California General Education Transfer Curriculum, because it prepares students for both UC and CSU transfers. It replaced the older IGETC certification in 2025. If you are applying to both UC and CSU, Cal-GETC can be a good way to satisfy lower-division **GE requirements at both systems**.

However, Cal-GETC comes with important **caveats**. It is not required for UC admission, not accepted by all UC campuses and programs, and its eleven courses go well beyond the seven-course breadth minimum. For example, Berkeley's Engineering and Business schools do not accept it, and neither does Riverside's Natural and Agricultural Sciences. Pursuing full certification on top of a demanding major preparation can stretch your schedule and hurt the grades that matter most for admission. If you plan to request certification, your CCC must submit it by **July 15** of your enrollment year. All courses must be passed with a C or higher.

Seven-Course Pattern vs. Cal-GETC

Area	Requirement	UC 7-Breadth Pattern	Cal-GETC
1A	English Composition	1 course	1 course
1B	Critical Thinking & Composition	1 course	1 course
1C	Oral Communication	—	1 course
2	Mathematical Concepts & Quantitative Reasoning	1 course	1 course
3	Arts & Humanities	4 courses total from at least 2 of Areas 3, 4, and 5	2 courses
4	Social & Behavioral Sciences	(see Area 3)	2 courses
5	Physical & Biological Sciences	(see Area 3)	2 courses
6	Ethnic Studies	—	1 course
Total		**7 courses**	**11 courses**

Pass/No Pass Limit

Pass/No Pass is a grading option that allows you to take a course without a letter grade. Instead of an A, B, or C, you either pass the course, or you do not. It is sometimes also called Credit/No Credit. Pass/No Pass courses carry **no grade point value** and are excluded from your UC transfer GPA calculation.

This cuts both ways: a Pass protects you from a lower grade hurting your GPA, but it also means a strong performance in that course does nothing for your GPA either. Use Pass/No Pass sparingly and never for a required major preparation course. Most UC campuses **require letter grades for major preparation**, and a Pass grade will not satisfy the requirement.

The UC caps Pass/No Pass coursework at a maximum of **14 semester units** (or 21 quarter units) across your entire transfer record. If you exceed that limit, you become ineligible for transfer. 21 quarter units are equivalent to just five courses. That limit fills up faster than many students expect, especially if you took Pass/No Pass courses early without tracking the total.

Planning Tools and Programs

Understanding your eligibility requirements is one thing, but **building a plan** that makes you a competitive applicant is another. The UC system provides tools and programs to help CCC students. Unfortunately, two completely different things share the abbreviation TAP: the UC Transfer Admission Planner, which is an online planning tool, and the Transfer Alliance Program, which are a set of campus-level programs. But let us first have a look at the most important planning tool.

ASSIST.org

ASSIST is the transfer student's best friend. It is the official database of **articulation agreements** between California community colleges and all UC campuses. Articulation is a formal agreement confirming that a specific course at a CCC satisfies a specific requirement at a specific UC campus. Without that agreement, a course may transfer for general credit but may not count toward your major.

> **Course transferability**
> Before registering for any CCC course, check the ASSIST database to make sure that course transfers to the UC.

On ASSIST, select your community college, your target UC campus, and your intended major. The result shows exactly which of your courses satisfy which requirements for that combination. The database updates every year, so check it at the start of each academic year and before you sign up for any new course.

Whenever possible, **complete a sequential series** like Calculus, Chemistry, or Physics at the **same community college**. Splitting a sequence between two colleges can create gaps where the articulation does not carry over cleanly from one course to the next.

If you are a **UC-to-UC transfer student**, ASSIST does not map your courses, but you can still use it to get a reasonable idea by working backwards. Find a CCC course on ASSIST that matches the UC course you took, then check whether it satisfies the requirement at your target UC. Discuss the mapping of your UC-to-UC course plan with the admissions office of your target UC. They can give you a definitive answer.

UC Transfer Admission Planner

Another useful transfer tool is the free UC Transfer Admission Planner[35], or UC TAP. It **tracks your progress** against UC eligibility requirements, flags gaps in your preparation, and maps your coursework against ASSIST articulation data. This way, you see which requirements your courses satisfy at your target campuses. Set it up in your first term and keep it updated as you go. To get the most out of the TAP, enter every course at every college you have attended, including dual enrollment, extension, summer, out-of-state, and international courses. Also enter all your grades including W and NP grades, and your AP and IB scores. The more complete your information, the more useful the tool becomes.

UC TAP is also the platform you will use to **file a TAG application**; the Transfer Admission Guarantee program covered in the next section. UC campuses also use UC TAP to send communications directly to prospective transfer students. When you submit your UC application, make sure the email on your UC TAP account matches the email on your application so your coursework data imports correctly.

TAG: The Transfer Admission Guarantee

TAG offers something that rarely exists in college admissions: a formal guarantee. It is an agreement between California community colleges and six UC campuses (Davis, Irvine, Merced, Riverside, Santa Barbara, and Santa Cruz) that **guarantees admission** in a stated major to any CCC student who meets the published requirements. UCLA, Berkeley, and UCSD do not offer TAG. For eligible majors, TAG turns UC transfer admissions into a checklist.

---

[35] uctap.universityofcalifornia.edu

Keep these key rules in mind:

TAG rules

- You may file **only one TAG** to exactly one campus (You 'TAG one school').
- TAG is not available for every major; impacted and capped programs are typically excluded. Confirm that your specific major is eligible.
- The filing window is September 1 to September 30 the year before you plan to transfer, through your UC TAP account.
- To remain eligible, you must meet the campus GPA requirement and complete all required GE and lower-division major preparation by the stated deadlines.
- Your TAG GPA is calculated from your transcript as of the end of the fall term before you apply and locks in at that point. If your GPA drops in winter or spring after filing, you can lose the guarantee.

Even with a TAG, you still must submit the full **UC transfer application** during the October 1 to November 30 window. The TAG guarantees the outcome of that application, provided you continue meeting all requirements.

UC Transfer Pathways and Pathways+

TAG secures your transfer to one of six campuses. But most transfer students are also aiming for Berkeley, UCLA, or UC San Diego, none of which offer TAG. That is where UC Transfer Pathways come in.

UC Transfer Pathways are **standardized preparation plans** for about 30 common majors. Each pathway identifies the lower-division courses you need for a specific major. Complete them and your preparation works at every UC campus offering that major. Some campuses may require fewer courses for admission, but none will require more. If your major has a published pathway, completing those courses means your preparation aligns with the expectations of every UC campus offering that major. Even when following a Transfer Pathway, you should still verify campus-specific requirements on ASSIST.

Pathways+ takes this one step further by combining a **Transfer Pathway with a TAG**. You file a TAG with one of the six TAG campuses, securing a guaranteed admission outcome. At the same time, you follow your major's Transfer Pathway, building a preparation record that works across the UC system. One outcome is guaranteed, and the same coursework prepares you to apply competitively to Berkeley, UCLA, UC San Diego, and any other campus offering the major.

Transfer Alliance Programs

Transfer Alliance Programs are campus-level programs designed to give students an edge in admissions. They do not guarantee that you get in, but they provide structured support and, at some campuses, a meaningful boost in how your application is reviewed. For example, **UCLA's Transfer Alliance Program** connects directly with approved honors programs. About half of all CCCs have a qualifying honors program, and students who complete it receive **enhanced consideration** in UCLA's transfer review. It is one of the most concrete steps you can take to strengthen your transfer application to UCLA. Check early whether your college's honors program qualifies and start it as soon as you can.

Other programs, such as Berkeley's Transfer Alliance Project, UC Davis's Transfer Opportunity Program, and UC Irvine's Transfer Prep Program, all **work with partner CCCs** to support transfer students. None of them guarantees admission, but all three offer structured help with coursework planning, major preparation, and the transfer application. Depending on the campus and program, you may also have access to workshops, mentoring, campus visits, and other enrichment activities. UC San Diego, UC Riverside, UC Santa Barbara, UC Santa Cruz, and UC Merced do not offer equivalent programs tied to admission review.

UC transfer strategy

The most effective transfer strategy combines TAG, TAP, and the Transfer Pathway.

A TAG with Davis or Santa Barbara secures a guaranteed outcome. An approved honors curriculum connects you to UCLA's Transfer Alliance Program. And the Transfer Pathway builds a major preparation record that holds up at every campus you apply to.

The Transfer Application

The UC transfer application uses the **same platform**[36] as the first-year application. The core sections remain the same, but several parts work differently for transfer applicants.

> **Academic history**
> Transfer applicants must report every college and every college course.

This includes courses from colleges you attended briefly, courses you withdrew from, and courses you did not pass. All UC-transferable courses from all institutions become part of your transfer record and are used to calculate your UC transfer GPA. You must also report all **AP, IB, and dual enrollment coursework** completed during high school because these may carry transferable credit. High school courses themselves are not reported. The UC verifies the courses you report against official transcripts from every college you attended.

Transfer applicants apply while still completing their final year at the CCC. The application therefore asks you to list courses currently in progress as well as courses you plan to take in winter and spring terms before transfer. If your plans change, you must update them in the **Transfer Academic Update** or notify the campus. Failing to complete required courses, or completing different ones than reported without approval, can lead to your admission being rescinded.

Major Selection

Transfer applicants apply directly to a **specific major** at each campus. Admission decisions are made within the context of that major and the preparation required for it. Some campuses may consider an alternate major if one is listed, but policies vary widely.

---

[36] admission.universityofcalifornia.edu/apply-now.html

Four Personal Insight Questions

Transfer applicants answer four PIQs: **one mandatory question** and three additional prompts. These essays provide context for your academic record and preparation. The role of PIQs in transfer admissions varies by campus and is discussed later in this chapter.

Activities and Awards

The application also includes the activities and awards section. For transfer applicants, this typically emphasizes **college-level experiences** such as jobs, internships, research, leadership roles, volunteer work, and family responsibilities. High school activities may still be reported if they remain relevant, but the focus should shift to what you have done since starting college.

Application Timeline

The filing window opens on **October 1** and closes on **November 30**. There is no early action, no early decision, and no advantage to submitting early. Two campuses also accept **mid-year** applications: UC Merced admits for the spring semester and UC Santa Cruz for the winter quarter.

Transfer Academic Update (TAU)

After fall grades are posted, transfer applicants must return to the UC application and submit the Transfer Academic Update between **mid-December and January 31**. In the TAU, you report your fall grades and confirm or revise your winter and spring course plans. Campuses rely on this update when reviewing transfer applications.

Date	Action
May 1 – 31	TAG filing period for Winter/Spring terms (Merced, UCSC)
July 1 - 31	Spring semester application filing period: UC Merced
July 1 – August 15	Winter quarter application filing period: UCSC
August 1	Application opens for Fall
September 1 - 30	TAG filing period through UC TAP (Fall applications)
October 1 – November 30	Fall application filing period
October 1 – March 2	FAFSA / CADAA / Cal Grant GPA Verification Form
December 15 – January 31	Transfer Academic Update priority filing
March - May	Fall admissions decisions released
June 1	Statement of Intent to Register deadline
July 1	Final official transcripts due

Non-CCC Transfers

Most UC transfers come from a California community college. But if you transfer from a private four-year university, another UC campus, an out-of-state community college, or an international institution, the general application process is the same. But you do not qualify for TAG, UC TAP's priority features, or the priority consideration that CCC students receive. In addition, ASSIST articulation agreements cover only California community colleges.

How Applications Are Reviewed

Like for first-year applications, each UC campus reviews transfer applications **independently**. There is no shared 'UC admissions pool,' and campuses do not coordinate their admissions process. A decision at one campus tells you nothing about what another will decide. Within each campus, applications are **evaluated by major**. You are competing against students who apply for the same program at the same campus. Understanding that independence is step one. The next is understanding how your application is evaluated.

Nine Comprehensive Review Factors

You may remember from the freshman chapter that first-year applicants are evaluated on thirteen factors. Transfer applicants are evaluated on nine. Why fewer? By the time you apply, the UC is not trying to predict whether you can handle university-level coursework. You have two years of college grades that answer that question already. The nine factors below are **less about potential** and more about what you have done during the first two years in college. A useful way to understand the nine factors is to group them by what they are measuring.

Readiness for Upper-Division Work in Your Major

- Completion of major preparation coursework (including UC Transfer Pathways, ADTs, or campus-specific prerequisites)
- GPA in all transferable courses, especially in major preparation
- Completion of general education or breadth requirements

This is the **foundation** of every transfer decision. The question is not general academic potential, but whether you have already built the lower-division foundation for your major and performed well in it.

> **Major preparation is key**
> At selective campuses and in many STEM majors, missing required preparation is often disqualifying. Grades in required major courses are the best signal of readiness for upper-division work.

Evidence of Rigor and Academic Initiative

- Participation in academically selective honors courses or programs
- Completion of special academic projects such as research or capstones
- Completion of a UC Transfer Pathway or an ADT

These factors show how you approached your coursework **beyond the minimum.** They signal structure, challenge, and initiative. However, some of this information, especially special projects, may only appear in the activities section or in the Personal Insight Questions. At campuses that do not use

PIQs in transfer selection, these elements may be less visible and therefore play a **smaller role** in the decision.

Context and Contribution

- Special talents, achievements, leadership, and extracurricular involvement
- Academic accomplishments in light of life experiences and special circumstances
- Location of your college and your residence

These factors help admissions readers understand your record in **context:** what you did, under what conditions, and what you bring to a campus. They are most visible at Berkeley, Irvine, and UCLA, the three campuses that use the PIQs. At the other campuses, they play a **limited role** and are not central to the admission decision.

Personal Insight Questions

Just like first-year applicants, transfer applicants submit four PIQs, each with a **350-word limit**. We already covered how to write strong PIQs in Chapter 8. This section focuses on what is different for transfer applicants.

You must answer one required question and choose three from seven optional prompts. The optional prompts are the same as those for first-year applicants, except for the 'academic subject that inspires you' (prompt number 6). In its place, transfer applicants answer a mandatory question focused on academic preparation.

> **Mandatory transfer PIQ**
> 'Please describe how you have prepared for your intended major, including your readiness to succeed in your upper-division courses once you enroll at the university.'

This prompt asks you to make a clear, evidence-based case that you are ready for upper-division work in your major. Focus on what you have done. Name specific courses and what they taught you, show progression from one course to the next, and highlight key skills or experiences that prepare you for advanced study. Then connect that preparation directly to what upper-division coursework in your field will demand.

The transfer PIQ is **not a general reflection** or a personal story. It is a focused academic argument to demonstrate that you have completed the right preparation, you understand what comes next, and you are ready for it.

Three Optional Prompts

The required question already covers your academic preparation, so use your three optional prompts wisely. Pick the ones that let you show sides of yourself that nothing else in your application captures. Transfer applicants often have richer material to work with than first-year students: real work experience, leadership in their community, barriers they have overcome, and responsibilities they have carried. Do not default to safe or generic stories.

If you **previously applied** as a first-year applicant, think carefully before recycling the same prompts and stories. You are a different person now. Two years of college, growth, and new experiences separate you from the 17-year-old who wrote that first application. Ideally, choose different prompts than you did two years ago and write from your current perspective. If you answer the same prompts, do not reuse the same story. **Show something new.**

What to Know About Each Campus

Every UC campus uses the same application, but they do not all review it the same way. Only **Berkeley, UCLA, and Irvine** conduct fully **holistic transfer reviews** in which PIQs, activities, achievements, and personal context play a direct role in selection. At the other six campuses, the decision is driven much more heavily by academic record and major preparation.

Transfer admission is decided at the **major level**, not the campus level. The campus admit rates below give you a general idea, but your actual odds depend on whether your GPA and preparation are competitive for your specific major. The UC's transfer data[37] lets you look that up by campus, major, and

[37] universityofcalifornia.edu/about-us/information-center/transfers-major

even community college. The UC also publishes transfer data broken down by community college and UC campus[38]. For the full picture on any individual campus, see the UC Campus Transfer Profiles in the Appendix.

Transfer Overview by Campus[39]

Campus	Admit Rate	Apps	TAG	TAP	PIQs	CCC
UCLA	22.2 %	30,645	No	Yes	Yes	92.3 %
UCB	20.0 %	26,216	No	Yes	Yes	91.5 %
UCI	36.4 %	27,038	Yes	Yes	Yes	94.8 %
UCSD	47.4 %	26,314	No	No	No	90.1 %
UCD	58.2 %	17,421	Yes	Yes	No	93.9 %
UCSB	61.6 %	18,866	Yes	No	No	91.5 %
UCR	70.4 %	14,753	Yes	No	No	94.3 %
UCSC	67.7 %	13,501	Yes	No	No	96.3 %
UCM	79.5 %	6,401	Yes	No	No	95.2 %

Admit Rate = Percentage of transfer applicants admitted (Fall 2026)
Apps = Number of transfer applications submitted for Fall 2026
TAG = Transfer Admission Guarantee program available (not all majors available)
TAP = Transfer preparation or honors partnership program available
PIQs = Personal Insight Questions used in the campus transfer admission review
CCC = Percentage of admitted transfer students from California community colleges (2025)

After You Apply

Understanding how each campus reviews transfer applicants helps you apply strategically. But submitting the application is only the midpoint. The months

[38] universityofcalifornia.edu/about-us/information-center/california-community-college-new-enrollments-uc

[39] Sources: University of California Transfer Admit Data (Fall 2026); Campus Transfer Admission Profiles; UC Preliminary Fall 2026 Application Counts; Quick Reference Guide to UC Admissions (August 2025)

that follow include several required updates and deadlines that can directly affect your admission outcome. Here is what you need to do and when.

The Transfer Academic Update (TAU)

In mid-December, the UC emails every transfer applicant with instructions to complete the Transfer Academic Update, or TAU, accessed through the Application Status page. Every transfer applicant **must complete** it, including students with no fall grades to report and no changes to their course plans. The deadline is **January 31**.

In the TAU, you report your **fall semester grades** and confirm or update your planned courses for winter and spring. Fall grades entered by January 31 factor into the transfer GPA calculation; winter and spring courses are excluded from the GPA calculation even if grades are available before January 31. But you should still report those grades since they give readers context about your progress. You can continue updating through **March 15**, but UC campuses do not commit to reviewing changes submitted after January 31.

Do not list planned **summer courses** unless you are fully committed to completing them. Some campuses treat planned summer coursework as a commitment, and listing a course you do not complete can result in a rescission. Failure to submit the TAU by January 31 can directly affect your admission decision.

Berkeley applicants must also complete a separate form by January 31, completely independent of the TAU. Submitting only the TAU and not the Berkeley form means your Berkeley application will not be reviewed. Log in to MAP@Berkeley as soon as the portal opens and check your to-do list.

Provisional Admission

Transfer decisions roll out between March and May. When you are admitted to more than one campus, you have until **June 1 to** submit a Statement of Intent to Register. You can only submit one SIR. Choosing one campus means releasing your spot at the others.

Transfer admission is always **provisional**. You are offered admission based on what you have done and what you have committed to completing. If either change, so can your acceptance offer. Two things most reliably trigger a review: earning a **grade below C** after your offer is issued, including in winter and spring courses taken after you applied, and **failing** to complete the **required major preparation** before your transfer date.

If you listed a required course as 'in progress' when you applied, it must be finished with a C or better. Rescissions happen more often than students expect. A single late-semester stumble has cost students their admission.

Since you are entering as a junior, you usually **cannot change your major** after you are admitted. Resolve any uncertainty about your major before you apply.

Post-Admission

By **July 1**, you need to have all final **official transcripts** sent directly from every college and high school you attended to your committed campus. By July 15, AP and IB score reports must be received, and Cal-GETC certification must be submitted if you are relying on it to clear lower-division GE requirements. After that, monitor your specific campus's post-admission checklist for housing deadlines, orientation registration, advising appointments, and placement assessments.

Putting It Together

Students who navigate UC transfer admission successfully share a few traits. They start early, build their coursework with specific major requirements in mind, and use every tool available to them. And they arrive at the application window with a strong academic record and a clear story: here is why I am ready for what comes next.

For students who did not get into a UC as freshmen, or who had a difficult start before finding their footing, the community college pathway offers something the freshman process does not: the chance to prove it on an actual record rather than a prediction. For students who are willing to plan carefully and execute well, the path to the UC is genuinely open.

We now look at the other major transfer destination in California: the California State University system. The CSU is the largest four-year university system in the country, and for many students it is the right fit academically, geographically, and financially. The next chapter covers how CSU transfer admission works and how to build a plan that gets you there.

14 | Transferring to the CSU

Affordable Route to a Four-Year Degree

Community college transfer is one of the strongest routes into the CSU. If your high school grades do not reflect your true abilities, this path gives you a real second chance. Maybe you needed more time to grow, faced challenges early on, or just were not ready. Transferring from a CCC allows you to make a fresh start in a system built to support you.

The CCC-to-CSU transfer is also one of the **most affordable** ways to earn a four-year degree. Spending two years at a community college costs much less than attending a CSU for four years, but you still end up with the same degree. For many students, the lower cost and priority admission make transferring a smart choice, not just a backup plan. That said, the path has specific rules and knowing them early is what separates successful transfer students from those struggling to transfer. Before we get into the details, it is important to understand what type of transfer you want to pursue, since the rules and requirements vary.

Types of Transfer Applicants

Lower-Division Transfer

Students with fewer than 60 transferable semester units (or less than 90 quarter units) at the time of enrollment are lower-division transfer applicants, arriving with **sophomore standing**. Because they have not yet completed two full years of college work, lower-division transfer applicants must still meet several requirements tied to **high school preparation**. To be considered, you need to have completed the A-G requirements in high school and graduated or earned a GED. You also need to meet the minimum CSU freshman admission eligibility standards, hold at least **a 2.0 GPA** across all transfer units attempted, and be in good academic standing at your last college. On top of that, you need to have completed English composition and a math or quantitative reasoning college course, each with a C-minus or better.

Lower-division transfer is not offered everywhere. At many CSU campuses, and in many majors, transfer admission is geared primarily toward upper-division applicants. It is also not a complete reset, since lower-division applicants are still **evaluated** in part on their **high school record and freshman** eligibility requirements.

Upper-Division Transfer

Most CCC students transfer as upper-division applicants, and if you are planning to spend two years at community college before transferring, this is almost certainly you. The threshold is **60 semester units (or 90 quarter units)** of transferable college work completed by the time you enroll. You are arriving with junior standing, which means two years of college are already behind you, and you are ready to begin upper-division work in your major.

You may have heard the term **'senior standing'** used for students with 90 or more semester units (135 quarter units). Senior transfers still apply as upper-division transfers. Applying with senior standing does not mean students will finish their degree in one year. CSU transfer planning is still built around completing upper-division coursework after the transfer. Students may still need up to two years to finish their major requirements, GE still owed at the CSU, campus graduation requirements, or residency requirements. Senior standing usually tells you more about **how many units** you have accumulated than about how quickly you will graduate.

This chapter primarily focuses on **upper-division transfer**. For almost every student, completing the full 60 transferable semester units is the right strategy. Once you reach the upper-division level, high school performance drops out of the review, your options expand, and your application is judged based on what you have done in college. Once you know which transfer category you are in, the next step is understanding exactly what the CSU requires for admission.

Transfer Routes Within the CSU

The CSU offers two programs supporting transfer students. The Associate Degree for Transfer offers a structured major-specific pathway, and the Transfer Success Pathway provides guaranteed admission.

Associate Degree for Transfer

The Associate Degree for Transfer, or ADT, comes in two forms: the Associate in Arts for Transfer (AA-T) and the Associate in Science for Transfer (AS-T), depending on your field of study.

> **Benefits of ADT**
> Students who complete a specific AA-T or AS-T degree aligning with their intended CSU major receive priority consideration, Cal-GETC certification, and a guarantee of no more than 60 units remaining after transfer.

If an eligible California-resident ADT student is not admitted to any CSU campus they applied to, they may be considered for **redirection** to another CSU campus. Pursuing a standard AA or AS degree without the transfer designation does not carry any of these benefits. Not every major has an ADT pathway, so check early before you commit to a course plan.

Here is where students get tripped up. Your ADT **must closely match** your intended CSU **major**, not just broadly relate to it. A student completing an AA-T in Business Administration who applies to Business at a CSU is in an aligned pathway and gets the full benefits. The same student applying to Computer Science with that AA-T is considered misaligned and forfeits those benefits entirely. The free CSU Transfer Planner app flags **misalignments** with a Similar/Dissimilar alert when you compare your ADT to your intended programs. Review that alert early, not after two years of coursework.

Transfer Success Pathway

The Transfer Success Pathway, or TSP, is a transfer program that allows students to enter into an agreement with a CSU campus that **guarantees admission** if all requirements are met. If you have read the UC transfer chapter, the TSP is comparable to the UC's Transfer Admission Guarantee. Both programs are early agreements that guarantee admission if all requirements are met. The key difference is timing. You enter a TSP at the very beginning of your community college journey, not at the end.

All CSU campuses participate in TSP, but **not all majors** and programs are open for a TSP agreement. Right at the start of your first community college semester, you sign an agreement with one specific CSU campus. That agreement commits both you and the campus. If you meet all transfer eligibility requirements and complete either an ADT or the campus's prescribed course of study within the agreed timeline, the campus **guarantees** your **admission to a specific major**. The TSP agreement cycle is published annually by the CSU. Check the official TSP page for the current terms. You still must apply through Cal State Apply during the standard filing period. Programs requiring auditions, portfolios, or clinical selection, such as Nursing, are typically excluded.

TSP and ADT are not alternatives to each other, and you can pursue both **simultaneously**. But if you do, the ADT major and the TSP major must match. If you are considering both, discuss with your transfer counselor.

Transfer Eligibility

To be eligible as an upper-division transfer applicant, you need to meet all required criteria by the end of the spring term before you enroll. Let us have a closer look at each requirement.

Transferable units

You must complete at least 60 CSU-transferable semester units (or 90 quarter units), including at least 30 semester units of GE coursework (or 45 quarter units).

Remedial or developmental courses, non-transferable vocational courses, and any course not on the CSU-transferable list do not count. There is also a ceiling on the other end. No matter how many units you accumulate at a community college, a **maximum of 70 semester units** (or 105 quarter units) can count toward your CSU bachelor's degree. Additional community college units above the 70-semester-unit cap may still be accepted for subject credit and used to meet GE or major-preparation requirements.

Good standing

You must be in good academic standing at your community college, meaning you are eligible to re-enroll there.

Being on academic probation or even disqualification will stop your transfer in its tracks if you do not address them. If you are on **probation**, you are still enrolled and still technically eligible to re-enroll, but your GPA is below 2.0, which means you are failing the transfer GPA requirement. You need to bring that GPA up before you apply.

Disqualification is more serious. If you have been academically disqualified, you are no longer eligible to re-enroll, which makes you ineligible to transfer until that status is resolved. If either situation applies to you, talk to a counselor before you do anything else.

Minimum GPA

You must maintain a minimum cumulative college GPA of 2.0, using all attempted transfer units.

The CSU states that nonresident transfer applicants are often held to higher admission standards. In practice, that means the GPA needs to be higher than the 2.0 eligibility floor, especially at impacted campuses and majors.

The CSU calculates your transfer GPA using **all your transfer units** you have attempted. This means that if all your community college courses are transferable, your transfer GPA will match your college GPA. The calculation only differs from your community college GPA when non-transferable courses appear on your record, because those are excluded from the CSU GPA. 'Pass/No Pass' grades are not included in the GPA calculation, though a passing grade still counts toward your unit total. A 'No Pass' grade earns no units and does not affect your GPA. A grade of 'WF,' meaning Withdrawn Failing, is treated as an F and brings down your GPA.

Repeated courses follow the grading policy of the institution where you took the course. If your community college excludes the original attempt from the institutional GPA because you repeated it, the CSU honors that policy. In Cal State Apply, you enter 'RP' for a repeated course excluded from the institutional GPA. If both attempts appear in your college's GPA, both appear in your transfer GPA calculation as well.

After entering all your coursework in the CSU application, use the 'Calculate my Transfer GPA' function to preview the GPA the system generates before you submit. Students who run this calculation may catch entry errors, courses with unchecked transferable flags, and omitted coursework while there is still time to fix them.

> **The Golden Four**
> Oral Communication, Written Communication, Critical Thinking, and Mathematics or Quantitative Reasoning must be completed with a C-minus or better before you transfer.

Missing even one course makes you ineligible, regardless of how strong the rest of your record is. For Oral Communication, you need a college-level public speaking or communication course. Written Communication requires a college-level English composition course. Critical Thinking requires a course explicitly focused on analytical reasoning, typically listed as Critical Thinking, Logic, or a related philosophy course. And for Mathematics or Quantitative Reasoning, you need a transferable math course at the level of Statistics, college algebra, or higher. Courses below college Algebra, including Arithmetic and Prealgebra, do not qualify, even if they carry college credit.

A D or F means you need to **retake the course** before you can transfer. AP exam scores may satisfy some Golden Four requirements depending on the campus and subject. Always verify which specific courses at your community college satisfy each Golden Four area through ASSIST or the CSU Transfer Planner; not every English or math course qualifies, even if the name suggests it should.

Keep this potential pitfall in mind. A C-minus is enough to satisfy the Golden Four requirement and make you eligible to transfer. But Cal-GETC, covered in the next section, has a stricter standard: every course requires a C or better. This means you can be eligible to transfer while still having an incomplete GE certification.

General Education: Cal-GETC

The Golden Four GE courses are only the minimum needed for CSU transfer eligibility. Most students, however, plan **beyond that minimum**, especially if they want to keep both the UC and CSU open. Arriving at a CSU without a completed lower-division GE pattern means taking those courses after the transfer, in addition to challenging upper-division coursework for your major. Completing more of your general education at community college, where tuition is lower and classes are smaller, usually saves both time and money.

Cal-GETC is now the standard **lower-division GE pathway** for CCC transferring to either a CSU or UC. Students who began before fall 2025 and maintained continuous enrollment may still complete the older IGETC under their earlier catalog rights.

Cal-GETC benefits
Every CSU campus accepts Cal-GETC certification.

Completing Cal-GETC before your transfer leaves more room in your schedule for upper-division coursework and a cleaner path to graduation. For ADT students, Cal-GETC certification is already built into the degree. For all other CSU transfer students, completing it is **strongly recommended**. To **receive certification**, you request it from your CCC, typically at the same time you request your transcript be sent to a CSU campus. Without formal certification, the CSU campus may not recognize your coursework as satisfying lower-division GE. Request it before you transfer.

Cal-GETC consists of **eleven courses** totaling a minimum of 34 semester units (or 51 quarter units) across six subject areas. Every course must be completed with a grade of **C or better**. That is a stricter standard than the Golden Four, where a C-minus is sufficient for transfer eligibility. AP and IB exam scores may be accepted. After you transfer, **nine units of upper-division GE** must still be completed at the CSU campus, regardless of Cal-GETC certification.

CSU Golden Four vs Cal-GETC

Area	Requirement	Golden Four	Cal-GETC
1A/A2	English Composition	1 course	1 course
1B/A3	Critical Thinking & Composition	1 course	1 course
1C/A1	Oral Communication	1 course	1 course
2/B4	Mathematical Concepts & Quantitative Reasoning	1 course	1 course
3	Arts & Humanities		2 courses
4	Social & Behavioral Sciences		2 courses
5	Physical & Biological Sciences		2 courses
6	Ethnic Studies	—	1 course
Total		**4 courses**	**11 courses**

When Cal-GETC Is Not the Right Path

For high-unit programs in Engineering, Computer Science, Architecture, and the sciences, completing all Cal-GETC courses on top of lower-division major preparation can push your unit count well beyond 60. For those majors, a targeted approach that covers the **Golden Four** and **selected GE areas** while **prioritizing major preparation** is often more efficient.

Once you know what you need to complete, the next question is how to track your progress and whether the classes will be recognized at your target campuses. That is where the CSU transfer tools come in handy.

CSU Transfer Tools

A successful transfer does not happen by accident. Most California community colleges have transfer centers staffed by counselors who specialize in CSU and UC planning. Meet with a transfer counselor regularly, not just once when application season arrives. Counselors, along with the tools covered in this section, help you figure out which courses count, how your plan lines up with your target campuses, and whether you are actually competitive for the major you have in mind.

ASSIST.org

ASSIST is the official statewide articulation database and the single **most important planning tool** in the transfer process. It shows exactly which courses at your community college satisfy the major-specific preparation requirements at each CSU campus, which community college courses are CSU-transferable, and how your coursework maps to Cal-GETC. Use it before you register for any classes.

Let us have a look at how you would use ASSIST. Say you are at Saddleback College, and you want to transfer to CSU Long Beach for Business Administration. You open the ASSIST database, select Saddleback as the sending institution and CSULB as the receiving institution, then select Business Administration as the major. ASSIST shows exactly which Saddleback courses fulfill each required and recommended requirement for that program. That list becomes the foundation of your two-year course plan. If a course does not appear on ASSIST as fulfilling a requirement for your target major, assume that it **does not count** toward major preparation. ASSIST tells you what each CSU campus requires. The next tool helps you keep track of how your own coursework lines up with those requirements over time.

CSU Transfer Planner

The CSU Transfer Planner is a free **online planning tool** available to all transfer bound students. Create an account as early as possible. The planner lets you log completed, in-progress, and planned coursework, track your total transferable units, including AP and IB test credit, monitor your Golden Four and Cal-GETC progress, and track ADT alignment status. If you attend multiple community colleges, counselors from each institution can access your record and communicate with you through the platform. But your own plan is only half the picture. Understanding how competitive your target campuses and majors are will help you gauge your chances more realistically, which is where impaction comes in.

Campus Impaction

Many CSU campuses publish statistics containing transfer admission criteria and competitive thresholds after each admission cycle. For example, at SJSU, you can find **post-cycle transfer impaction results** by major, showing the minimum GPA at which students were admitted and how thresholds shifted based on preparation coursework completed. Other campuses may publish major-specific transfer criteria, minimum preparation requirements, or impacted-program admissions data on multiple pages rather than a single one.

As there is no system-wide centralized source, you must go directly to each campus's admissions website. These **thresholds usually shift** from cycle to cycle based on applicant volume, seat availability, and how many fully prepared students apply each year. Historical data tells you the range and direction of competition. Use it to calibrate your CSU campus list.

By now, we understand the minimum requirements and the tools that help you plan your CSU transfer. What comes next is your application strategy.

Transfer admission depends not just on eligibility, but on how well your GPA, completed major preparation, and overall profile line up with your target major.

CSU Transfer Admission Factors

> **GPA and major preparation**
> Eligibility gets you to the door. A competitive GPA and completed major preparation get you through it.

Every CSU campus spells out exactly which lower-division courses it expects you to have completed for each major. These are accessible through ASSIST and each campus's admissions website. The CSU evaluates both **how many of those courses** you completed and **how well you performed** in them. Missing required preparation can raise the GPA requirements, eliminate you from consideration entirely, or mean you are only reviewed if space remains after all fully prepared applicants have been admitted. And at the most competitive programs, that remaining space is typically zero.

How well you **performed** in those courses matters too, not just whether you completed them. For competitive programs, a C in a required preparation course can raise questions about your readiness for upper-division work, even if your overall GPA is strong. Some programs specify minimum grades in preparation courses as part of their stated requirements.

Check the major-specific requirements for each of your target programs on ASSIST and on each campus's admissions page. But even a strong record may not be competitive, depending on where you apply. That is where impaction starts to matter.

Impaction
At SDSU, SJSU, Cal Poly SLO, Cal State Fullerton, and Cal State Long Beach, all programs are impacted for upper-division transfer applicants.

At other campuses, impaction may apply only to certain majors. Sacramento State, for example, is not impacted campus-wide, but some majors have additional requirements and higher competition. A student applying to History may face a very different level of competition from a student applying to Business Administration, Nursing, or Psychology. But how do impacted campuses and programs decide between similarly qualified students?

Local preference
Attending a CCC that is local to a specific campus may give you an advantage at that campus.

The CSU system allows campuses to give preference to students from nearby community colleges, particularly at impacted campuses. For example, SJSU gives local transfer applicants a **GPA boost** if they completed most of their units at a nearby community college.

Major preparation is also critical. When applicants have similar GPAs, campuses often prioritize students who have **completed more** of the **required lower-division coursework** for the major. The takeaway is that major choice shapes more than your academic path. It directly affects how **competitive** your application will be.

Switching Your Major

Transfer students arrive with **junior standing**, meaning fewer semesters remain than for freshmen, and attempting to switch into a different impacted major can make it impossible to complete that program within a standard graduation timeline. In addition, changing your major at an impacted campus is genuinely **difficult**. Cal Poly SLO warns students to choose their major carefully because, after admission, it cannot guarantee a change of major.

Formal change-of-major processes at impacted programs across the CSU typically require meeting strict GPA minimums, completing prerequisites, and surviving a competitive review process similar to the original admission process. Do not count on switching after you arrive. With that in mind, the next task is building a list that matches the reality of your options.

Building a Realistic Transfer List

Building a strong transfer list requires the same honest assessment as the freshman list, with one meaningful advantage: you have time to shape your profile before you apply. Every semester at a community college is an opportunity to raise your GPA, complete more required preparation courses, and strengthen your position.

Start by **identifying the impaction status** of every program you are considering. The CSU publishes an impaction matrix, a campus-by-campus, major-by-major table showing which programs are impacted. You can find it at calstate.edu/apply, or search 'CSU Impaction Matrix' along with the current year to make sure you are looking at the most recent version. Separate your targeted CSU schools into campus-wide impacted and program-level impacted, since the competitive standard differs significantly between the two.

For each target campus and major, **use ASSIST** to map out the required and recommended preparation and calculate how many you can realistically complete before you apply. Then check each campus's transfer criteria pages for the **historical minimum GPA** and **preparation profile** expected for your intended major. If your projected GPA and coursework do not clear that threshold, either adjust your targets or use your remaining semesters to close the gap.

Local admission area preference is worth factoring in. Research whether the campuses on your list give preference to students from community colleges in their service area and factor that into how you assess your own chances.

A strong CSU transfer list
Make sure to have at least one or two programs where your profile is well above the historical threshold, two or three targets where you are competitive, and perhaps one or two reach schools.

Every program on the list should be one you would genuinely attend if it were your only offer. Once your list reflects your GPA, major preparation, impaction, and local preference, the next step is entering that plan accurately into the CSU application itself.

Filling Out the Application

The transfer application follows the same basic structure as the freshman CSU application, so if you have read that chapter, much of this will feel familiar. What follows covers the parts that are different for transfer students, and a few places where small mistakes can cause real problems.

Application Timeline

Application dates **vary by term and cycle**, so always check the CSU webpage before applying. Not all campuses accept applications for every term, and not every program is available each term.

Spring transfer admission is more limited than fall. Most competitive and impacted programs are not available for spring entry, and many campuses do not accept spring transfer applications at all. For students targeting competitive majors, fall is the pathway to plan around. Some programs stop accepting applications before the priority deadline due to high demand, so apply **as early as possible** once the application opens.

What to have ready

- Unofficial transcripts from every college attended
- Social Security number
- Credit card for the $70 per campus application fee (up to four fee waivers are available if you qualify)
- Annual household income
- Your CCCID and campus ID
- Applicants to EOP need their parents' employment background and contact information for two recommenders.

Extended Profile

Complete the 'Extended Profile' first. Your answers determine which sections appear throughout the application. Select the correct **transfer type** based on how many transferable units you will have by the time you enroll (not at the time you apply). For example, a student applying in October with 52 units who will complete 8 more by the following spring is an upper-division applicant.

If you select 'Copy Application Data' from a previous year's application, any data entered previously will be carried forward, and all information will be editable. If you are completing an ADT, identify your specific AA-T or AS-T degree in the 'Extended Profile.' Do not select ADT options if you are earning a standard AA or AS degree.

Colleges Attended

Report all colleges attended, including international colleges. For each college, select the correct term type from your transcript: quarter, semester, or trimester. Attendance dates must be accurate. Incorrect dates will block you from entering coursework for that college. If you attended a college **outside the United States**, you can upload an unofficial copy of your transcript directly within Cal State Apply. Students with an official WES or ECE evaluation can connect their account to Cal State Apply so the evaluation can be provided directly to CSU campuses. Neither is required, but both can expedite review.

College Coursework

Complete the 'College Coursework' section by entering **all college courses** you have taken, have in progress, or have planned. This includes non-transferable courses and repeated courses. Course codes, titles, credits, and grades must match your transcript exactly. Do not enter a space between the subject prefix and the course number. For example, enter 'BIO2', not 'BIO 2.'

Some courses will **populate automatically** from a dropdown as you type, pulled from ASSIST data. Select from the dropdown whenever possible. For courses that do not populate, enter the course code and title manually exactly as they appear on your transcript. If your grades are listed as BA, CB, or DC, you must list them as AB, BC, and CD for the system to recognize them. Put the higher grade first. For Pass/No Pass grading, enter P for a passed course. For Credit/No Credit, enter CR. For repeated courses excluded from the institutional GPA, enter RP. For academic renewal, enter AR.

The **transferable course toggle** is unchecked by default and must be manually checked to note that the course is transferable. Leaving it unchecked is one of the **most common errors** in the application and can cause your unit count to appear below 60 even when your actual total is higher. Once all coursework is entered, confirm that you have completed everything correctly and click 'Save Your Transcript.' If you go back and edit coursework after saving, be sure to save again. After entering all coursework, use the 'Calculate my Transfer GPA' function to preview your GPA before submitting.

In-Progress and Planned Coursework

When you list a course as 'in progress' or 'planned,' you are committing to completing it. Your admission offer is conditional on finishing all reported courses with satisfactory grades. Dropping a required course, earning a D or F in a required course, or making significant schedule changes after being admitted puts that offer at risk. If anything in your spring schedule changes after you submit, contact the admissions office at each campus you applied to proactively.

General Education Matching

In the 'General Education' section, match your courses to the Golden Four areas using the dropdown menus. Courses from a CCC should **prepopulate** for approved GE categories based on ASSIST data. If they do not prepopulate, use ASSIST or GE category notations on your transcript to match them manually. After making any changes, you must go back into the 'General Education' section, review the courses matched to the GE areas, and click 'Save and Continue' to successfully complete your academic updates. Skipping this step means the system will not register your updates as complete.

Standardized Tests

Self-report any AP or IB scores in the 'Standardized Tests' section. ACT and SAT test scores will not be used for any admission purposes, and applicants are not required to submit these scores. **AP and IB scores count** toward your total transfer units earned to help meet the 60-unit threshold. After you enroll, send official AP scores to your campus using College Board code 3594, which covers all CSU campuses in a single submission. IB scores go directly from IB to your campus.

Educational Opportunity Program

The Educational Opportunity Program includes a dedicated advisor, priority registration at many campuses, a summer bridge program, emergency financial assistance, and a peer community. In the '**Supporting Information**' section, you will report whether you are currently in an EOP&S program and indicate whether you will be applying to the CSU's EOP. Only California residents and AB 540-eligible students who are both first-generation and low-income are eligible.

The EOP application for transfer students follows the **same structure** as for freshman applicants described in the previous chapter: autobiographical questions, detailed family and financial background information, and two letters of recommendation. That guidance applies equally here.

Technically, EOP can admit transfer students on an exceptional basis who fall below standard eligibility requirements but demonstrate the potential to succeed with support. However, this pathway is genuinely rare and should not be counted on as a backup for a weak academic record. EOP is a support program for students who meet eligibility and need additional resources, not an alternative admissions track.

Note that **EOPS**, the Extended Opportunity Programs and Services, is the community college version of this program. Participating in EOPS at your community college does **not automatically connect** you to CSU EOP, but your EOPS counselor can help you prepare a strong application. EOP deadlines at most campuses typically fall in mid-January, with a system-wide deadline of **January 31**. Start the EOP application early. It requires time and preparation and should not be left as an afterthought.

Unlike CSU freshman applicants, transfer applicants do **not report** any **extracurricular or work** activities. The 'Supporting Information' section is used mainly for items such as EOP&S status, the EOP application, ADT-related information, and certain campus- or program-specific questions.

International Coursework

If you have only college coursework from outside the United States, you will not enter those courses individually in Cal State Apply. Instead, CSU campuses review your international coursework based on official transcripts, required translations, and, in some cases, a course-by-course credential evaluation (such as WES or ECE). Admission is typically conditional until these documents are submitted and verified by the campus.

Program Materials

Each program you apply to has its own tile in the 'Program Materials 'section, where you complete any required questions or documents. You cannot submit your application if you do not complete all the information in this section. Some campuses review whether you have completed all required prerequisites. If yours does, you will see a **'Prerequisites'** section where you match your completed courses to each requirement. You must complete the 'Academic History' section before you can access this. The **housing** question in 'Program Materials' is used for financial aid planning purposes and does not affect your admission decision.

Before You Submit

Review the summary page carefully before submitting. Note any warnings that may require you to update your application before submitting. Once submitted, your application **cannot be changed** (minor exceptions apply). There are no refunds if you make a mistake.

A common issue for transfer applicants is the **upper-division unit warning**, which appears when your reported transferable unit count falls below 60. If you receive it, review your 'College Coursework' entries and confirm the **transferable course toggle is checked** for all eligible courses. Also, make sure you entered all in-progress and planned coursework.

Campus Portals

As soon as you submit your application, set up your **applicant portal** for every campus you applied to. These portals are separate from Cal State Apply and are where each campus communicates with you from this point forward, including document requests, supplemental application instructions, admission decisions, financial aid information, and housing applications. Check them (and your email account and spam folder) regularly from the moment you submit.

Academic Update

The Academic Update is the second part of the CSU transfer application, not just a follow-up. Between **January 1 and January 31**, you must return to Cal State Apply and report your final fall grades and confirm your spring coursework. Without this, campuses may not have the information they need to complete your review, and in competitive majors, that can cost you an offer. There is one exception: if you are a **returning student** applying back to the same CSU campus you previously attended, you do not need to complete the academic history update.

Use your unofficial transcripts to **enter grades exactly** as they appear. The update brings your application in line with what happened after you submitted it. You must report final fall grades, confirm or revise planned and in-progress coursework, add new colleges or coursework if needed, add standardized test scores, and update courses matched to prerequisites. Keep in mind that completed course titles and course numbers cannot be changed, and colleges and standardized test scores already listed cannot be deleted.

Fall grades are the part you need to handle most carefully. To report them, you must change the term from 'in progress' or 'planned' to '**completed**.' Once you do that and save it, you cannot change that term back or remove courses from it. Go slowly and check everything before you save. If you make an error, Cal State Apply support cannot fix it, so you would need to contact every CSU campus you applied to directly.

There is one step here that is **easy to miss**. If you make any changes in 'College Coursework,' you must also return to the **'General Education'** section, review the courses matched to the GE areas, and save that section again. If you skip that step, the system may not register your update as complete even though you entered the new information.

Download the PDF version of your application (in the 'Check status' tab) and make sure your fall grades match your transcript, the fall term now shows as completed, and your Golden Four courses are still matched correctly in General Education. That PDF is what admissions offices will review.

After submitting the TAU

Some campuses require additional, campus-specific steps after submitting the TAU. Keep checking your email and applicant portal regularly.

These additional steps are not part of Cal State Apply and will be communicated **directly by the campus**. For example, SJSU requires transfer applicants to complete a separate 'Supplemental Application' after the TAU. This form is used in SJSU's admission and impaction review, so missing it can affect your application. Requirements vary by campus, but the key takeaway is that the **application process may continue** even after the TAU is submitted.

Residency and AB 540

Residency classification at the CSU follows the same framework discussed earlier in the UC and freshman CSU chapters and applies equally to transfer students. One important transfer-specific detail is that AB 540 status **does not carry over automatically** from a community college to a CSU campus. If you were AB 540-eligible at your community college, you still must submit the AB 540 nonresident tuition exemption form to each CSU campus, along with the required transcripts or attendance records. Submit it as early as possible after admission, since you may be charged nonresident fees until your eligibility is confirmed.

After You Are Admitted

Conditional Offers

Every CSU transfer offer comes with conditions attached. You need to finish your remaining semester the way you described it in your application. Earning a D or F in a required course, dropping a required course, or making significant schedule changes can result in your offer being withdrawn. If anything changes unexpectedly, contact the admissions office right away rather than hoping no one notices.

Intent to Enroll

After receiving an offer, you commit to one CSU school through the campus portal, not through Cal State Apply. There is **no systemwide Intent to Enroll deadline** for transfer students. Each campus sets its own and communicates it in the admission offer. Read the offer carefully and respond by the campus-specified deadline. Missing it forfeits the offer.

Final Transcripts

Submit official final transcripts from every college you attended by the deadline. Transcripts must show all completed coursework, any degrees, and confirm your eligibility conditions. If you completed an ADT, your community college must officially post the degree to your transcript before you request it. Any discrepancy between what you reported in the application and what official transcripts show can result in rescission.

Redirection

CSU redirection may be available to CSU-eligible California residents who apply as upper-division transfer or ADT applicants and are not admitted to any CSU campus to which they applied. Redirection does not mean admission to the original campus or major; it gives eligible applicants a chance to be considered by another CSU campus with available space.

From Public Pathways to Private Colleges

The community college transfer pathway is one of the most **underappreciated** options in California's higher education landscape. Students who take this path seriously do the work up front. They build their coursework around what their target programs require, complete Cal-GETC alongside major preparation where it makes sense, and submit a complete and accurate application. Those students consistently reach programs that may not have been accessible to them straight out of high school. The degree at the end is identical; only the path is different.

With that, this closes the public university pathways in California: direct entry to the University of California and the California State University and transfer pathways through the California's community colleges. The next section turns to private colleges, where the rules, timelines, and evaluation process work very differently, and where the parts of the application that the CSU largely ignores become much more important.

California Private Colleges

15 | Private Colleges

Independence and Variability

When people think of California colleges, a few names come to mind immediately: Berkeley, UCLA, and, of course, Stanford. Stanford University is one of the most recognizable brand names in the world, alongside Harvard and Yale. But California's private colleges extend far beyond Stanford. The state has dozens of private institutions, from small liberal arts colleges in the foothills to large research universities in Los Angeles. These schools operate entirely outside California's public university system.

This chapter focuses on nonprofit, regionally accredited private institutions. California also has multiple for-profit colleges that operate under profit-driven business models. Students considering any private institution should confirm that it holds regional accreditation through the Western Association of Schools and Colleges (WASC), which serves as the baseline quality.

Outside the Public System

Private colleges operate on their own terms. They receive no direct funding from the State of California and answer to independent boards rather than public officials. They face no requirement to prioritize California residents or publish their admissions formulas. This lets them shape their classes based on their **own goals and needs**. This freedom extends to international enrollment. Public universities face political and practical limitations on the number of international students they can enroll. Private colleges are not bound by the same enrollment limits. At Stanford, for example, more than one-fifth of the student population are international students.

For students, the financial independence of private colleges cuts both ways. It allows for smaller classes, distinctive academic models, and generous financial aid at a few wealthy institutions. But it also means admissions decisions are even **less predictable.**

Selectivity as a Choice

Private colleges in California vary widely in how selective they are. At the extreme end sit Stanford University and the California Institute of Technology (Caltech).

Highly selective

Stanford admits roughly 3–4 percent of applicants, and Caltech accepts around 2–3 percent.

Both schools enroll very small undergraduate populations. Caltech has fewer than 1,000 undergraduates, and Stanford enrolls about 8,000. Their applicant pools are high-performing, global, and self-selecting.

Other selective institutions include Pomona College and Harvey Mudd College, both admitting well under 10 percent. Mid-tier privates admit more students: Loyola Marymount, Santa Clara, Pepperdine, Chapman, Occidental, and the University of San Diego all have higher acceptance rates. Once you move outside major metropolitan areas, acceptance rates climb further. Simpson University in Redding, for example, admits around two-thirds of its applicants.

The University of California must admit top California graduates by state mandate. Private colleges do not face such constraints and can decide how selective they want to be. Many remain **small by design**. Being hard to get into helps with college rankings, keeps admitted students more likely to enroll, and makes alumni feel their degrees are more valuable. A low acceptance rate is often an institutional choice, not necessarily a reflection of academic quality.

Financial Strength

Financial stability varies across California's private colleges, and those differences directly shape the student experience. Some private schools have large investment funds, called **endowments**, that support scholarships, faculty hiring, research, student services, and long-term financial stability. Stanford's endowment exceeds $40 billion[40]! That level of wealth allows them to offer generous financial aid packages, fund undergraduate research, and maintain small class sizes.

It also gives Stanford the freedom to absorb policy decisions without changing their admissions priorities. For example, Stanford considers **legacy status** as one factor in admissions, giving preference to applicants whose parents attended the school. When California banned this practice at institutions receiving state aid, Stanford chose to withdraw from the Cal Grant program rather than change its admissions policies. Cal Grants are state-funded scholarships for California residents. Stanford gave up this state funding and replaced it with its own money, covering the equivalent amount for affected students. That decision was possible only because of Stanford's unique financial position.

However, most California private colleges operate under different financial constraints. These schools do not have large endowments and therefore, **depend on tuition revenue** to fund their operations. Schools such as Loyola Marymount, Santa Clara, Pepperdine, Chapman, and the University of San Diego fall into this category.

That reliance directly impacts the student experience. Financial aid budgets must be carefully managed, which can mean less scholarship money available and a preference for students who can **pay the full tuition**. Programs may be

[40] news.stanford.edu/stories/2025/10/report-investment-portfolio-value-endowment

cut if enrollment drops, and majors with low enrollment may disappear completely. These financial realities also affect class sizes, faculty hiring, and campus facilities.

Sticker Price vs. Net Price

Private colleges publish a list price (or sticker price) that may exceed $60,000 per year. The University of Southern California (USC), for example, has a total cost of attendance of roughly $100,000 per year! While those numbers are real, many students do not pay the sticker price. What you see as the official list price may not be what your family will pay. Often, private colleges reduce costs through financial aid, which comes in two forms: need-based aid and merit aid. Need-based aid depends on your family's financial situation. Merit aid depends on your grades, test scores, or other achievements, regardless of whether you need the money.

Chasing Merit Aid

Here is where it gets strategic. Less selective and tuition-dependent colleges often use merit aid to attract strong students and fill seats. They are competing for talented students. If you have a strong profile and are looking for merit aid, it is better to **expand your list** beyond the most selective schools. Look at colleges one tier below where your academic profile puts you at the top of their applicant pool. That is where receiving merit aid is most likely. Highly selective private colleges such as Stanford do not offer merit aid because every applicant is a highly talented student. Instead, they focus on need-based aid.

Need-Based Aid

Virtually all colleges offer some need-based financial aid, but the amount varies widely. Only a handful of wealthy private colleges meet the full demonstrated financial need for every admitted student.

> **Meeting full demonstrated need**
> Stanford, Caltech, Pomona College, Claremont McKenna, Harvey Mudd, Scripps, and Pitzer fully cover the gap between what your family can pay and their total cost of attendance.

However, here is the problem: what colleges consider financial need often differs from what families feel they can afford. Each college calculates demonstrated need **using its own formula**. These calculations may factor in home equity, retirement accounts, or income assumptions that do not reflect your family's actual budget. Two colleges can look at the same family and come up with very different numbers. You might get a generous aid package from one school and a smaller package from another, even if both claim to meet full need.

This is why the **Net Price Calculator** (NPC) is essential. Every college is required to publish one on its financial aid website. Based on your family's financials, the NPC estimates what your family would likely pay after grants and scholarships. Comparing net prices across colleges is far more telling than comparing sticker prices. This applies to public universities as well. Always use the NPC before assuming you can or cannot afford a school.

Cost and aid policies are only one part of the picture. The **type of college** also matters, because different schools offer different academic environments and student experiences to undergraduate education.

Small Liberal Arts Colleges

California is home to some of the strongest small liberal arts colleges (SLACs) in the country. A liberal arts education emphasizes broad **learning across disciplines** rather than narrow professional training. All students take courses in humanities, social sciences, natural sciences, and arts regardless of their major. The goal is to develop critical thinking, writing, and analytical skills that apply across fields.

At liberal arts colleges, **undergraduate education** is the central mission. Classes are discussion-based, and writing is emphasized across disciplines, including math and science. Graduate teaching assistants are rare; professors teach their own courses. With enrollments sometimes under 2,000 students, they know students by name. Feedback is constant, and there is little anonymity. For some students, this creates exceptional mentorship. For others, it feels like there is no place to hide.

The **Claremont Consortium** is California's best-known liberal arts institution. The group consists of five separate institutions, Pomona, Claremont McKenna, Harvey Mudd, Scripps, and Pitzer, that share libraries, dining halls, and some classes. They each maintain their own admissions processes and campus cultures.

However, the liberal arts model is **not for everyone**. Particularly, STEM students may be surprised by the amount of writing required, even in technical courses. Students who want to focus narrowly on their major may find the breadth requirements of SLACs frustrating.

Private Research Universities

California has several private research universities classified as **R1 institutions**. This classification means they conduct the highest level of research activity. By research budget, Stanford and Caltech rank among the top research universities nationwide. The University of Southern California operates differently, combining large undergraduate enrollment with extensive professional schools and research infrastructure.

At private research universities, undergraduates may do research earlier than at the UCs. But a larger student body at USC may also mean **larger classes** and more administrative complexity. Like public flagships, these universities often prioritize faculty research productivity, graduate programs, and grant funding. The difference is that they answer to trustees and donors, not state legislatures or the public.

Students considering private research universities should ask specific questions. How often do undergraduates participate in research? How is advising structured? Do faculty incentives reward teaching or focus primarily on securing grants?

Religious Schools

Many California private colleges have religious affiliations. How much does that matter? It depends entirely on the school. Some maintain historical ties to a religious tradition but function as secular institutions. Others weave faith into every part of campus life. Religious affiliation **shapes student experience** more than many applicants expect.

Take Jesuit universities like Santa Clara University, Loyola Marymount, and the University of San Francisco. They emphasize ethics, service, and educating the whole person. You will take theology courses as part of the standard curriculum. But campus culture tends to be open and pluralistic, welcoming students of all faiths and no faith.

Other faith-based schools go further. At Pepperdine or Biola, students agree to community standards that regulate alcohol use, visitation policies, and religious participation. Chapel attendance may be required. For students seeking faith-centered communities, these environments offer deep support. For those who are not, they can feel restrictive. Student handbooks and housing policies show you what daily life looks like. Read them before you apply, not after you enroll.

Nontraditional Colleges

Not all colleges fit neatly into categories. Some colleges reimagine where and how learning takes place. At **Minerva University**, headquartered in San Francisco, students take small, discussion-based seminars online and rotate through multiple global cities over four years. The result is an experience that is international and highly structured but lacks the traditional campus experience.

Others are built around a fixed intellectual framework rather than open-ended choice. **Thomas Aquinas College** in Santa Paula follows a Great Books curriculum in which students read original texts. Students move through a shared program rather than selecting from a specific major. This approach creates a deeply coherent academic experience, but it also limits flexibility.

Some colleges integrate academic life with daily responsibilities in ways that fundamentally change the student experience. **Deep Springs College**, located in a remote valley in eastern California, combines academics with required labor on a working ranch. With an extremely small student body and an isolated setting, it offers a unique environment. The common thread is that these colleges ask students to opt into a specific way of learning. That can be appealing for students who know what they want and are energized by a clearly defined environment.

Holistic Admissions and Institutional Priorities

Private colleges usually use holistic admissions. Applications are **reviewed in context** rather than by formulaic GPA cutoffs. Grades and rigor matter, but they are not the only factors. Private universities want to see the applicant holistically, including extracurricular activities, personality traits, and writing skills. The UCs also consider applicants in a comprehensive way, but admissions at private schools is further driven by **institutional priorities**: enrollment targets, academic balance, geographic distribution, financial aid constraints, alumni influence, athletics, and legacy status.

Two students with similar academic profiles can receive **different outcomes**. It depends on how they fit into the class that a college is building. A student with a high GPA applying from an overrepresented region or major may be denied. Another applicant with a slightly lower GPA but different academic interests or background may be admitted. Internal priorities influence private college admissions decisions, turning the outcomes unpredictable for the applicants.

Alumni Networks and Career Outcomes

One of the strongest advantages of private colleges is their alumni engagement. Smaller institutions often maintain tight alumni networks. They offer more active mentorship. They have stronger involvement in internships and hiring. Alumni connections can **open doors** that applications alone cannot: internships at family businesses, referrals at competitive firms, or introductions to industry contacts.

Private colleges also differ in how they prepare students for **graduate education**. Highly selective private colleges send large shares of graduates to PhD, MD, JD, and MBA programs. At institutions such as Caltech and Pomona, graduate school placement is an explicit goal. Other private colleges focus more heavily on workforce entry and professional preparation. Students aiming for research-intensive graduate programs should look for undergraduate research access and faculty mentorship. Students targeting industry should examine internship pipelines, employer relationships, and alumni placement in their field.

Structural Limitations of Private Colleges

Smaller private colleges offer unique environments, but their structure also creates constraints, for example in their academic offerings. Many smaller private colleges offer a **limited number of majors**. That can be a strength for students who arrive with clear goals, but it reduces flexibility. Changing majors is common in college, yet at a small institution, the alternative major may not exist, or required courses may be offered only once per year, making late changes difficult or time-consuming. **Course depth** is another potential limitation. Instead of many elective options, students may follow a single pathway designed by the department. This supports coherence and close faculty guidance, but leaves less room for specialization, niche interests, or combining fields in unconventional ways.

Facilities and research infrastructure also vary widely. Some small private colleges support undergraduate research, but opportunities can be limited. Specialized labs, advanced equipment, or large research teams may not be available. Access often depends on individual mentorship rather than institutional capacity.

Financial structure also matters. Many private colleges rely heavily on tuition revenue and annual fundraising. Without large endowments, they have less margin for error. Over time, this can affect course availability, staffing levels, or the pace at which programs expand or adapt. These pressures are rarely visible during the admissions process, but they shape the academic experience students ultimately have. Researching and understanding these limitations helps students choose private colleges for the reasons they work best, rather than assuming every private campus offers unlimited flexibility.

Making Sense of the Variability

Private colleges can feel confusing because there is no single model. Each one sets its own rules, priorities, and expectations. Two schools can offer very different academic experiences, campus cultures, and costs. California's public universities operate within shared structures and constraints; private colleges do not. That difference affects admissions decisions, financial aid, class size, housing, advising, and student life.

16 | Applying to Private Colleges

Fit and Depth

Earlier, we looked at what makes an application strong in general. Chapter 4 outlined the **Three Pillars**: academic performance, extracurricular engagement, and personal qualities. This chapter picks up from there. Once a private college has received your application, how does that school turn your file into a decision? And because private colleges vary so much, how do you build an application strategy that works across a list of different schools while still being specific enough to matter at each one?

California's private colleges include highly selective research universities, a nationally recognized liberal arts consortium, faith-based institutions, and smaller colleges that differ widely in culture and purpose. When you apply to several of them, you are not just sending the same application to different addresses. You are moving through several different admissions processes at once. Understanding how those processes work is one of the most useful things you can do before you start.

How Colleges Build Their Class

Private colleges do not all use the admissions process, and they do not publish a simple admissions flowchart. Even so, enough information is public knowledge to show the **broad patterns**. At many selective private colleges, your file is not simply read once by one person and decided on the spot. It may be read first by one admissions officer and then reviewed by another or read by a regional officer and then carried into **committee**.

At some schools, separate category ratings help structure later discussion. Stanford states that admissions decisions are made by committee rather than by any one admissions officer acting alone. At schools receiving many applications, an initial read may last **only a few minutes**. Volume shapes the process, and a file must make sense quickly. The student's academic record, main areas of engagement, and overall direction need to come through clearly enough that a reader can carry them forward.

This is where **coherence** becomes practical. A file where the transcript, activities, essays, and supplements point in the same general direction is easier to explain and advocate for. A file where different parts suggest different versions of the student loses momentum. One reader often summarizes the applicant and presents the file to the admissions committee. The clearer the application, the easier that task becomes.

Most colleges also use some form of **rubric** or **rating system** to organize the review process. The exact structure varies, but the goal is consistent: to compare students who are strong in different ways. Ratings help organize discussion, but they do not replace judgment. Once a file reaches the admissions committee, the question shifts. It is no longer just whether a student is strong but how that student fits into the overall incoming class the college is building. Colleges refer to this process as 'shaping the class.'

No application is evaluated in isolation. Colleges are **shaping the class** with set constraints: academic balance across majors, geographic distribution, institutional programs, and enrollment targets. This is also where certain groups receive additional consideration. Recruited athletes fill roster needs. Some institutions consider legacy status. Many prioritize first-generation or lower-income students as part of access goals. Others have specific institutional needs, such as musicians for ensembles or students for particular academic programs.

Enrollment management adds another layer. Colleges are not only selecting strong students. They are also selecting students who are likely to enroll. Highly selective colleges have more flexibility here. When you receive an offer from Caltech or Stanford, you are less likely to turn it down, and those institutions know it. Their prestige largely takes care of yield on its own, which is why early application programs matter more as a tool for shaping a class than for securing it.

Less selective colleges face a harder version of this problem. Their yield is lower. More admitted students will choose another school, and the consequences of coming up short are real. They still must fill a class, hit tuition targets, and manage the gap between how many students they admit and how many actually show up.

Demonstrated interest exists at many of these institutions for exactly that reason. Tracking whether you have visited, emailed, or attended an info session is a way of reducing uncertainty and identifying students who are most likely to enroll. Later in the process, colleges often manage enrollment through their **waitlist**, releasing spots in small batches and giving applicants only a few days to decide. By repeating this process multiple times, colleges gradually fill their class while adjusting for students who decline or committed elsewhere.

These layers explain why strong students sometimes receive different results from similar schools. A file can be compelling and still land in the middle of a highly competitive pool. That outcome reflects how the class is being shaped, not a failure of the application.

What Selective Colleges Look For

By the time you are applying to selective private colleges, basic competence across the Three Pillars is assumed. Strong grades, rigorous courses, and meaningful activities are the starting point. They do not separate applicants on their own. They create a large pool of applicants who are all able and competitive.

What separates applicants in that pool is the structure within the application. Admissions readers are not ranking you in a vacuum. They are trying to understand your application quickly. A file that feels scattered is harder to interpret, whereas a file with a clear center is easier to carry into the admissions committee. What often makes the difference in that pool is referred to as a **spike.**

What helps stand out?
A spike is a clear, sustained area of depth that gives your application a center of gravity and makes you easy to remember and advocate for in committee.

A spike shows up not as a single impressive line on a résumé, but as a student's pattern of depth and development. Going **deep into one area of interest** on top of being well-rounded sends a different kind of signal than doing many unrelated things at a moderate level. A student who has taken increasingly advanced coursework in a subject, pursued independent work, engaged outside the classroom, and reflected on that interest in writing presents a profile with a clear center of gravity.

The same logic applies **outside of academics**. Long-term involvement with increasing responsibility, leadership that grows out of genuine commitment rather than title-chasing, and projects that show initiative over time create a sense of continuity. That continuity allows a reader to understand what you really care about.

Balance still matters; a one-dimensional application without academic strength or engagement beyond the classroom will not hold up. In highly selective pools, though, the difference between applicants is rarely the absence of a pillar. The presence of a clear spike is what tends to move a file forward. How applications get discussed in committee reflects this. A reader needs to describe you in a way that others can grasp quickly. 'Strong student with good grades and activities' does not carry much weight. 'Student deeply engaged in X, with sustained work and clearly defined impact' is easier to argue for.

Research, national awards, publications, competitions, and independent projects can all **add weight** to a spike. The stronger they connect to a clear story-line in the application, the more convincing they are. An applicant with one or two serious commitments often reads more convincingly than someone who appears to have tried everything without going far in anything. Essays are one of the clearest places where your spike, or the absence of one, becomes visible.

Essays

In Chapter 4, we discussed what makes essays effective in general. Keep in mind that the essay is the only place where the admissions reader directly hears **your voice** and starts to imagine you as a real person rather than a file. A transcript demonstrates discipline and aptitude, and activities show how you spend your time. Essays, however, help the reader understand who you are and what you value.

Traditionally, essays also carried a second function. They gave colleges a direct sample of an applicant's **writing ability**. Recently, that function has become less stable. With generative AI and outside editing widely available, admissions offices can no longer assume that the final product cleanly reflects a student's unassisted writing. In 2024, Duke University stopped assigning numerical ratings to applicants' essays, attributing that change largely to AI-generated writing and highly edited essays by paid consultants. They still require short essays, so the writing has not disappeared from their process, but essays matter less in the admissions process.

These trends do not mean essays are going away but their function is **likely to shift**. In large, competitive applicant pools, many students look similar on paper and essays help readers distinguish between them. They clarify how a student thinks, what they value, and how the rest of the application fits together. They also make it easier for a reader to present the applicant to a committee.

Private college essays also diverge across institutions in ways that public systems do not. The personal statement is only one piece. Most private colleges add their own **supplemental questions**, often several per school. A student applying to eight or ten private colleges may end up writing dozens of additional responses.

Many students underestimate this workload. They think the personal statement is the main task and that supplements will fall into place afterward. In reality, supplements take as much care as the main essay. When they are left to the final weeks, quality drops. Schools begin to blur together, and responses start sounding interchangeable. This is one of the most common ways a strong application weakens.

Supplemental essays function as tests of fit and understanding. Each response should connect what you have already done, what you want to do next, and why that next step makes sense at that particular school. Specificity carries the argument. Naming a particular academic approach, program structure, research style, or campus environment is more persuasive than describing the school in broad terms.

Different colleges signal **different priorities** through their prompts. For example, USC emphasizes scale, resources, and urban opportunity. Pomona emphasizes small classes, close faculty relationships, collaborative learning, and undergraduate research. Pitzer's public language is unusually explicit about values. Stanford's questions ask about intellectual liveliness, self-awareness, and personality. The strongest supplements are tailored, not recycled.

What about AI?

Students apply in a time when AI tools are widely available (and used), but college policies are not uniform. Some colleges have published detailed guidance, while others refer to academic-integrity expectations. Keep in mind that more and more colleges use tools to check essays for AI-generated writing or plagiarism.

Generally, **AI can be helpful** in the early stages of the essay writing process. It can support brainstorming, early organization, and clarity checks. Those uses are similar to other forms of college counseling support. The line is crossed when the tool starts replacing the student's own thinking and writing. The risk is not only ethical but practical. Essays that rely heavily on generated language often lose specificity and voice. They read as polished but hollow. Admissions readers are looking for evidence of how a student thinks and engages with the world. When the writing becomes generic, that evidence weakens.

The safest rule is simple. Use AI as an **early support tool**, not as a substitute. Brainstorm with it. Use it to help organize ideas. But do not let it generate the essay for you. Essays work best when the reader can clearly hear a real person behind the words.

Common App

Most California private colleges use centralized application platforms. For most students, that means the **Common App**[41]. It now serves more than 1,100 colleges, which is why it has become the practical center of the application process for many applicants. You complete the shared core once, then add each college's supplemental questions, essays, and requirements. The alternative to the Common App is **Scoir**[42] (formerly known as Coalition App). It is used by some high schools as a college-planning platform and now supports applications to over 100 colleges.

The main advantage of platforms like Common App and Scoir is not just **convenience** for students. It is **coordination**. Counselors and teachers submit transcripts, school reports, and letters of recommendation through the same system. Instead of sending documents separately to each college, materials are uploaded once and distributed across multiple applications. This reduces missing documents, duplicate requests, and last-minute confusion. But the Common App and Score are not the only pathways for applications. Many colleges allow students to **apply directly** through their own application portals on their websites.

Regardless of the application platform, some colleges require you to enter your full academic record course by course into a separate portal called **STARS** (Self-reported Transcript and Academic Record System)[43].

Common App's Direct Admissions Program

The Common App recently introduced its Direct Admissions program. The core idea is simple: you receive an **acceptance before even applying.**

41 commonapp.org/

42 happ.scoir.com/signin

43 srar.selfreportedtranscript.com/Login.aspx

Participating colleges review your information and accept you based on your profile. In practical terms, you know early that you already have a spot at a college.

For many students, especially those who are anxious, getting an early acceptance can significantly **reduce stress**. The question shifts from 'Can I get in?' to 'Is this a school I actually want to attend?' These offers are still conditional, and students must complete the remaining steps. But the psychological shift is real. Having an acceptance early can make it easier to approach the rest of your applications. In California, Direct Admissions includes Saint Mary's College, Whittier College, and the University of the Pacific, and the list is likely to grow.

Application Plans

One key aspect of your overall application strategy is when to apply. Application plans do more than change deadlines. They **change the pool** you are applying in, the level of commitment you signal, and sometimes your chances of getting in.

Application plans also matter for a more **practical reason**. College application season can become exhausting very quickly, especially when supplements for private schools multiply. If you apply to every college with the same regular deadline, the quality of your application may drop. Essays get rushed, schools start sounding interchangeable, and you may burn out at when you need to be most thoughtful. Understanding different application windows lets you spread out the work, making sure you deliver high quality throughout.

Applying in chunks

Apply to a few schools early, then focus on UC and CSU in October and November, and work on a few more private colleges in December and January.

That pacing usually produces better writing and less panic. Let us have a closer look at the different application plans.

Early Action

Early Action (EA) is **nonbinding**. You apply early (typically in November), hear back in December, and keep the freedom to compare all college offers. For students who are ready in fall, this can be useful because it spreads out the work and brings some decisions forward. EA can also have strategic value even when it is not formally an admissions boost. At some colleges, applying early is the only way to remain eligible for major **merit scholarships** or special programs. That means the early deadline may matter financially, even if it is not dramatically changing your odds of admission. For example, USC states that the Early Action deadline serves also as the merit scholarship deadline.

An EA decision usually comes in one of three forms: admit, deny, or defer. A **deferral** means the college wants to compare you with the larger applicant pool before making a final call. That is disappointing, but it is still an active application. Follow the college's instructions. Some welcome a brief update; others want nothing.

Early Decision I

Early Decision I (ED I) is **binding** and typically has deadlines in early November. You can only apply to one school via ED. If admitted in December, you are expected to enroll at that school and withdraw all other early applications. That makes ED useful only when one school is clearly your first choice and your family is comfortable committing before comparing financial aid offers from multiple colleges. Before applying ED, run the Net Price Calculator and check that you can **afford to pay** the amount stated. Do not assume that you get additional scholarships beyond the NPC.

You may have heard that applying ED **improves your odds**. And often, it does. However, the reality is more nuanced. At some schools, ED does provide a meaningful advantage. But the early pool is not always a smaller version of the regular pool. Students applying ED usually are top achievers, making the **applicant pool very competitive**. Also, at smaller private colleges with significant athletic recruitment, a noticeable share of the early pool may be reserved for recruited athletes. At some schools, legacy applicants get priority. Consequently, an apparently higher ED admit rate does not automatically translate into the same advantage for every unhooked applicant.

Early Decision II

Early Decision II (ED II) is the **later binding round**, usually in early January. It works much like ED I but gives students more time to prepare. This option can be useful for students who did not apply or were denied in ED I, or who only later realized that one school had become their top choice. The commitment, however, is the same. If admitted, you are expected to enroll. Students should treat ED II with the same financial caution as ED I.

Restrictive Early Action

Restrictive Early Action (REA) is **nonbinding**, but it limits where else you can apply. For example, Stanford's REA applicants cannot apply to other private colleges under EA, REA, or ED plans. Stanford also evaluates REA and regular applications the same, which means REA does not come with a hidden admissions boost. It is better understood as a timing and signaling choice.

Stanford and USC
Stanford explicitly permits applying early to USC, since USC's early program is nonbinding and required for merit scholarship consideration.

Regular Decision

Applying in the Regular Decision (RD) window remains the main route for most students. It gives them more time to revise essays, include fall grades, and build a more thoughtful college list. But it also places them into the broadest and often most crowded pool. That does not make it a bad option. For many students, especially those whose writing improves with more time or whose list is still taking shape through the fall, applying RD is the better choice.

Rolling Admission

Rolling admission works differently. Instead of waiting for one large decision release, colleges review applications as they are submitted and release

decisions continuously. Applying earlier gives you an advantage as the college has more spots to fill. Some less selective private colleges use rolling or near-rolling models, and this can be strategically useful. Getting an early acceptance can reduce pressure and make the rest of the season easier to handle.

Being Waitlisted

Sometimes, students receive neither an acceptance nor a rejection but are waitlisted. A waitlist offer is an invitation to stay in the college's wait pool while the school sees how many admitted students enroll. Waitlist movement varies enormously from year to year and school to school. In some years, a college may admit many students from the waitlist. Some years, it may admit almost none.

If you are waitlisted at a school that you genuinely want to attend, accept the spot and send a short, specific **letter of continued interest**. A good LoCI does three things well. It confirms that you are still seriously interested. It gives the college any meaningful new information, such as stronger grades, a significant award, or an important update. And it reminds the reader why the match is real, usually in a way that lines up with the school's values or priorities. If the college considers demonstrated interest, a thoughtful LOCI can reinforce that interest. Keep the letter brief, usually one page is enough. Be specific. If you would genuinely enroll if admitted, say so. And always read the college's instructions first. Some colleges welcome additional material. Others do not.

At the same time, do not put your life on hold for a waitlist. **Commit** to another school **by the May 1** deadline and treat it as your plan going forward. If the waitlist moves later, you can make a new decision then. Staying on the waitlist while committing somewhere else protects you while leaving the door open.

Waitlists are a reminder that the admissions process and the college-choice process are not the same thing. Even before admissions decisions arrive, you need a way to think about which private colleges make sense for you.

Fit by Student Type

The question of fit at California's private colleges is genuinely complex. Let me introduce a framework helping you to categorize your options and guide the questions and tradeoffs you should be considering.

> **Chasing merit aid**
> If you are chasing merit scholarships, your college list needs to skew toward schools where your academic profile makes you a top candidate.

Highly selective colleges generally do not offer merit scholarships. Schools like Stanford and Caltech can fill their incoming class many times over, which means they have no strategic reason to offer merit awards. Their financial aid is almost entirely need-based.

The colleges where merit aid is most available tend to be **one tier below the most selective colleges**. These colleges attract top students by offering generous scholarships. Building a merit-focused college list means including schools where your GPA and test scores are clearly strong relative to admitted students. It also means looking for schools where merit scholarships are available and substantial, and where the school is still a good fit for you. Run the Net Price Calculator for each school and look at merit award patterns in the Common Data Set.

> **Discussion-driven learner**
> A student who thrives in discussion-heavy seminars, values close feedback, and wants faculty mentorship is a good fit for a small liberal arts college.

Do you come alive in a seminar room, where ideas get debated, challenged, and built on in real time? If so, a small liberal arts college may be the right fit. The emphasis is on developing your critical thinking over mastering a body of facts. Learning happens through discussion, not lecture. You will be assessed through papers, presentations, and seminars rather than multiple choice exams. Faculty are accessible, classes are small, and mentorship is part of the culture. Schools like Pomona, Occidental, and Claremont McKenna are good examples.

Planning for graduate school

For students planning to pursue a PhD, MD, or other research-intensive graduate program, access to undergraduate research is critical.

At private universities like Stanford, Caltech, and USC, undergraduates can often work in faculty labs earlier than at large public universities. At liberal arts colleges, undergraduate research can be strong but looks different. Fewer labs and projects exist, but when opportunities are available, undergraduates often have more direct access since they are not competing with graduate students.

Pomona, Harvey Mudd, and Scripps all have strong undergraduate research reputations, and faculty mentorship is often built directly into the student experience. If you plan to go on to graduate school, the practical questions are departmental, not just institutional: how many undergraduates work on faculty research, how are positions assigned, are there funded summer opportunities, and where do graduates go afterward?

Career-focused student

The right private colleges are the ones whose networks, resources, and opportunities match the career path you want to pursue.

For the student with a specific career in mind, that goal shapes how they evaluate colleges. A student targeting consulting, finance, or tech may find that a larger university like USC offers stronger recruiting pipelines and internship access. A pre-med, pre-law, or PhD-track student needs to focus on research access, advising quality, and graduate school preparation. A student in arts or design may care more about specialized programs than general prestige.

The practical questions matter most: Where do alumni in your targeted field work? Does the school have structured recruiting relationships? How strong is the advising for your intended path? Are internships, research positions, or portfolio opportunities easy to access?

Faith-centered student
California's private colleges include many religiously affiliated institutions, and how much faith shapes campus life varies widely.

Campus culture at Jesuit schools tends to be open and pluralistic. Schools like Pepperdine or Biola regulate aspects of daily life more directly, and the religious dimension is often more visible in policy and student experience. For students seeking a community where faith and academics are deeply integrated, these environments can offer real support. For other students, these schools can feel restrictive in ways that are hard to anticipate.

Anxious student
Building a realistic list, using data instead of assumptions, and securing an early acceptance are effective ways to lower stress.

Some students need realistic options that arrive early enough to reduce stress. If that describes you, start by building a list that prioritizes **rolling admissions** and Direct Admissions programs, which can get decisions into your hands sooner. From there, let data do some of the work. Looking up actual admit rates and digging into sources like the Common Data Set or Naviance replaces anxiety with facts. If test scores are a source of stress, focus on test-optional schools.

Smaller colleges, schools **closer to home**, or campuses where you already have a connection are also worth taking seriously. They can feel more approachable. And if you are genuinely uncertain about the path, community college with a transfer plan may be a path with less stress.

Undecided student

For undecided students, the right college offers broad options, flexible structure, strong advising, and a clear path to switching direction if needed.

Some students are not ready to choose a narrow path, and that is fine. Problems can arise when they choose a college that assumes they already know what they want. **Liberal arts colleges** generally work well for students who enjoy breadth. Larger universities can also work if changing direction is not too difficult. Be careful with highly specialized institutions or fixed curricula where switching paths is hard. At many larger universities, popular majors like Business, Computer Science, or Nursing may be capped, and getting in undeclared with the intention of switching later is not always possible. The real question is not whether it is okay to be undecided but how well a college **supports you** in finding the right direction over time.

Putting It Together

Applying to private colleges requires more than sending the same application to multiple schools. The process works best when you build your list with all three dimensions of fit in mind from the beginning: academic, personal, and financial. From there, the task is to understand how each school operates. Check the Common Data Set to see whether a college tracks demonstrated interest. Some schools use early application deadlines strategically for scholarships or enrollment management. Others rely heavily on supplements to judge fit. Sending the same application everywhere, with minor edits, is one of the most common mistakes.

This also means being realistic about how you plan the work. Private college applications become overwhelming because the **writing load** is easy to underestimate. A strong personal statement is only the start. Supplemental essays take time, and it can weaken your application when you leave them to the end or recycle your answers across schools.

One way to manage your workload is to tackle applications in **batches.** Rather than working on everything at once, use early and regular decision deadlines strategically to spread your workload. **Start earlier** than you think you need to, give yourself plenty of time to revise, and treat school-specific questions as important. Keep the logistical side organized too by tracking portals, requirements, and deadlines carefully across schools.

Once all your applications are submitted, the process is not over. Senior year grades and the midyear report still count, and a meaningful update can make a difference if something genuinely new strengthens your file. But by that point, most of the work is done.

That still leaves the question that often shapes the final decision. A college can be a strong fit academically and personally, and still be the wrong choice if the finances do not work out. The most expensive private colleges can cost up to $100,000 a year, which adds up to $400,000 for a four-year degree. Unless money genuinely is not a concern for your family, affordability is not a detail to sort out later. The next chapter looks at ways how you can interpret financial aid offers and ways to finance your college education.

The Bottom Line

17 | Paying for College

Understanding Costs and Financial Aid

Four hundred thousand dollars. That is what four years at California's most expensive private colleges can cost. Some families see that number and assume college is out of reach, or they think it comes down to picking the cheapest option. Neither is true. For many families, a college's sticker price is not what they end up paying. For others, particularly middle-income households that earn too much to qualify for need-based aid but cannot easily cash-flow college costs, the published price is closer to reality than they hoped.

This chapter walks you through the full financial picture: what to include in college costs, how financial aid works, and how to read an award letter. Understanding the financial side of the decision puts you in a strong position to choose a college your family can realistically sustain for four years.

Understanding College Costs

Cost of Attendance

Every college is required to publish their Cost of Attendance, or COA. This is the total estimated cost of going to that school for one year. It is the complete financial picture, made up of two parts. The first part includes **direct costs**, such as tuition and fees, room and board if you live on campus, and sometimes health insurance. In most cases, these are the charges the college will **bill you** directly. Health insurance may be waived if you can show qualifying outside coverage, such as staying on your parents' health insurance.

The second part of COA are the **indirect costs.** These are estimated expenses that the college does **not bill you** for but expects you to have. Books and supplies, transportation, and personal expenses. These are real costs, but you have some **control over them**. A student who commutes from home may spend less on housing than the estimate assumes. A student living off campus in an expensive city might spend more. Two students at the same college can end up with different total costs depending on how and where they live and how carefully they manage their money.

Sticker vs Net Price

The published Cost of Attendance, often called the sticker price, is not necessarily what your family will pay. What you pay depends on your financial profile and the aid you receive. Families who qualify for need-based or merit aid will pay less (sometimes significantly) than the published price. Families who do not qualify will pay close to the sticker price. Either way, the number that matters is **your net price**: what remains after grants and scholarships are subtracted.

Net price
= Cost of Attendance minus financial aid, grants, and scholarships

Focus on the net price when comparing schools, not the sticker price. Two colleges that look very different on paper can end up costing nearly the same after aid, or have a dramatic difference in cost, depending entirely on your financial profile and what each school offers. The only way to know is to run the numbers for your specific situation at each school. Every college offers a **Net Price Calculator** on its website. Use it early, before you invest significant time in applications.

The UCs require students to have health insurance and automatically enroll you in the university plan if you cannot show proof of existing coverage. The cost runs between $3,000 and $5,000 per year. If you are covered under a parent's plan, you can submit a waiver to opt out and avoid that charge.

Let us first have a look at the different systems a college may use to determine how much financial aid they offer you.

Financial Aid Systems

FAFSA

For most families, the financial aid process starts with filing the FAFSA, the Free Application for Federal Student Aid[44]. One of the most persistent misconceptions about the FAFSA is that it gives money on top of whatever the college offers. FAFSA is the government's process to collect detailed financial information about your family and use it to calculate a number called the **Student Aid Index**, or SAI.

FAFSA is **not a source of money**; it is the form that kicks off the financial aid process. Once submitted, your financial information is shared with the colleges you select, and each school uses it to determine what aid to offer you. That aid comes from three places: the federal government, the state of California, and the college itself. This is the formula that colleges usually use to determine your financial need:

> **Demonstrated financial need**
> = Cost of Attendance minus Student Aid Index

A lower SAI means greater financial need and tends to lead to more need-based aid. The lowest possible SAI is -1,500, which reflects the highest level of financial need. A higher SAI suggests less financial need. The federal government states that the SAI is not the amount your family is expected to pay but simply an index that colleges use when calculating aid. That said, many colleges consider it a **rough estimate** of your expected family contribution.

[44] studentaid.gov/fsa-id/sign-in/landing

Very few colleges meet your **full demonstrated need**, and the ones that do are not all doing it in the same way. In California, only Stanford, Caltech, Pomona, Claremont McKenna, Harvey Mudd, Pitzer, Scripps, Occidental, and USC commit to meeting 100 percent of a student's demonstrated need. But that promise means different things at different schools. For example, Stanford meets full need without loans, whereas Caltech and Harvey Mudd may include loans and work-study in their offer. The UC does not make blanket commitments to meet full demonstrated need, leaving a gap for many families. The gap between what colleges offer and what your family can afford to pay (also known as **unmet need**), must be covered through loans, work, savings, or outside scholarships.

Even if your **SAI** is **too high** for need-based aid, you should still file the FAFSA. Some colleges require it to be considered for merit scholarships. In addition, federal student loans, which carry better terms than private loans, and work-study are only accessible through the FAFSA process. Filing costs nothing (well, it does cost your time) and can be completed in a single sitting if you have your financial documents ready.

What is FAFSA based on?
FAFSA uses your family's income from two years ago (based on IRS tax data) and your assets as they stand on the day you submit the form.

For example, the 2027 FAFSA will use the 2025 taxed earnings and the assets on the day you file it. FAFSA does not count the value of the home your family lives in, retirement accounts, or some family businesses and farms. Even so, families can still feel squeezed by the amount the formula says they *should* be able to pay. If that happens, your family has had a real change in circumstances, or there is important context the FAFSA does not reflect well, that can be a valid reason to appeal your financial aid offer later.

FAFSA Deadline

Usually, the FAFSA opens on October 1 for the following academic year. To get California state aid, the deadline to submit your FAFSA is **March 2**. Missing that date means losing eligibility for Cal Grants, which can represent up to $15,588 per year in free money. Many colleges also have their own institutional aid priority deadlines that fall before March 2. Filing as early as possible after October 1 gives colleges the most time to build your financial aid package and gives you enough time to compare offers before the May 1 enrollment deadline.

Divorce, Separation, and Non-Traditional Families

When parents are divorced or separated, the FAFSA does not automatically require information from both biological parents. Instead, a dependent student reports financial information for the parent who provided the greater share of the student's financial support during the past twelve months. If both parents provided the same amount of support, the FAFSA uses the parent with the greater income and assets. If that parent has remarried, the stepparent's information is generally included as well. If your parents are divorced, remarried, separated, or in a more complicated family arrangement, check the Federal Student Aid website for current guidance.

Verification

After you submit the FAFSA, a college may require verification, which means their financial aid office wants to confirm certain information before finalizing your aid package. This does not mean you did anything wrong. Students can be selected randomly, and some colleges verify all students. If you are selected, follow the college's instructions carefully and submit the requested documents as soon as possible.

> **File every year**
> You must submit the FAFSA (or CADAA) every year, and award amounts can change based on family income, assets, and financial aid rules.

CSS Profile

In addition to the FAFSA, many **private colleges** require a second financial aid form called the College Scholarship Service Profile[45], administered by the College Board. While the FAFSA is the federal tool for calculating aid eligibility, the CSS Profile is the college's own, **more detailed version**. It

[45] cssprofile.collegeboard.org/

collects information that the FAFSA does not include. Colleges use it to determine eligibility for their own institutional aid, meaning grants funded by the college's own money rather than by federal or state programs.

The CSS Profile is **not free** ($25 for the first school and $16 for each additional school), but fee waivers are available for eligible students. Deadlines vary by school and are often earlier than you expect, sometimes as early as November 1 for Early Decision applicants. Check the deadline for each school.

Because it **collects more data**, the CSS Profile can produce different results. Two families with the same SAI can receive different aid offers, based on factors that the CSS Profile uses but the FAFSA ignores. If a private college is on your list, find out early whether they require the CSS Profile and be prepared for the possibility that their aid calculation differs from what you expected.

California Dream Act Application

Students who are not eligible for FAFSA, including **undocumented students** and members of mixed-status families, can file the California Dream Act Application, known as CADAA[46]. This is a separate system with its own portal but the same **March 2** deadline. CADAA provides access to California state aid, including Cal Grants, institutional aid at many California colleges, and California Dream Loans. Students fill out either the **FAFSA or CADAA**, but not both.

CADAA limitations

CADAA applicants do not have access to federal aid: no Pell Grants, no federal student loans, and no federal work-study.

Once the financial aid systems, FAFSA, CSS Profile, and CADAA, have collected your family's financial information and shared it with your colleges, the next question is what free money exists. Let us first take a closer look at what the federal government and the state of California offer.

---

[46] dream.csac.ca.gov/landing

Free Federal and State Aid

Federal Grants

Federal grants are generally need-based, meaning the amount you receive depends on your family's financial situation. The most significant federal grant is the **Pell Grant**. For 2026-27, the maximum Pell Grant is $7,395 per year. The amount you receive depends on your SAI, with students showing the greatest financial need receiving the most aid. Pell Grants can be used at community colleges as well as four-year institutions, and you can draw on them for **up to six years** as long as you are making satisfactory academic progress. Pell Grants are only available through FAFSA; CADAA filers are not eligible.

Starting in 2026, you must be enrolled in at least **15 credits** per semester to receive the full Pell Grant, and students enrolled in fewer than 7 credits will receive nothing. When planning your course load, keep these thresholds in mind. The new rules also add a firm cutoff for Pell Grant eligibility, so some families in the $60,000 to $80,000 income range may no longer receive a Pell Grant, depending on family size and financials.

California State Aid

California's main financial aid program is the **Cal Grant**. For many students, this is the biggest source of free money in their financial aid package. Cal Grants are available to both FAFSA and CADAA filers. Keep in mind that Cal Grants are only available if you attend a college located in California. If you enroll at an out-of-state school, you forfeit your Cal Grant. Students confirm their eligibility and manage their California state aid in the **WebGrants4Students**[47] portal. Create your account and check it regularly. Cal Grants can be accessed **up to four years**.

For most California applicants, **March 2** is the key deadline for state grants. Some California community colleges use a later deadline beginning of September, but for students applying to four-year colleges, missing March 2 can mean losing out on California's state aid.

---

[47] mygrantinfo.csac.ca.gov/

The two main types, Cal Grant A and Cal Grant B, have **different eligibility** requirements. Based on your GPA and your family's income, you may qualify for either Cal Grant A or Cal Grant B, but not both. The award amounts also differ by the type of school you attend.

Cal Grant A

The Cal Grant A requires a minimum 3.0 GPA. Eligibility also depends on income and asset ceilings that vary by family size.

For 2026–27, a family of four can earn up to $144,700 and hold assets up to $111,900, not including retirement accounts[48]. If your family's income or assets exceed those limits, Cal Grant A is not available to you.

The **grant amounts** depend on where you enroll. At UC and CSU campuses, Cal Grant A covers a large share of the systemwide tuition: up to $15,588 at a UC and up to $6,838 at a CSU. At a qualifying California private nonprofit college, Cal Grant A pays up to $9,358. For students starting at a community college, the Cal Grant A is held in reserve for up to two academic years and activated when you transfer to a tuition-charging four-year school.

If your GPA is below 3.0, you are ineligible for the Cal Grant A, but the Cal Grant B may still be an option.

Cal Grant B

The Cal Grant B requires a minimum GPA of 2.0 but has lower income and asset thresholds than the Cal Grant A.

For 2026–27, the household income ceiling for a family of four is $76,100, with an asset ceiling of $111,900. Across the four years, the Cal Grant B is structured differently from the Cal Grant A.

48 csac.ca.gov/sites/default/files/2025-07/2026-27-Income-and-Asset-Ceiling.pdf

In your first year, Cal Grant B provides only a **stipend of $1,648** for books and supplies. From year two onward, you receive that stipend plus a tuition grant matching the Cal Grant A amounts: $15,588 at a UC, $6,838 at a CSU, $9,358 at a qualifying private nonprofit. The **first-year gap** is real: a Cal Grant B recipient at a CSU gets $1,648 instead of $6,838, a difference of over $5,000 that needs to be accounted for in your first-year budget. Some schools offer limited first-year grants to fill this gap, but those funds are first-come, first-served.

Cal Grant B covers a maximum of **four years**, and that clock starts the moment you begin using it. At a **California community college**, the grant pays a $1,672 living allowance for books but does not cover tuition until you transfer to a four-year school. This matters because every year you draw the living allowance at a community college is one less year of tuition coverage available after you transfer. If you plan to transfer to a UC or CSU, think carefully about whether the book allowance now is worth losing tuition coverage later.

The Middle Class Scholarship

California also offers the Middle Class Scholarship[49] for students attending a UC or CSU campus. For 2026-27, the income and asset ceiling is $250,000 for a family of four. The state allocates a fixed amount of money for the program each year and divides it among all eligible students, so the award **amount varies** annually and is typically under $2,000.

Cal KIDS Scholarship

If you attended a California public school during the 2021-22 school year and received free or reduced-price lunch, you may have a Cal KIDS scholarship[50] waiting for you. Low-income students are eligible for $500, with additional funds available for foster or homeless youth. Check your eligibility using your State Student ID on your high school transcript. It is a small amount, but it is free money that many eligible students never claim simply because they did not know about it. Now that we have covered free money from the

[49] csac.ca.gov/middle-class-scholarship

[50] calkids.org

government, let us turn to another way students can offset college costs: working.

Part-Time Work

Federal Work-Study

As part of the federal financial aid, some students are invited to the work-study program. This is a federally **subsidized program** that allows students to earn money through part-time jobs, often on campus. Eligibility is based on financial need as determined by the FAFSA. 'Subsidized' means the federal government helps cover part of the wages, which is why colleges can offer these jobs specifically to students with financial need.

However, being offered work-study does not mean that a job is already waiting for you. You still must find and apply for open positions. Slots tend to fill up quickly, so apply as early as possible once you arrive on campus. At most schools, student work hours are capped at 20 per week or less during the term. The earnings go directly to you and are meant to help cover day-to-day living expenses. Earnings may be **taxable income**. There is currently no comparable California work program for CADAA filers.

Regular Campus Jobs

Even if you are not offered work-study, most colleges have campus jobs available to any enrolled student. These positions are not subsidized by the federal government, but they are usually flexible and more understanding of student schedules than off-campus employers tend to be. Working **10 to 15 hours per week** during the school year is manageable for most students once they have settled into the academic rhythm. Working significantly more than that risks that you do not have the time needed for your classes.

Free Institutional Aid

In addition to free federal and state aid, students may receive grants and scholarships **directly from the college**, funded by its endowment or operating budget. Because private colleges have more flexibility in how they award their own money, a private school with a high sticker price can sometimes end up being just as affordable as a public university.

Institutional aid
Colleges offer need-based grants, determined by your SAI and CSS Profile, and merit scholarships based on academic achievement (GPA, SAT/ACT).

Keep in mind that highly selective colleges like Stanford rarely give merit aid. At schools one tier below, merit scholarships can be substantial as colleges use them to attract high performing students. If merit aid is central to your plan, look for schools where your academic profile puts you in the top range of admitted students. In addition, wait until late April before committing. Some schools **improve their financial offer** in the final weeks before May 1, and committing early forfeits that potential leverage.

Institutional scholarships are usually renewable but come with **conditions** like a minimum GPA, continued full-time enrollment, or satisfactory academic progress. Find out what those conditions are and what happens to your award if you do not meet them before you commit. The UC and CSU offer limited institutional aid; their lower tuition is the main benefit for in-state students.

Outside Scholarships

Private scholarships can come from foundations, community groups, corporations, local businesses, professional associations, and civic organizations. They range from a few hundred dollars to full-tuition awards.

Look for **local scholarships** that tend to have smaller applicant pools, which increases your odds. Your school counselor likely keeps a list of local awards that students in your area have won. Ask for it early in senior year. National scholarships like the Coca-Cola Scholars Program or the Gates Scholarship are worth a shot if your profile is competitive, but do not build your financial plan around winning one.

However, winning an outside scholarship does not always lower what you pay out of pocket. Some colleges reduce their own grant aid when you receive an outside award. That practice is called **scholarship displacement.** In California, students who are eligible for a Pell Grant, a Cal Grant, or aid through the California Dream Act are protected from this kind of dollar-for-dollar reduction in institutional gift aid, unless their total gift aid goes above the school's cost of attendance. Ask the financial aid office exactly how an outside scholarship will be applied to your award.

QuestBridge

If you are a high-achieving student from a low-income background, you should know about QuestBridge[51]. This national nonprofit organization partners with 55 selective colleges to offer **full four-year scholarships** covering tuition, housing, food, books, and travel, with no loans and no parental contribution. The scholarship is worth over $325,000.

Students apply through QuestBridge in September of their senior year, using a **separate application portal**. Those selected as Finalists rank up to 15 participating colleges. In early December, students find out if they have been matched. This means they were admitted early with the full scholarship to the highest-ranked school on their list that also selected them. Like ED, matching is binding. Students who are not matched in the early round can still apply to partner colleges through QuestBridge Regular Decision. The application is free.

QuestBridge partners in California
Caltech, Claremont McKenna, Pomona, Scripps, Stanford, and the University of Southern California

529 Savings Plans and Family Savings

If your family has been saving for college, that money is an important part of your financial picture, even though it will not appear on any award letter. The

[51] questbridge.org

most common savings tool is a 529 plan, a **tax-advantaged account** where money grows tax-free and withdrawals are tax-free when used for qualified education expenses (tuition, room and board, fees, books, and required technology). California's version is called ScholarShare 529. California does not offer a state tax deduction for contributions, but qualified withdrawals are free from both federal and California income tax.

On the financial aid side, a 529 account held by a parent is reported as a parent asset on the FAFSA. Parent assets affect your SAI at a much smaller rate than you might expect. A $50,000 529 account, for example, would increase your SAI by a few thousand dollars at most, not by $50,000. Factor your 529 and any other potential savings into your four-year budget alongside grants, scholarships, and work earnings. Money saved for college is money you do not have to borrow, and borrowing less is almost always the better strategy.

Loans

Federal Student Loans

Federal student loans are the most common form of borrowing for college, and they come in several types. Not all student loans are equal and understanding the differences before you borrow matters more than most students realize. There are two types of federal loans, subsidized and unsubsidized ones.

Subsidized federal loans
The federal government pays the interest on the loan while you are in school. Eligible students can take a maximum of $3,500 in their first year.

Subsidized loans are the best type of federal student loan available. They are need-based, and students qualify based on their SAI. Interest does not accumulate while you are in school, which means the amount you owe when you graduate is the same as the amount you originally borrowed. The interest rate for 2025-26 is 6.39 percent, and the standard repayment plan is ten years.

Unsubsidized federal loans
Regardless of financial need, all students can take out unsubsidized loans.

Interest begins accumulating from the moment you borrow, including while you are still in school. If you do not pay the interest while enrolled, it gets added to your loan balance. You then pay interest on a larger amount, and the debt grows faster than most students expect when they first sign the promissory note.

Annual Limits

College students can no longer take out unlimited student loans. Over four years, dependent students can take out **up to $27,000**. The combined annual limits for subsidized and unsubsidized federal loans increase every year as you advance. In your first year, you can borrow up to **$5,500 total** (up to $3,500 subsidized and $2,000 unsubsidized). In your second year, the ceiling rises to $6,500 (up to $4,500 subsidized and $2,000 unsubsidized). From your third year onward, the limit is $7,500 per year (up to $5,500 subsidized and $2,000 unsubsidized). If you qualify for less than the full subsidized amount in any given year, the remaining borrowing capacity shifts to unsubsidized.

Early Repayment, Reducing Interest

Even though regular repayment usually begins after you leave school, you are allowed to make payments earlier. This matters most for unsubsidized loans, because interest starts building as soon as the loan is disbursed. If you can pay some of that interest while you are still in college, your loan will cost less in the long run. Federal loans also have **no prepayment penalties**, which means you are not charged extra for paying early. If you earn money from a part-time job, receive an outside scholarship, or realize you do not need as much loan money as expected, you can use some of that money to reduce your loan balance while still in school.

What Else to Know

You do not have to accept the full loan amount you are offered. Borrowing less now is one of the easiest ways to keep your future payments manageable. If you qualify for both subsidized and unsubsidized loans, **start** with the **subsidized loan** because interest does not build while you are enrolled.

Also remember that the interest rate is not the only cost. Federal loans include an **origination fee**. Federal student loans usually have a six-month grace period after you graduate, leave school, or drop below half-time enrollment. Dropping below half-time or not meeting academic progress requirements can affect your aid eligibility and can trigger repayment.

Before taking out a loan, you should test a few financial scenarios with a **student loan calculator**[52]. You can simulate what happens if you borrow the full amount, borrow less, make small payments while in school, or wait until after graduation.

Federal Parent PLUS Loans

Since students are limited in how much they can borrow, parents may want to help. Parent PLUS Loans are federal loans **taken out by the parents**, not the student. They carry a higher interest rate, 8.94 percent (in 2025-26), and have fewer income-driven repayment protections than student loans. Parents can request a deferment so that repayment does not begin while their child is in school, but interest still accumulates during that deferment period.

> **Maximum Parent PLUS loans**
> Parent PLUS loans are capped at $20,000 per year, up to $65,000 total per child.

California Dream Loans

For students who file the CADAA and are not eligible for federal loans, California offers Dream Loans as an alternative. Dream Loans function similarly to subsidized federal loans. You do not have to begin repayment while enrolled at least half-time, and the interest rate for 2025-26 is 6.39 percent. The maximum loan amount is **$4,000 per year** with a lifetime cap of

[52] For example: calculator.net/student-loan-calculator.html

$20,000. Availability is subject to state funding levels, which means it is not guaranteed from year to year.

Private Loans

Private loans from banks and other lenders should be treated as an absolute last resort. They carry higher interest rates than federal loans; the rates are often variable (not fixed), and eligibility depends on the borrower's credit score. Most students do not qualify for private loans on their own and will need a parent or other adult to **co-sign**. A co-signed loan means the co-signer is equally responsible for the debt. If payments are missed, it damages both the student's and the co-signer's credit history and financial standing for years.

Private loans also lack the flexible repayment options, income-driven plans, deferment protections, and forgiveness programs available with federal loans. If federal aid, state aid, institutional aid, part-time work, and family savings are not enough to cover your costs at a particular school, the honest answer is usually to reconsider whether that school is the right financial fit.

Rule of thumb

Your total student loan balance at graduation should not exceed your expected first year salary.

Graduate School Loans

If you plan to pursue graduate or professional school, keep in mind that federal borrowing rules are shifting beginning in July 2026 for new borrowers. The Department of Education has announced the end of the Grad PLUS program and new borrowing limits. Graduate students will be limited to **$20,500 per year in federal loans**, with lifetime caps of $100,000 for graduate programs and $200,000 for professional degrees like law or medicine.

If graduate, medical, or law school is part of your long-term plan, be conservative about undergraduate borrowing now. A heavy undergraduate debt load can limit your flexibility later, especially if graduate borrowing becomes more restricted.

The Right Order for Funding

When you think about how to piece together funding for college, the order matters significantly. Start with grants and scholarships, because they are free money and do not have to be paid back. Add work-study or other part-time work if you can balance it with your academic course load. Check if your family can contribute to your college budget. If there is still a gap, consider federal subsidized loans, followed by federal unsubsidized loans. Parent PLUS Loans come only after all other sources are exhausted and if your parents are willing to co-sign. Private loans should be the absolute last resort, and only after a serious conversation about whether the school is truly affordable for your family.

Special Situations

Western Undergraduate Exchange

The Western Undergraduate Exchange, or WUE, allows students from participating Western states to enroll in certain out-of-state public college programs at **150 percent** of the host school's **in-state tuition**. Participating states include Alaska, Arizona, California, Colorado, Hawaii, Idaho, Montana, Nevada, New Mexico, North Dakota, Oregon, South Dakota, Utah, Washington, and Wyoming. Participation is program-specific, so verify eligibility for your specific **major** in writing before relying on it in your budget. The WICHE website[53] at has a searchable database of eligible programs.

However, for California residents, the tuition savings often do not hold up once you factor in that you **lose the Cal Grant**. Choosing an out-of-state WUE school over a California public school means forfeiting up to $15,588 per year in free money. For students who do not qualify for a Cal Grant or who need a program that does not exist in California, the math may look different, but it still requires a full financial comparison.

---

[53] wiche.edu/tuition-savings/wue

For **out-of-state students** looking at California colleges, many CSU campuses participate in WUE. UC Merced is currently the only UC campus participating.

International Students

International students are **not eligible** for U.S. **federal aid,** such as Pell Grants, federal student loans, or work-study, or the Cal Grants. Public universities in California are less likely to offer substantial need-based aid than private colleges. To apply for institutional aid, you may need to submit separate forms, such as the **CSS Profile,** the **ISFAA**, or the college's own financial aid form. Also, do not confuse a financial aid application with a proof-of-finances form required for visa documents like the I-20. Check each college's website early to see whether it offers aid to international students and what form it requires.

By now we have a solid understanding of how financial aid works: the systems that collect your family's information, the federal and state grants, scholarships, work-study, and loans that make up a typical package. The next step is understanding what your actual financial aid letter says and what it means for your family. What looks generous on the surface is not always what it seems.

Interpreting Award Letters

Once you are admitted, each college will send you a personalized financial aid offer. These letters are not standardized, and different schools present the same information in completely different formats, which makes comparing them harder than it should be.

The key is to separate free money from borrowed money. Grants and scholarships do not need to be repaid. Loans do. Work-study is potential earnings from a job you still must find and work, not a deposit into your bank account. Some award letters bundle all three into one total, making the offer **look more generous** than it is.

A typical financial aid offer starts with the school's estimated cost of attendance, then lists the aid offered to help cover that cost. The example below shows common categories you may see like grants and scholarships, work-study, student loans, and parent loans. The student did not qualify for a Pell Grant.

Cost of Attendance

Tuition and Fees	$ 18,000
Food and Housing	$ 22,000
Books, Personal, Transportation	$ 5,000
Health Insurance	$ 3,000
Cost of Attendance	**$ 48,000**

Financial Aid Offer

	How the school presents it	**The Reality**
Cal Grant A	$ 15,000	$ 15,000 (free)
Institutional Grant	$ 12,000	$ 12,000 (free)
CA Middle Class Scholarship	$ 2,000	$ 2,000 (free)
Federal Work-Study	$ 5,000	Must be earned
Subsidized loan	$ 3,500	Must be repaid
Unsubsidized loan	$ 2,000	Must be repaid
Parent PLUS loan	$ 8,500	Must be repaid
Total	**$ 48,000 covered**	**$ 29,000 truly free**
Gap	**$ 0**	**$ 19,000**

This shows why a financial aid offer that appears to cover the full cost may still leave a significant gap. This college presents the financial aid package as covering the full $48,000 cost of attendance, but only $29,000 is truly free money. The $5,000 in work-study must be earned through a part-time job, and the $14,000 in loans must be repaid with interest.

Your College Bill

What the school bills you usually covers only part of the full cost of attendance. Most colleges **bill you directly** for tuition, fees, on-campus housing, and health insurance if not waived. Everything else, books, personal expenses, and transportation, is an estimate of what you will spend throughout the year, not a charge that appears on your college bill.

In our example, the direct costs before aid are $43,000. After subtracting $29,000 in grants and scholarships, the direct college bill comes to $14,000 per year. At a semester school, that breaks into two payments of $7,000 each, due in August and January. Many colleges offer monthly payment plans that spread each semester bill across several months, typically for a small enrollment fee.

Appealing a Financial Aid Offer

If your financial aid offer does not reflect your family's real situation, you can appeal. A job loss, a drop in income, or major medical expenses since the tax year the FAFSA reflects are all valid grounds. Explain the situation in writing with documentation and politely **ask for a review**. Financial aid offices have more flexibility than most families realize. If another comparable school has offered significantly more, attach the offer and ask whether they can do better. Some will. Some will not. But it costs nothing to ask. Keep in mind that appeals are not always resolved before May 1.

Taxes on Financial Aid

One thing that catches many families off guard is that scholarships and grants may be **taxable**. Aid used for tuition, required fees, and required course materials is generally tax-free. But aid used for other expenses, such as room and board, may be taxable depending on how the package is structured. If you receive a large aid package that includes living expenses, keep taxes in mind. Make sure to plan for any tax payments in your annual budget.

Building a Four-Year Budget

A common mistake is evaluating college costs based only on the first year. College is a **four-year commitment**, and the numbers can change more than families expect. Tuition may rise each year, housing costs may shift depending on whether you live on campus, off campus, or at home, and the aid package you receive in year three may not look the same as the one you received in year one.

For each school you are seriously considering, build a year-by-year estimate instead of relying on a single first-year number. Start with the full cost of attendance, including tuition and fees, housing and food, books and supplies, transportation, health insurance, and personal expenses. Then adjust those numbers based on your **actual plans**. If you expect to move off campus after freshman year, look up typical rents near campus and account for utilities, groceries, transportation, and other day-to-day costs. For private colleges, it is also wise to assume that tuition may increase by about two to four percent per year. Think through **personal expenses** such as clothing, phone plans, toiletries, laundry, dining out, social outings, and occasional larger purchases like a new laptop.

Next, look carefully at the **funding side**. Some aid is predictable, but some is not. A Cal Grant may stay relatively consistent, while Cal Grant B works differently in the first year than in later years. **Scholarships** may be renewable only if you meet certain GPA, enrollment, or progress requirements. Some scholarships are one-time awards that help in year one and then disappear. **Family savings** also need to be spread across the full college timeline. A 529 plan or savings account that makes the first year affordable may not solve the problem if it runs out halfway through college.

Work income should also be treated realistically. A part-time job can help cover personal expenses, books, or transportation, but it usually cannot erase a large affordability gap. Before counting on work income, consider your course load and whether you will need time for internships or research.

After you subtract grants, scholarships, family contributions, savings, reasonable work income, and any loans you are willing to take, the remaining amount is the **real funding gap**. That gap matters most when you look at it across all four years. A school may look affordable in year one but become difficult by year three if tuition rises, a scholarship expires, or savings run out. If the numbers remain manageable across the full timeline, the college may be a viable financial option. If the plan depends on hoping that something will work out later, pause before committing. 'We will figure it out later' is rarely a good strategy.

Making the Decision

Working through the financial details can be tedious and even uncomfortable, but it is worth doing carefully. By the end, you should understand not only what each college costs, but what your family is committing to. A few principles are worth keeping in mind as you make the final decision.

Take away

- **Compare net costs**, not sticker prices or aid packages. A school that offers $40,000 in aid may still be unaffordable if the cost of attendance is $80,000. The number that matters is what your family will pay after free money is subtracted.

- **Think across four years**, not just year one. A strong first-year offer that evaporates in year two because a one-time scholarship expires is not a solid offer.

- **Borrow thoughtfully**. Federal student loans are a reasonable tool when used in proportion to your expected earnings after graduation. Borrowing more than your future income can realistically support can limit your choices for years.

- Do not commit to a school until you have **compared** all the **schools** that admitted you. Use the time between receiving your admission offers and May 1 to check all offers for affordability.

For many families, college is one of the largest financial commitments. A school that is a strong academic and personal fit can still be the wrong choice if the cost does not work out. The good news is that there are many schools that are a good fit for you, academically, personally, *and* financially. The goal of this chapter was to help you find them.

18 | Bringing It All Together

By now, we have covered a lot of ground: how the California college landscape differs from the rest of the country, how to build a balanced college list, how colleges evaluate applications, and finally, how to pay for it all. For many families, money is the most stressful part of the college process, and understandably so. At the same time, this is also the area where good information can make the biggest difference.

Stepping back, though, the **bigger lesson** of this book is not just how to apply. It is how to think about the whole process. A strong college decision is not about chasing prestige, getting attached to a dream school, or trying to 'win' the admissions game. It is about understanding your options well enough to make a smart, grounded choice that fits you academically, personally, and financially.

That starts with the list itself. Build a **best-fit college list based on facts**, not prestige or guesswork. Use sources like the Common Data Set, Naviance, and admission statistics by school and major to understand where each college realistically fits. A strong list has a real spread of schools, not a list weighted toward reaches with a couple of likely schools thrown in. Every school on your list should be one you would be happy to attend and makes sense for you on multiple levels. This is what best fit means.

It also means understanding that college admissions is **more nuanced** than most students realize. It is not just about grades and test scores. The Three Pillars of a competitive application rest on academics, extracurriculars, and the personality traits that shine through in your writing. Context is woven throughout. Admissions officers are trying to understand the whole student, not just a number. That is why **starting early** matters. The student who begins thinking about their story and their writing in junior year is in a fundamentally different position from the one who starts in September of senior year.

Just as important, this process gets much easier to handle when you stop seeing California through a narrow prestige lens. The University of California campuses are competitive, but they are not impossible to get into. What they are is a **numbers game**. There are more qualified applicants than there are available seats, and that is true even for students who have done everything right. Some campuses and programs are significantly more selective than others. A student who is a middle-of-the pack applicant for UCLA or Berkeley may be a very competitive applicant at Santa Cruz, Riverside, or Merced. Understanding the **full range of the UC system**, rather than fixating on the two most famous campuses, opens up real options.

And once you **widen that lens** even more, the bigger picture comes into focus. California gives you more solid options than almost any other state. The University of California is among the finest public university systems in the world. The CSU system trains more of California's teachers, engineers, nurses, and public servants than any other institution. The community college pathway can get you to a UC or CSU at a fraction of the cost. Private colleges in California range from small liberal arts gems to major research universities, many with genuine financial resources to make attendance affordable for qualifying families. Students in many other states do not have this extensive range of options. As a California student, you do. Consider all of them.

One of the most useful things you can do in this process is stop trying to predict every admissions outcome and focus instead on understanding the system. The students who navigate this process best are usually not the ones trying to guess what a college 'really wants.' They are the ones who learn how the **system works** and **use that information well**. They build balanced lists. They analyze the data carefully. They think realistically about selectivity. They understand that college choice and major choice are connected, especially in California, where a highly selective major can change your admission chances in a dramatic way.

That is also why I would urge you **not to get hung up on prestige** or the idea of a dream school. Dream schools create a lot of unnecessary anxiety, and they can keep students from seeing the full range of places where they could thrive. Brand names matter far less than most students think. What matters is whether you are in an environment where you will be challenged, supported, and engaged, and whether you will graduate with the skills, relationships, and credentials to build the career and life you want. That can happen at a UC, a CSU, a private college, or start at a community college.

And then there is the **financial side**, which must be part of the conversation from the beginning, not something you deal with after the admissions decisions arrive. Have the uncomfortable **budget discussion** with your family early in the process, ideally before you build your college list, not after the acceptance letters come in. Knowing what your family can realistically sustain across four years changes which schools belong on your list in the first place. Finding out in April that your first-choice school is unaffordable is one of the most heartbreaking outcomes in this process, and it is usually avoidable.

The right school, then, is not just the one where you can genuinely thrive academically and personally. It is also the one where the financial commitment is something your family can afford across four years without debt that constrains your choices for a decade after graduation. Fit and financial sustainability must be evaluated together, not separately.

Which brings us to the most important reframe of this book.

Getting into college is not the goal. It is just the beginning. The goal is what you do once you are there. College is what you make of it. The skills you build, the relationships you form, the thinking you develop, and the work you put in will shape your future far more than the name on the sweatshirt. Two students at the same institution can have radically different outcomes based on how intentionally they engage with the experience. The school opens the door. What happens next is up to you.

That is why there is **never just one** perfect school, and why no one admission decision defines your future. College admissions season can make everything feel bigger and more final than it really is. It can make students (and parents) feel as if one acceptance, one rejection, or one school name will determine the rest of their lives. It will not. What matters is making a thoughtful decision with full information and choosing a place where you can grow.

So, as you move forward, keep the **big picture** in mind. Build a best fit college list. Choose your major thoughtfully. Apply strategically. Compare award letters carefully before you commit. Remember that the May 1 deadline is your deadline, not the school's. You are making the decision. Make it with full information, not wishful thinking. And make it knowing that the point is not to collect the most impressive acceptance. The point is to choose a path that gives you the **strongest foundation** for the next four years and beyond.

I hope this book has helped you make the college application process feel clearer and a little less overwhelming. The goal is not just to get into college. It is to choose a place where you can grow and make the most of the opportunity.

Enjoy the ride!

Appendix

Appendix A: California Community Colleges

Bay Area & Peninsula

Berkeley City College (Berkeley) • Cañada College (Redwood City) • Chabot College (Hayward) • College of Alameda (Alameda) • College of Marin (Kentfield) • College of San Mateo (San Mateo) • Contra Costa College (San Pablo) • De Anza College (Cupertino) • Diablo Valley College (Pleasant Hill) • Evergreen Valley College (San Jose) • Foothill College (Los Altos Hills) • Gavilan College (Gilroy) • Laney College (Oakland) • Las Positas College (Livermore) • Los Medanos College (Pittsburg) • Merritt College (Oakland) • Mission College (Santa Clara) • Napa Valley College (Napa) • Ohlone College (Fremont) • City College of San Francisco (San Francisco) • San Jose City College (San Jose) • Skyline College (San Bruno) • Solano Community College (Fairfield) • Santa Rosa Junior College (Santa Rosa) • West Valley College (Saratoga)

Sacramento & Sierra Foothills

American River College (Sacramento) • Cosumnes River College (Sacramento) • Folsom Lake College (Folsom) • Sacramento City College (Sacramento) • Sierra College (Rocklin) • Woodland Community College (Woodland) • Yuba College (Marysville)

Los Angeles County

Antelope Valley College (Lancaster) • Cerritos College (Norwalk) • Citrus College (Glendora) • College of the Canyons (Santa Clarita) • Compton College (Compton) • East Los Angeles College (Monterey Park) • El Camino College (Torrance) • Glendale Community College (Glendale) • Los Angeles City College (Los Angeles) • Los Angeles Harbor College (Wilmington) • Los Angeles Mission College (Sylmar) • Los Angeles Pierce College (Woodland Hills) • Los Angeles Southwest College (Los Angeles) • Los Angeles Trade-Technical College (Los Angeles) • Los Angeles Valley College (Valley Glen) • Long Beach City College (Long Beach) • Mt. San Antonio College (Walnut) • Pasadena City College (Pasadena) • Rio Hondo College (Whittier) • Santa Monica College (Santa Monica) • West Los Angeles College (Culver City)

Orange County

Coastline College (Fountain Valley) • Cypress College (Cypress) • Fullerton College (Fullerton) • Golden West College (Huntington Beach) • Irvine Valley College

(Irvine) • Orange Coast College (Costa Mesa) • Saddleback College (Mission Viejo) • Santa Ana College (Santa Ana) • Santiago Canyon College (Orange)

Inland Empire & Desert

Barstow Community College (Barstow) • Chaffey College (Rancho Cucamonga) • College of the Desert (Palm Desert) • Copper Mountain College (Joshua Tree) • Crafton Hills College (Yucaipa) • Moreno Valley College (Moreno Valley) • Mt. San Jacinto College (San Jacinto) • Norco College (Norco) • Palo Verde College (Blythe) • Riverside City College (Riverside) • San Bernardino Valley College (San Bernardino) • Victor Valley College (Victorville)

San Diego & Imperial

Cuyamaca College (El Cajon) • Grossmont College (El Cajon) • Imperial Valley College (Imperial) • MiraCosta College (Oceanside) • Palomar College (San Marcos) • San Diego City College (San Diego) • San Diego Mesa College (San Diego) • San Diego Miramar College (San Diego) • Southwestern College (Chula Vista)

Central Coast & Ventura County

Allan Hancock College (Santa Maria) • Cabrillo College (Aptos) • Cuesta College (San Luis Obispo) • Hartnell College (Salinas) • Monterey Peninsula College (Monterey) • Moorpark College (Moorpark) • Oxnard College (Oxnard) • Santa Barbara City College (Santa Barbara) • Ventura College (Ventura)

Central Valley

Bakersfield College (Bakersfield) • Cerro Coso Community College (Ridgecrest) • Clovis Community College (Fresno) • College of the Sequoias (Visalia) • Fresno City College (Fresno) • Madera Community College (Madera) • Merced College (Merced) • Modesto Junior College (Modesto) • Porterville College (Porterville) • Reedley College (Reedley) • San Joaquin Delta College (Stockton) • Taft College (Taft) • Coalinga College (Coalinga) • Lemoore College (Lemoore)

Northern & Rural California

Butte College (Oroville) • College of the Redwoods (Eureka) • College of the Siskiyous (Weed) • Columbia College (Sonora) • Feather River College (Quincy) • Lake Tahoe Community College (South Lake Tahoe) • Lassen Community College (Susanville) • Mendocino College (Ukiah) • Shasta College (Redding)

Statewide / Online

Calbright College (Online)

Appendix B: UC Application Checklist

Before you start

☐ Unofficial transcript for every high school & college attended

☐ List of current and planned senior year courses

☐ Draft activities list with dates and hours per week

☐ Accurate household size and income information ready for fee waiver calculation

☐ Social Security number ready if applicable

☐ California Statewide Student ID (SSID) located and ready

☐ Draft PIQ responses written in a separate document

Personal information

☐ Email address is personal, not school-issued; same address across all applications

☐ Social Security number entered if applicable; if none, left blank

☐ California Statewide Student ID (SSID) confirmed in application

☐ Income entered accurately

☐ Fee waiver accepted on the billing screen if eligible

☐ Statement of Legal Residence completed accurately

Campuses and majors

☐ Sample four-year course plans reviewed for intended majors

☐ Researched Common Data Set, Net Price Calculator, Naviance, and admit data

☐ Campuses selected intentionally

☐ Major selections align with the story the application tells

☐ Alternate majors listed where campus policy allows

Academic history

☐ Course titles and grades match transcripts exactly

☐ Every school attended is listed

☐ Repeated courses are reported fully and accurately

☐ A-G eligibility confirmed at https://hs-articulation.ucop.edu/agcourselist

☐ Dual enrollment: A-G eligible courses in college coursework section

☐ Entered non-eligible courses in 'Other coursework' under 'Activities and Awards'

☐ Senior year planned courses entered correctly

☐ Out-of-state students: only AP and IB exams receive honors GPA boost

Activities and awards

☐ Work experience and family responsibilities included

☐ Independent projects and community commitments included

☐ Descriptions show action, responsibility, and impact, not just titles

☐ Hours per week and weeks per year are realistic and honest

☐ All entries are verifiable

Personal Insight Questions

☐ Four prompts answered

☐ Four PIQs show different aspects of who I am, not the same story

☐ Each PIQ includes effect and perspective, not just narrative

☐ PIQs written personally

Additional comments

☐ Used only to clarify specific academic issues

☐ Not used as an extra essay

Final submission

☐ Every section reviewed before signing

☐ Statement of Integrity read and understood

☐ Application is subject to verification

☐ Confirmation number and UC application ID saved

After you submit

☐ FAFSA or CADAA submitted by March 2

☐ WebGrants4Students account created to track Cal Grant award status

☐ Campus-specific applicant portal created for each UC campus applied to

☐ Email folder created for UC correspondence

☐ Check portals and email weekly

Appendix C: Activities Word Bank

Use these tips when drafting your Activities and Awards entries. Strong descriptions use specific, active language and follow a simple structure: what you did, what you were responsible for, and what it produced or changed.

Leadership and ownership

coordinated, created, delegated, designed, directed, facilitated, founded, implemented, initiated, launched, led, managed, mentored, organized, oversaw, recruited, scheduled, supervised, trained

Building and producing

built, coded, composed, curated, developed, drafted, edited, engineered, iterated, produced, prototyped, published, refined, repaired, tested, wrote

Collaboration and teamwork

assisted, collaborated, communicated, connected, contributed, coordinated with, mediated, partnered, planned with, served alongside, supported

Learning and growth

applied, attended training, completed workshops, deepened, expanded, explored, gained skills in, practiced, researched, strengthened, studied

Community service

advocated, assisted families, coached, coordinated volunteers, delivered, distributed, organized drives, provided care for, served, staffed events, supported community members, translated, tutored

Work and professional habits

ensured safety, handled transactions, improved workflow, maintained inventory, managed schedules, met deadlines, operated equipment, resolved issues, served customers, trained new staff

Impact words

accelerated, contributed to, enabled, expanded, improved, increased, raised, reduced, resulted in, streamlined, strengthened, supported

Appendix D: UC Campus Transfer Profiles

UC Berkeley

Berkeley is one of the most selective transfer campuses in the UC system. It uses a genuinely holistic review for transfer applicants, expects strong major preparation, follows its own additional post-application process, and leaves very little room for missing prerequisites.

Transfer applications (Fall 2026): 26,216
Admit rate (Fall 2026): 20.0 percent
TAG: No
PIQs: Used as part of holistic review.
How Berkeley reviews transfers: Berkeley does not consider alternate majors for transfer applicants. Every major has specific lower-division preparation requirements, and all major preparation courses must be taken for a letter grade.

Timing rules: The seven-course breadth pattern must be completed by the end of the spring term before enrollment. Berkeley also expects students to complete major preparation by the end of spring. For Engineering, all required core courses must be finished by then as well, and applicants must complete both English 1A and 1B.

Additional Berkeley step: Berkeley requires a supplemental form through MAP@Berkeley in addition to the systemwide Transfer Academic Update. You will receive an email in January when the form becomes available. For the colleges that require it, this form includes a section where you can explain why Berkeley is the right fit for you and your goals.

Colleges requiring MAP@Berkeley major prerequisite form: Chemistry, Engineering, Environmental Design, Natural Resources, and Haas School of Business. Applicants to Letters and Science or Computing, Data Science, and Society do not complete the prerequisite form, but should still verify all major requirements on ASSIST and in the Berkeley Academic Guide.

Deadline: Both the TAU and the MAP@Berkeley form should be completed by January 31. Missing the MAP@Berkeley form may mean your application is not reviewed. If your coursework plans change after January 31, contact the relevant Berkeley college directly.

Minimum major prep GPA: 3.0 for Chemistry, Computing, Data Science, and Society, and Letters and Science; 3.5 for Engineering. Business, Environmental Design, and Natural Resources complete a full review of applicants who meet course requirements regardless of GPA.

Highly selective majors: Most majors in Business, Computing, Data Science, and Society, Engineering, and Natural Resources, plus in Letters and Science: Art Practice, Analytics, Political Economy, Public Health, and Social Welfare.

Cal-GETC / IGETC: Letters and Science accepts full IGETC or Cal-GETC for breadth. Computing, Data Science, and Society accepts full IGETC or Cal-GETC or the college's own requirements. Chemistry may use full certification to satisfy English reading and composition, but not the full breadth requirement. Environmental Design accepts full IGETC or Cal-GETC for breadth. Natural Resources accepts IGETC or Cal-GETC, but lower-division major requirements must still be completed separately. Engineering and Business do not accept IGETC or Cal-GETC. Berkeley does not accept partial IGETC or Cal-GETC certification.

UC Davis

UC Davis is one of the most transfer-friendly campuses in the UC system. PIQs are not used in the transfer decision.

Transfer applications (Fall 2026): 17,421
Admit rate (Fall 2026): 58.2 percent
TAG: Yes
PIQs: Not used in transfer review.

How UC Davis reviews transfers: You are admitted to a specific major. If you list a valid alternate major, it may be considered on a case-by-case basis.

Timing rules: The seven-course pattern must be completed by the end of the spring term before enrollment. UC Davis gives the highest priority to applicants who complete selective major requirements by the end of spring term prior to fall enrollment. Major preparation courses must be taken for a letter grade.

Minimum major prep GPA: 2.8 for Agricultural and Environmental Sciences, 2.8 for Biological Sciences, 3.1 for Engineering, and 2.8 for Letters and Science. The guide also notes that a higher GPA is required for a UC Davis TAG and usually for selection, depending on enrollment targets.

Highly selective majors: All majors in Biological Sciences and Engineering; in Agricultural and Environmental Sciences: Biotechnology, Managerial Economics, and

Viticulture and Enology; and in Letters and Science: Applied Mathematics, Applied Physics, Computer Science, Data Science, Economics, Mathematical Analytic and Operations Research, Mathematical and Science Computation, Mathematics, Physics, and Psychology.

Cal-GETC / IGETC: All UC Davis undergraduate colleges accept IGETC and Cal-GETC. For selective majors, students should prioritize required lower-division major preparation and selection criteria first. UC Davis accepts partial IGETC and Cal-GETC certification if no more than two requirements are missing; students then have one year to complete them and must notify the college.

UC Irvine

UC Irvine reviews transfer applicants holistically. Your PIQs are read and considered in the decision.

Transfer applications (Fall 2026): 27,038
Admit rate (Fall 2026): 36.4 percent
TAG: Yes
PIQs: Used as part of holistic review.

How UC Irvine reviews transfers: You are admitted to a specific major. If you do not meet the criteria for your first-choice major, you may be considered for an alternate major on a case-by-case basis if you meet that major's criteria and space is available. Nursing Science and Business Administration will not be considered as alternate majors.

Timing rules: All majors require students to complete major coursework by the end of the spring term prior to fall enrollment. Major preparation courses must be taken for a letter grade.

Minimum major prep GPA: 2.7 to 3.0 by major.

Highly selective majors: Business Administration; all majors in the Donald Bren School of Information and Computer Sciences; Aerospace Engineering and Mechanical Engineering; Nursing Science; and in the School of Social Sciences: Business Economics, Cognitive Sciences, Economics, Psychology, and Quantitative Economics.

Cal-GETC / IGETC: All UCI schools accept IGETC and Cal-GETC. UC Irvine also accepts partial IGETC and Cal-GETC certification.

UCLA

UCLA receives more transfer applications than any other campus in the system and reviews them holistically. Your PIQs are read and considered in the decision.

Transfer applications (Fall 2026): 30,645
Admit rate (Fall 2026): 22.2 percent
TAG: No
PIQs: Used as part of holistic review.

How UCLA reviews transfers: You are admitted to a specific major, and in general, applicants are not considered for alternate majors. All majors except Education and Social Transformation and some majors in the School of Arts and Architecture have specific lower-division preparation requirements, and major preparation courses must be taken for a letter grade.

Timing rules: The seven-course breadth pattern and major preparation should be completed by the end of the spring term before transfer.

Transfer Alliance Program: If your community college has an honors program connected to UCLA's Transfer Alliance Program, completing it gives you enhanced consideration in the review.

Minimum major prep GPA: 3.0 for Arts and Architecture; 3.7 for Communication; 3.2 for Education and Social Transformation; 3.4 for Engineering and Applied Science; 3.2 for Letters and Science; 3.5 for Nursing; 3.2 for Music, Public Affairs, and Theater, Film and Television.

Highly selective majors: All majors in Engineering and Applied Science, Arts and Architecture, Nursing, Music, Public Affairs, and Theater, Film and Television, plus in Letters and Science: Biochemistry, Biology, Business Economics, Communication, Economics, Financial Actuarial Mathematics, Global Studies, Human Biology and Society (B.A./B.S.), International Development Studies, Mathematics/Economics, Political Science, Psychology, Sociology, and Statistics.

Cal-GETC / IGETC: All UCLA schools accept IGETC and Cal-GETC, though neither is recommended for applicants to the School of Engineering and Applied Science. UCLA accepts partial IGETC/Cal-GETC for all schools except Engineering and Applied Science, Nursing, and Theater, Film and Television.

UC Merced

UC Merced does not use PIQs in the transfer decision. It admits transfer students to a specific major, and applicants who meet the qualifications may also be offered an alternate major.

Transfer applications (Fall 2026): 6,401
Admit rate (Fall 2026): 79.5 percent
TAG: Yes
PIQs: Not used in transfer review.
How UC Merced reviews transfers: For fall transfer, the seven-course pattern must be completed by the end of the spring term before enrollment. For spring transfer, the guide says it is recommended that math and English be completed by the end of the summer term before enrollment. Selective majors require major preparation coursework by the end of spring for fall transfer and by the end of fall for spring transfer. Major preparation courses are advised to be taken for letter grades, and departments decide whether Credit/No Credit coursework can satisfy lower-division major requirements.

Spring term note: UC Merced accepts spring transfer applications in addition to fall applications. The spring application filing period is July 1 to July 31, and the TAG filing period for winter/spring applicants is May 1 to May 31.

Minimum major prep GPA: 2.4 for Engineering, 2.8 for Natural Sciences, and 2.4 for Social Sciences, Humanities and Arts, except Public Health, which is 3.0.

Cal-GETC / IGETC: Public Health requires IGETC or Cal-GETC prior to enrollment. In Engineering, IGETC and Cal-GETC are strongly discouraged but accepted. In Natural Sciences, they are not recommended but accepted. In Social Sciences, Humanities and Arts, they are recommended. UC Merced does not accept partial IGETC or Cal-GETC certification.

UC Riverside

UC Riverside offers TAG for eligible majors and evaluates transfer applicants primarily through academic record and major preparation. PIQs are not used in the transfer decision.

Transfer applications (Fall 2026): 14,753
Admit rate (Fall 2026): 70.4 percent

TAG: Yes
PIQs: Not used in transfer review.

How UC Riverside reviews transfers: You are admitted to a specific major. If you list a valid alternate major, it may be considered on a case-by-case basis.
Timing rules: The seven-course pattern must be completed by the end of the spring term before enrollment. Selective majors require major preparation coursework to be completed by the end of spring before transfer. Major preparation courses must be taken for a letter grade.

Minimum major prep GPA: 2.4 to 3.1 by major.
Majors requiring specific major prep: Business Economics, Economics, Economics/Administrative Studies, Neuroscience, Psychology, all majors in the Bourns College of Engineering, all majors in the College of Natural and Agricultural Sciences, and all majors in the School of Business.

Cal-GETC / IGETC: Business Administration highly recommends IGETC or Cal-GETC. Education, Humanities, Arts and Social Sciences, and Public Policy recommend it. Engineering accepts it, though additional coursework may be required after enrollment. Natural and Agricultural Sciences does not accept IGETC or Cal-GETC. UC Riverside accepts partial IGETC and Cal-GETC certification except in the College of Natural and Agricultural Sciences.

UC San Diego

UC San Diego evaluates transfer applicants primarily through academic record and major preparation. PIQs are not part of the transfer review.

Transfer applications (Fall 2026): 26,314
Admit rate (Fall 2026): 47.4 percent
TAG: No
PIQs: Not used in transfer review.

How UC San Diego reviews transfers: UC San Diego admits transfer students to a specific major and does not admit them as Undeclared. If your first-choice major is selective or requires minimum major preparation and you do not meet those requirements, you may be considered for your alternate major if there is space.

Timing rules: The seven-course pattern must be completed by the end of the spring term before enrollment. For majors that require major preparation, students must complete the minimum major preparation courses by the end of spring term prior to fall enrollment to be considered for admission. Major preparation courses must be taken for a letter grade. Summer work before fall enrollment may be used to complete IGETC or campus GE requirements, but not the minimum major preparation required for admission.

Minimum major prep GPA: 2.8 to 4.0 by program.

Selective majors: Bioengineering, Computer Science, Computer Engineering, Data Science, Electrical and Computer Engineering, Mechanical and Aerospace Engineering, and Public Health. Some majors are very popular but not yet formally selective, including Biological Sciences, Cognitive Science, Business Economics, Economics, Mathematics, and Psychology.

Cal-GETC / IGETC: At Muir, Warren, Roosevelt, Marshall, Sixth, Seventh, and Eighth Colleges, IGETC or Cal-GETC clears all lower-division GE requirements, though some upper-division courses are still required after enrollment. At Revelle, IGETC and Cal-GETC are acceptable, but lower-division GE may not be fully cleared. UC San Diego accepts partial IGETC and Cal-GETC certification.

UC Santa Barbara

UC Santa Barbara offers TAG for eligible majors and admits transfer students to a major or pre-major. PIQs are not used in the transfer decision.

Transfer applications (Fall 2026): 18,866
Admit rate (Fall 2026): 61.6 percent
TAG: Yes
PIQs: Not used in transfer review.

How UC Santa Barbara reviews transfers: Applicants may be considered for an alternate major if a valid alternate is listed and space is available. Engineering majors are not available as alternate majors. Students applying to the College of Creative Studies are encouraged to choose an alternate major in the College of Letters and Science. UC Santa Barbara does not admit transfer students as Undeclared.

Timing rules: The seven-course pattern must be completed by the end of the spring term before enrollment. Priority consideration goes to students who complete the mathematics requirement and at least one English composition course by the end of fall prior to enrollment. Summer work before fall enrollment may be used to complete IGETC, campus GE requirements, and non-required major preparation. For majors that require major preparation, courses must be completed by the end of spring before fall enrollment, and for selective majors the major preparation GPA is calculated using required major preparation courses completed through the fall term. Major preparation courses are advised to be taken for a letter grade.

Major preparation requirements: Preparation is required for Biological Sciences, Chemistry and Biochemistry, Computer Science, all Economics majors, all Engineering majors, all Mathematics majors, Physics, and all majors in the College of Creative Studies. The College of Creative Studies requires a supplemental application.

Minimum major prep GPA: 3.0 for Creative Studies, 3.4 for Engineering, and 2.7 to 3.0 depending on major in Letters and Science.
Highly selective majors: All Engineering majors, Biological Sciences, Chemistry and Biochemistry, Computer Science, Economics, Mathematics, Physics, Psychological and Brain Sciences, Statistics and Data Science, Dance B.A., Music B.M., and all Creative Studies majors.

Cal-GETC / IGETC: Letters and Science and Creative Studies accept IGETC and Cal-GETC. For Engineering, students are encouraged to prioritize major preparation, though IGETC or Cal-GETC may be used to satisfy GE requirements. UC Santa Barbara accepts partial IGETC and Cal-GETC certification.

UC Santa Cruz

UC Santa Cruz offers TAG for eligible majors and has a more flexible transfer structure than most UC campuses. PIQs are not used in the transfer decision.

Transfer applications (Fall 2026): 13,501
Admit rate (Fall 2026): 67.7 percent
TAG: Yes
PIQs: Not used in transfer review.

How UC Santa Cruz reviews transfers: You are admitted to a **proposed major**, not directly to a declared major. Students officially declare the major after meeting the qualification requirements. If you do not meet the criteria for your first-choice major, an alternate may be considered if you meet the alternate-major criteria as well.

Timing rules: The seven-course pattern must be completed by the end of the spring term, or the last regular term, before enrollment. Summer work before fall enrollment may be used to complete IGETC, additional major preparation, and campus GE requirements. UC Santa Cruz advises students to complete as much lower-division prerequisite coursework in the major as possible before enrolling, since most majors screen for major preparation. Major preparation courses are advised to be taken for a letter grade.

TAG note: TAG is available for fall quarter only. Computer Science B.A. and B.S. are excluded from TAG.

Minimum major prep GPA: 2.4 to 2.8 by major.

Highly selective major: Computer Science B.A. and B.S.
Cal-GETC / IGETC: IGETC and Cal-GETC are not recommended for Engineering and the physical and biological sciences. UC Santa Cruz accepts partial IGETC and Cal-GETC certification.

Appendix E: Glossary of Admissions Terms

Admission/Acceptance/Admit Rate: Percentage of applicants a college admits.
A-G Requirements: The 15 high school courses students must complete with grades of C or better to meet UC and CSU admission requirements.
AB 540: A California policy that allows some students, including eligible undocumented students, to pay in-state tuition at California public colleges if they meet specific requirements.
ACT: A standardized college admission test. UC and CSU campuses do not use ACT scores for admission decisions, but some private require or consider them.
Admission by Exception: A UC policy that allows campuses to admit a small number of students who do not meet standard freshman eligibility requirements but show strong potential.
ADT: Associate Degree for Transfer. A California community college transfer pathway designed for students planning to transfer to the CSU system.
Advanced Placement, AP: College-level high school courses and exams offered by the College Board.
Alternate Major: A second-choice major listed on some applications.
Appeal: A formal request asking a college to reconsider an admission decision.
Articulation Agreement: An agreement showing how courses at one college satisfy requirements at another college.
ASSIST: The official California transfer articulation database.
CADAA, California Dream Act Application: A financial aid application for eligible undocumented students who may qualify for California state aid.
Cal Grant: A California state financial aid program for eligible California residents and certain eligible nonresidents.

Cal-GETC: California General Education Transfer Curriculum. A general education pattern for California community college students planning to transfer to UC or CSU.
Campus Impaction: A CSU term used when a campus receives more qualified applicants than it can admit.
Capped Weighted GPA: A GPA calculation that gives extra points for approved honors, AP, IB, or college courses but limits how many extra points count.
Common Application: Common App. A shared application used by many private and out-of-state colleges.
College Credit: Credit a student earns toward a college degree.
Common Data Set, CDS: A standardized report colleges publish with information about admission, enrollment, financial aid, student demographics, and academic profile.
Cost Gap: The amount left for the family to cover after grants, scholarships, reasonable work income, planned loans, and family contribution are considered.
Cost of Attendance, COA: The college's estimate of the total cost to attend for one year. It usually includes tuition and fees, housing and food, books and supplies, transportation, personal expenses, and sometimes health insurance.
CSS Profile: A financial aid application used by some private colleges and scholarship programs to award institutional aid.
Deferred Admission: Permission from a college to delay enrollment after being admitted. Policies vary by campus.
Degree Requirement: A course, credit, GPA, or other requirement needed to graduate.
Demonstrated Interest: Actions that show a student's interest in a college, such as visiting, opening emails, attending events, or contacting admissions.
Direct Admit: When a student is admitted directly into a specific major, college, or program.
Early Action, EA: An option where students apply early and receive an earlier decision.
Early Decision, ED: A binding early application option.
ELC, Eligibility in the Local Context: A UC program that identifies top-performing California students based on their academic record within their own high school.
EOP, Educational Opportunity Program: A support program for students who have faced educational or economic barriers.
Enrollment Deposit: Money a student pays to reserve their spot after accepting an admission offer.
FAFSA: The Free Application for Federal Student Aid. U.S. citizens and eligible noncitizens use it to apply for federal, state, and institutional financial aid.
Federal Work-Study: A program that allows eligible students to earn money through part-time work. It is not free money because students must work to receive it.

Financial Aid Offer: A college's summary of the grants, scholarships, loans, and work-study offered to a student.

First-Generation Student: A student whose parents did not complete a four-year college degree.

Freshman Applicant: A student applying to enter college directly after high school.

Fully Weighted GPA: A GPA calculation that gives extra points for all eligible approved honors, AP, IB, and college courses without cap.

General Education: A set of broad courses outside the major that students must complete.

Golden Four: Four core CSU transfer requirements in oral communication, written communication, critical thinking, and quantitative reasoning.

Holistic Review: An admissions process that considers the whole applicant, including academic preparation, activities, essays, context, recommendations if used, and other factors. The UC often uses the term comprehensive review.

Impacted Major: A major that receives more qualified applicants than there is space to admit. Impacted majors can be much more selective than the overall campus.

Impaction Threshold: The GPA, points, or ranking level needed for admission to an impacted CSU campus or major in a particular year.

Institutional Aid: Financial aid given by the college itself.

Likely School: A college where the student has a strong chance of admission based on academic profile, major, residency status, and the school's admission patterns.

Lower-Division Courses: Introductory college courses usually taken during the first two years of college.

Major Change: A request to switch from one intended or declared major to another.

Major Preparation: Courses required or strongly recommended before applying to a major, especially as a transfer student.

Major-Level Selectivity: How difficult it is to get into a specific major at a campus.

Median: The middle value in a data set.

Merit Aid: Financial aid awarded for achievement, talent, or other qualities.

Middle 50th Percentile Range: The range between the 25th and 75th percentile. In admissions, this often shows the middle half of admitted students' GPA or test scores.

Middle Class Scholarship: A California financial aid program that may provide aid to eligible students attending UC or CSU campuses.

Minimum Eligibility: The basic requirements a student must meet to be considered for admission.

Need-Based Aid: Financial aid based on a family's financial circumstances. It may include grants, scholarships, loans, and work-study.

Net Cost: The amount a family pays after grants and scholarships are subtracted from the cost of attendance.

Net Price Calculator: An online tool that colleges provide to estimate a family's cost after financial aid.

Nonresident Applicant: A student who is not considered a California resident.

Parent PLUS Loan: A federal loan parents can use to help pay college costs. It must be repaid with interest.

Pell Grant: A federal grant for students with financial need, based on FAFSA information.

Percentile: A way to show where a number falls compared with a group. For example, the 75th percentile GPA means 75 percent of students had that GPA or lower, while 25 percent had a higher GPA.

Personal Insight Questions, PIQs: The short-answer questions required in the UC application.

Placement Tests: Assessments used to determine a student's appropriate level of coursework in subjects such as math, writing, or foreign language.

Pre-Major: A status where students enter with an intended major but must complete certain courses or GPA requirements before being officially admitted to the major.

Prerequisite: A course or requirement that must be completed before taking another course or entering a program.

Program Impaction: A major that gets more qualified applicants than it can admit.

Provisional Admission: Admission that depends on completing senior-year coursework, maintaining grades, submitting final transcripts, and meeting all stated conditions.

Reach School: A school where admission is uncertain or unlikely based on the student's profile, the school's selectivity, the major, and the applicant pool.

Regular Decision, RD: A common private-college application plan with deadlines often in January and decisions usually released in spring.

Rescind: When a college withdraws an admission offer.

Resident Applicant: A student considered a California resident for admission or tuition purposes.

Rolling Admission: An admission process where applications are reviewed as they are received. Some colleges make decisions throughout the cycle rather than waiting for one deadline.

SAI, Student Aid Index: The number calculated from the FAFSA and used to help determine financial aid eligibility. A lower SAI generally indicates greater financial need.

SAT: A standardized college admission test.

Scholarship Displacement: When outside scholarships reduce other financial aid instead of reducing the family's remaining cost.

Self-Reported Academic Record: A system where students enter their own courses and grades into an application.

SIR, Statement of Intent to Register: The official step used to accept an admission offer at UC and CSU campuses.

Subsidized Loan: A federal student loan for eligible students where the government pays the interest while the student is in school at least half-time.

Supplemental Materials: Additional items submitted with or after an application.

TAG, Transfer Admission Guarantee: A UC transfer pathway that offers guaranteed admission to participating UC campuses.

TAP: A transfer support or priority consideration program offered by some UC campuses.

Target School: A school where the student's academic profile and admission context suggest a reasonable chance of admission.

Test-Blind: A policy where a college does not consider test scores, even if submitted.

Test-Optional: A policy where students can choose whether to submit test scores.

Transcript: Official record of a student's courses, grades, credits, and GPA.

Transferable Course: A college course that can count for credit at another college.

Transfer Applicant: A student applying to a four-year college after completing college coursework elsewhere, often at a community college.

UC Transfer Admission Planner: An online UC tool that helps students plan their transfer.

UC Transfer Pathway: A set of major preparation recommendations for transfer students in certain popular majors.

Uncapped Weighted GPA: A GPA calculation that gives extra weight for all eligible advanced courses without the same cap.

Unmet Need: The remaining financial need after aid is awarded.

Unsubsidized Loan: A federal student loan that begins accruing interest immediately, even while the student is in school.

Unweighted GPA: A GPA based on courses without extra points for honors, AP, IB, or college courses.

Upper-Division Courses: Advanced college courses usually taken after completing lower-division requirements, often in the student's major.

Waitlist: A list of applicants who are not initially offered admission but may be admitted later if space becomes available.

Yield Rate: The percentage of admitted students who enroll.

Sources

ACT (2026). ACT / SAT Concordance. https://www.act.org/content/act/en/products-and-services/the-act/scores/act-sat-concordance.html

AICCU (2026). Member institutions. https://aiccu.edu/page/memberinstitutions

AICCU (2026). Transfer students. https://aiccu.edu/page/transferstudents

ASSIST (2026). The official course transfer and articulation system for California colleges and universities. https://assist.org/

California Community Colleges. I Can Go To College. (2026). Associate Degree for Transfer. https://icangotocollege.com/associate-degree-for-transfer

California Community Colleges Chancellor's Office. (2026). Key facts. https://www.cccco.edu/about-us/key-facts

California Community Colleges Chancellor's Office. (2026). Participating independent non-profit universities. https://www.cccco.edu/Students/Transfer/participating-ca-independent-non-profit-universities

California Community Colleges Chancellor's Office. (2026). Transfer. https://www.cccco.edu/Students/Transfer

California Community Colleges Chancellor's Office. (2026). Transfer and Articulation Program. https://www.cccco.edu/About-Us/Chancellors-Office/Divisions/Educational-Services-and-Support/Transfer-and-Articulation-Program

California Community Colleges Chancellor's Office. (2025). Cal-GETC Standards, Version 1.2. https://www.cccco.edu/-/media/CCCCO-Website/docs/curriculum/calgetcstandards122024a11y.pdf

California Legislative Information. (2024). Assembly Bill No. 1780. Independent institutions of higher education: legacy and donor preference in admissions. https://leginfo.legislature.ca.gov/faces/billNavClient.xhtml?bill_id=202320240AB1780

California State University. (2026). Access and Impaction at the CSU. https://www.calstate.edu/attend/impaction-at-the-csu

California State University. (2026). Associate Degree for Transfer. https://www.calstate.edu/apply/transfer/pages/ccc-associate-degree-for-transfer.aspx

California State University. (2026). Cal State Apply. Freshman. https://www.calstate.edu/apply/freshman

California State University. (2026). Cal State Apply. Transfer. https://www.calstate.edu/apply/transfer

California State University. (2026). Cal State Apply Freshman Application Guide 2026–2027. https://www.calstate.edu/apply/freshman/Documents/cal-state-apply-freshman-application-guide.pdf

California State University. (2026). Cal State Apply Transfer Application Guide 2026–2027. https://www.calstate.edu/apply/transfer/Documents/cal-state-apply-transfer-application-guide.pdf

California State University. (2026). CSU Admission Handbook 2026–2027. https://www.calstate.edu/attend/student-services/Documents/csu-admission-handbook.pdf

California State University. (2024). CSU Transfer Planner. https://www.calstate.edu/apply/transfer/Documents/CSU-Transfer-Planner-Info-Flyer-2024.pdf

California State University. (2025). Fall 2025 Counselor Conference. Supporting Students Through the Educational Opportunity Program. https://www.calstate.edu/apply/counselor-resources/counselor-conferences/Documents/2025-presentations/EOP%20Counselor%20Conferences%20Fall%202025%20FINAL.pdf

California State University. (2025). First-time Freshman Supplemental Admission Factors Summary 2025–2026. https://www.calstate.edu/apply/counselor-resources/Documents/First-time-Freshman-Supplemental-Admission-Factors-Summary.pdf

California State University. (2026). Golden Four Completion. https://www.calstate.edu/apply/casper/Pages/golden-four.aspx

California State University. (2026). Impacted Undergraduate Majors and Universities, 2026–2027. https://www.calstate.edu/attend/degrees-certificates-credentials/Pages/impacted-degrees.aspx

California State University. (2026). Lower-Division Transfer. https://www.calstate.edu/apply/transfer/Pages/lower-division-transfer.aspx

California State University. (2026). Redirection. https://www.calstate.edu/apply/redirection

California State University. (2026). Transfer Success Pathway. https://www.calstate.edu/apply/transfer/Pages/transfer-success-pathway.aspx

California State University. (2026). Upper-Division Transfer. https://www.calstate.edu/apply/transfer/Pages/upper-division-transfer.aspx

California State University. (2026). 2026–2027 Estimated Undergraduate Cost of Attendance. https://www.calstate.edu/apply/paying-for-college/Documents/cost-of-attendance.pdf

California State University (2026). Freshman: Admission Requirement. https://www.calstate.edu/apply/freshman/getting_into_the_csu/Pages/admission-requirements.aspx

California State University. (2026). 2026–2027 Impaction Matrix. https://www.calstate.edu/attend/impaction-at-the-csu/Documents/ImpactedProgramsMatrix.pdf

California Student Aid Commission. (2026). California Dream Act Application. https://dream.csac.ca.gov/

California Student Aid Commission. (2026). California Dream Act Application and eligibility. https://csac.ca.gov/cadaa-and-eligibility

California Student Aid Commission. (2026). Cal Grant Award Amounts by Segment and Term. https://www.csac.ca.gov/post/cal-grant-award-amounts-segment-and-term

California Student Aid Commission. (2026). Cal Grant Community College Entitlement Award. https://www.csac.ca.gov/post/cal-grant-community-college-entitlement-award

California Student Aid Commission. (2026). Middle Class Scholarship. https://www.csac.ca.gov/middle-class-scholarship

California Student Aid Commission. (2026). WebGrants 4 Students. https://mygrantinfo.csac.ca.gov/

California Student Aid Commission. (2026). What are the Cal Grant Award Amounts? https://www.csac.ca.gov/post/what-are-cal-grant-award-amounts

California Student Aid Commission. (2026). 2026–2027 Cal Grant Income and Asset Ceilings. https://www.csac.ca.gov/sites/default/files/2025-07/2026-27-Income-and-Asset-Ceiling.pdf

California Student Aid Commission. (2026). California Student Aid Commission. https://www.csac.ca.gov/

Caltech. (2026). Undergraduate admissions. https://www.admissions.caltech.edu/afford

Claremont McKenna College. (2026). Financial aid. https://www.cmc.edu/financial-aid

Coalition for College. (2026). Apply Coalition on Scoir. https://www.coalitionforcollegeaccess.org/apply-coalition-on-scoir

College Board. (2018). Guide to the 2018 ACT/SAT Concordance. https://satsuite.collegeboard.org/media/pdf/guide-2018-act-sat-concordance.pdf

College Board. (2026). CSS Profile. https://cssprofile.collegeboard.org/

Common App. (2026). Application guide for first-year students. https://www.commonapp.org/apply/first-year-students/

Common App. (2026). Requirements grid. https://content.commonapp.org/Files/ReqGrid.pdf

Common Data Set Initiative. (2026). Common Data Set. https://commondataset.org/

Duke University. (2024). Duke no longer giving numerical rating to standardized testing, essays in undergraduate admissions. *The Chronicle.* https://www.dukechronicle.com/article/2024/02/duke-university-undergraduate-admissions-changes-numerical-rating-standardized-testing-essays-covid-test-optional-ai-generated-college-consultants

Federal Student Aid. (2025). 2026–2027 Student Aid Index and Pell Grant Eligibility Guide. https://fsapartners.ed.gov/knowledge-center/library/handbooks-manuals-or-guides/2025-06-13/2026-27-student-aid-index-sai-and-pell-grant-eligibility-guide-updated-aug-25-2025

Federal Student Aid. (2026). 2026–2027 FAFSA. https://studentaid.gov/h/apply-for-aid/fafsa

Federal Student Aid. (2026). FAFSA Submission Summary: What You Need To Know. https://studentaid.gov/articles/fafsa-submission-summary/

Federal Student Aid. (2026). How To Evaluate Your Aid Offers. https://studentaid.gov/articles/evaluating-financial-aid-offers/

Federal Student Aid. (2026). Manage and Repay Your Federal Student Loans. https://studentaid.gov

Federal Student Aid. (2026). Student Aid Index Explained. https://studentaid.gov/sites/default/files/sai-explained.pdf

Federal Student Aid. (2026). 7 Things To Do After Submitting Your FAFSA Form. https://studentaid.gov/articles/things-after-fafsa/

Harvey Mudd College. (2026). Determining Your Eligibility. https://www.hmc.edu/admission/afford/determining-your-eligibility/

Hees, Christine. (2024). *Mission: Accepted! U.S. College Admissions for International Students.* Periwinkle Tide Publishing.

Internal Revenue Service. (2026). Publication 970: Tax Benefits for Education. https://www.irs.gov/publications/p970

Internal Revenue Service. (2026). Topic No. 313: Qualified Tuition Programs. https://www.irs.gov/taxtopics/tc313

Kaleem, J. (2026). Citing 'severe' math deficits, UC faculty demand a return to SAT tests for STEM applicants. Los Angeles Times. https://www.latimes.com/california/story/2026-05-27/uc-math-professors-demand-return-of-sat-for-stem-admissions

Mission Accepted! College Counseling (2026). https://www.missionaccepted.international

National Association for College Admission Counseling. (2023). Factors in the Admission Decision. https://www.nacacnet.org/factors-in-the-admission-decision/

National Center for Education Statistics. (2026). College Navigator. https://nces.ed.gov/collegenavigator/

National Center for Education Statistics. (2026). Integrated Postsecondary Education Data System. https://nces.ed.gov/ipeds

Occidental College. (2026). Occidental Affordability Promise. https://www.oxy.edu/admission-aid/affordability/promise

Pitzer College. (2026). Financial Aid Information. https://www.pitzer.edu/admission-aid/financial-aid-information

Pomona College. (2026). Financial Aid. https://www.pomona.edu/financial-aid

ScholarShare 529. (2026). California 529 Plan: Options & Benefits. https://www.scholarshare529.com/why/benefits

ScholarShare 529. (2026). Frequently Asked Questions. https://www.scholarshare529.com/resources/faq

Scoir. (2026). Apply Coalition with Scoir. https://www.scoir.com/students/apply-with-scoir

Scoir. (2026). The Full Guide to First-Year Coalition College Applications. https://www.scoir.com/students/first-year-applications

Scripps College. (2026). Apply for Financial Aid. https://www.scrippscollege.edu/financialaid/apply-for-financial-aid

Stanford University. (2026). Financial Aid: Undergraduate Basics. https://financialaid.stanford.edu/undergrad/

Stanford University. (2026). Undergraduate Admission: Decision FAQs. https://admission.stanford.edu/faqs/decision.html

University of California. (2024). Accountability Report. https://accountability.universityofcalifornia.edu/2024/chapters/chapter-3.html

University of California. (2025). Accountability Report. https://accountability.universityofcalifornia.edu/2025/welcome.html

University of California. (2025). California Community College new enrollments at UC. https://www.universityofcalifornia.edu/about-us/information-center/california-community-college-new-enrollments-uc

University of California. (2026). Fact Sheet: Fall 2026 First-Year and Transfer Admissions. https://www.ucop.edu/institutional-research-academic-planning/_files/factsheets/2026/admissions-fact-sheet-data-tables.pdf

University of California. (2025). High School Counselor Conference. https://admission.universityofcalifornia.edu/counselors/events/counselor-conference.html

University of California. (2025). More than 77 percent of California applicants were offered UC admission for fall 2025. https://www.universityofcalifornia.edu/news/more-77-percent-california-applicants-were-offered-uc-admission-fall-2025

University of California. (2025). Quick Reference Guide to UC Admissions. https://admission.universityofcalifornia.edu/counselors/_files/documents/quick-reference-guide-to-uc-admissions.pdf

University of California. (2025). Senate-Administration Workgroup on Admissions Final Report. https://senate.ucsd.edu/media/740347/sawg-report-on-admissions-review-docs.pdf

University of California. (2026). A-G Course List. https://hs-articulation.ucop.edu/agcourselist

University of California. (2026). Admissions. https://admission.universityofcalifornia.edu/

University of California. (2026). Admissions decisions. First-year applicants. https://admission.universityofcalifornia.edu/how-to-apply/applying-as-a-first-year/after-you-apply/admissions-decisions.html

University of California. (2026). Admissions decisions. Transfer applicants. https://admission.universityofcalifornia.edu/how-to-apply/applying-as-a-transfer/after-you-apply/admissions-decisions.html

University of California. (2026). Counselors. https://admission.universityofcalifornia.edu/counselors

University of California. (2026). Fall 2026 Preliminary Application Tables. https://ucop.edu/institutional-research-academic-planning/content-analysis/ug-admissions/ug-pages/applications.html

University of California. (2026). Filling out the application. First-year applicants. https://admission.universityofcalifornia.edu/how-to-apply/applying-as-a-first-year/filling-out-the-application.html

University of California. (2026). Filling out the application. Transfer applicants. https://admission.universityofcalifornia.edu/how-to-apply/applying-as-a-transfer/filling-out-the-application.html

University of California. (2026). Freshman Admission by Discipline. https://www.universityofcalifornia.edu/about-us/information-center/freshman-admission-discipline

University of California. (2026). How applications are reviewed. First-year applicants. https://admission.universityofcalifornia.edu/how-to-apply/applying-as-a-first-year/how-applications-are-reviewed.html

University of California. (2026). How applications are reviewed. Transfer applicants. https://admission.universityofcalifornia.edu/how-to-apply/applying-as-a-transfer/how-applications-are-reviewed.html

University of California. (2026). Information Center. https://www.universityofcalifornia.edu/about-us/information-center

University of California. (2026). Personal Insight Questions. First-year applicants. https://admission.universityofcalifornia.edu/how-to-apply/applying-as-a-first-year/personal-insight-questions.html

University of California. (2026). Personal Insight Questions. Transfer applicants. https://admission.universityofcalifornia.edu/how-to-apply/applying-as-a-transfer/personal-insight-questions.html

University of California. (2026). Transfer Academic Update. https://admission.universityofcalifornia.edu/how-to-apply/applying-as-a-transfer/after-you-apply/transfer-academic-update.html

University of California. (2026). Transfer Admit Data. https://admission.universityofcalifornia.edu/campuses-majors/transfer-admit-data.html

University of California. (2026). Transfer by Major. https://www.universityofcalifornia.edu/about-us/information-center/transfers-major

University of California. (2026). Transfer Pathways. https://admission.universityofcalifornia.edu/admission-requirements/transfer-requirements/transfer-pathways/

University of California. (2026). Transfer planning tools. https://admission.universityofcalifornia.edu/admission-requirements/transfer-requirements/transfer-planning-tools/

University of California. (2026). Transfer requirements. https://admission.universityofcalifornia.edu/admission-requirements/transfer-requirements/

University of California. (2026). UC Transfer Admission Guarantee for students applying for 2026–2027 admission. https://admission.universityofcalifornia.edu/_assets/files/transfer-requirements/uc-tag-matrix_2026-2027.pdf

University of California. (2026). UC Transfer Admission Planner. https://admission.universityofcalifornia.edu/admission-requirements/transfer-requirements/transfer-planning-tools/uc-transfer-admission-planner.html

University of California. (2026). UC Transfer Admission Planner. https://uctap.universityofcalifornia.edu/students/

University of California Berkeley. (2026). Management, Entrepreneurship, and Technology Admissions. https://met.berkeley.edu/admissions/

University of California Berkeley. (2026). Office of Undergraduate Admissions. https://www.admissions.berkeley.edu/

University of California Board of Regents. (2022). Regents Policy 2110: Policy on Augmented Review in Undergraduate Admissions. https://regents.universityofcalifornia.edu/governance/policies/2110.html

University of California Davis. (2026). Undergraduate Admissions. https://www.ucdavis.edu/admissions/undergraduate

University of California Irvine. (2026). Office of Undergraduate Admissions. https://admissions.uci.edu/

University of California Los Angeles. (2026). Undergraduate Admission. https://admission.ucla.edu/

University of California Los Angeles (2026). Common Data Set. https://apb.ucla.edu/file/d1ab04b3-ee89-4cf2-9124-8dc0471b5e5a

University of California Merced. (2026). Admissions. https://admissions.ucmerced.edu/

University of California Merced. (2026). MAAP Test. https://admissions.ucmerced.edu/node/6046

University of California San Diego. (2026). Undergraduate Admissions. https://admissions.ucsd.edu/

University of California Santa Barbara. (2026). Office of Admissions. https://admissions.sa.ucsb.edu/

University of California Santa Cruz. (2026). Undergraduate Admissions. https://admissions.ucsc.edu/

University of Southern California. (2026). Financial Aid at USC. https://financialaid.usc.edu/undergraduate-financial-aid/prospective-students/financial-aid-at-usc/

University of Southern California. (2026). Undergraduate Admission. https://admission.usc.edu/

U.S. Department of Education. (2026). College Scorecard. https://collegescorecard.ed.gov/

About the Author

Christine Hees is a California-based independent college counselor and the author of *Mission: Accepted! U.S. College Admissions for International Students.* Before moving into college counseling, she had a corporate career at a Fortune 500 company in marketing. Today, Christine is a passionate advocate for making higher education more accessible and works with both domestic and international students.

Her work focuses on helping students develop strong application strategies and present their experiences effectively. In addition to her private counseling work, Christine supports first-generation students through pro bono advising at local high schools.

Christine also serves as an application reader for the University of California and holds a College Counseling Certificate from the University of California San Diego. She is originally from Germany and lived in France and Austria before moving to California.

www.ingramcontent.com/pod-product-compliance
Lightning Source LLC
LaVergne TN
LVHW020530100826
845148LV00010B/1409